# RAF Bomber Command Profiles

# 630 Squadron

# RAF Bomber Command Profiles

# 630 Squadron

Chris Ward

www.aviationbooks.org

This edition first published 2024 by Aviation Books Ltd., 25 Cromwell Street, Merthyr Tydfil, CF47 8RY.

Copyright 2024 © Chris Ward.

The right of Chris Ward to be identified as Author of this work is asserted by him in accordance with the Copyright, Designs and Patents Act 1988.

The original Operational Record Book of 630 Squadron RAF and the Bomber Command Night Raid Reports are Crown Copyright and stored in microfiche and digital format by the National Archives. Material is reproduced under Open Licence v. 3.0.

All rights reserved. No part of this publication may be reproduced, stored in a retrieval system, transmitted in any form or by any means, electronic, mechanical, or photocopied, recorded or otherwise, without the written permission of the copyright owners.

This squadron profile has been researched, compiled and written by its author, who has made every effort to ensure the accuracy of the information contained in it. The author will not be liable for any damages caused, or alleged to be caused, by any information contained in this book. E. & O.E.

Every effort is made to trace the copyright holders of photographs and we apologise in advance for any unintentional omissions. These and other errors brought to our attention will be corrected in subsequent editions of this Profile.

Cover design: Topics - The Creative Partnership www.topicsdesign.co.uk

Photos and captions: Clare Bennett

A CIP catalogue reference for this book is available from the British Library.

ISBN 9781915335432

## Also by Chris Ward from Bomber Command Books:

*Casualty of War: Letters Home from Flight Lieutenant Bill Astell DFC*

*Dambuster Deering: The Life and Death of an Unsung Hero*

*Dambusters : The Complete WWII History of 617 Squadron*
(with Andy Lee and Andreas Wachtel)

## Other RAF Bomber Command Profiles:

*IX Squadron*
*10 Squadron* (with Ian MacMillan)
*35 (Madras Presidency) Squadron*
*44 (Rhodesia) Squadron*
*49 Squadron*
*50 Squadron*
*57 Squadron*
*75(NZ) Squadron* (with Chris Newey)
*83 Squadron*
*90 Squadron (*with Shannon Taylor*)*
*101 Squadron*
*102 (Ceylon) Squadron*
*103 Squadron* (with David Fell)
*106 Squadron* (with Herman Bijlard)
*115 Squadron*
*138 Squadron* (with Piotr Hodyra)
*207 Squadron* (with Raymond Glynne-Owen)
*300 Squadron* (with Grzegorz Korcz)
*301, 304 and 305 Squadrons* (with Grzegorz Korcz)
*405 (Vancouver) Squadron RCAF*
*408 (Goose) Squadron RCAF*
*455, 458, 462,464 Squadrons RAAF*
*460 Squadron RAAF*
*467 Squadron RAAF*
*514 Squadron* (with Simon Hepworth)
*619 Squadron*

## Table of Contents

| | |
|---|---:|
| Introduction | 9 |
| Dedication | 11 |
| Narrative History | 11 |
| November 1943 | 13 |
| December 1943 | 20 |
| January 1944 | 26 |
| February 1944 | 34 |
| March 1944 | 40 |
| April 1944 | 49 |
| May 1944 | 80 |
| June 1944 | 89 |
| July 1944 | 98 |
| August 1944 | 110 |
| September 1944 | 150 |
| October 1944 | 157 |
| November 1944 | 165 |
| December 1944 | 170 |
| January 1945 | 176 |
| February 1945 | 182 |
| March 1945 | 189 |
| April 1945 | 195 |
| Postscript to the Story of P/O Barnes | 201 |
| Roll of Honour | 203 |
| Station | 212 |
| Commanding Officers | 212 |
| Aircraft | 213 |
| Operational Record | 213 |
| Aircraft Histories | 215 |

# Introduction

RAF Bomber Command Squadron Profiles first appeared in the late nineties and proved to be very popular with enthusiasts of RAF Bomber Command during the Second World War. They became a useful research tool, particularly for those whose family members had served and were no longer around. The original purpose was to provide a point of reference for all of the gallant men and women who had fought the war, either in the air, or on the ground in a support capacity, and for whom no written history of their unit or station existed. I wanted to provide them with something they could hold up, point to and say, "this was my unit, this is what I did in the war". Many veterans were reticent to talk about their time on bombers, partly because of modesty, but perhaps mostly because the majority of those with whom they came into contact had no notion of what it was to be a "Bomber Boy", to face the prospect of death every time they took to the air, whether during training or on operations. Only those who shared the experience really understood what it was to go to war in bombers, which is why reunions were so important. As they approached the end of their lives, many veterans began to speak openly for the first time about their life in wartime Bomber Command, and most were hurt by the callous treatment they received at the hands of successive governments with regard to the lack of recognition of their contribution to victory. It is sad that this recognition in the form of a national memorial and the granting of a campaign medal came too late for the majority. Now this inspirational, noble generation, the like of which will probably never grace this earth again, has all but departed from us, and the world will be a poorer place as a result.

RAF Bomber Command Squadron Profiles are back. The basic format remains, but, where needed, additional information has been provided. Squadron Profiles do not claim to be comprehensive histories, but rather detailed overviews of the activities of the squadron. There is insufficient space to mention as many names as one would like, but all aircraft losses are accompanied by the name of the pilot. Fundamentally, the narrative section is an account of Bomber Command's war from the perspective of the bomber group under which the individual squadron served, and the deeds of the squadron are interwoven into this story. Information has been drawn from official records, such as group, squadron and station ORBs, and from the many, like me, amateur enthusiasts, who dedicate much of their time to researching individual units and become unrivalled authorities on them. I am grateful for their generous contributions, and their names will appear in the appropriate Profiles. The statistics quoted in this series are taken from The Bomber Command War Diaries, that indispensable tome written by Martin Middlebrook and Chris Everitt, and I am indebted to Martin for his kind permission to use them.

Finally, let me apologize in advance for the inevitable errors, for no matter how hard I and other authors try to write "nothing but the truth", there is no such thing as a definitive account of history, and there will always be room for disagreement and debate. Official records are notoriously unreliable tools, and yet we have little choice but to put our faith in them. It is not my intention to misrepresent any person or Bomber Command unit, and I ask my readers to understand the enormity of the task I have undertaken. It is relatively easy to become an authority on single units or even a bomber group, but I chose to write about them all, idiot that I am, which means 128 squadrons serving operationally in Bomber Command at some time between the 3$^{rd}$ of September 1939 and the 8$^{th}$ of May 1945. I am dealing with eight bomber groups, in which some 120,000 airmen served, and I am juggling around 28,000 aircraft serial numbers, code letters and details of provenance and fate. I ask not for your sympathy, it was, after all, my choice, but rather your understanding should you find something with which you disagree. My thanks to you, my readers, for making the original series of RAF Bomber Command Squadron Profiles so popular, and I hope you receive this new incarnation equally enthusiastically.

My thanks are due to Louise Bush at the Lincolnshire Aviation Heritage Centre for providing most of the photographs, and to Amanda Burrows for the images and details of her father, Len Barnes. As always, thanks to my gang members, Andreas Wachtel, photo editor, Clare Bennett, Steve Smith and Greg Korcz for their unstinting support, without which my Profiles would be the poorer. Finally, my appreciation to my publisher, Simon Hepworth of Aviation Books Ltd, formerly Mention the War Publications, for his belief in my work, untiring efforts to promote it, and for the stress I put him through to bring my books to publication.

Chris Ward. Skegness, Lincolnshire. October 2024.

# Dedication

This WWII history of 630 Squadron is dedicated to the memory of
P/O Len Barnes, who served as a pilot from January to March 1944,
before failing to return from an operation to Stuttgart and evading capture.

He represents all who served with 630 Squadron at East Kirkby in the air and on
the ground during its operational career between November 1943 and May 1945.

# Narrative History

## November 1943

Unlike most Bomber Command squadrons, which boasted a sometimes long and varied history stretching back to an initial formation in the Great War, 630 Squadron had no such heritage and tradition when it was formed as a brand-new unit on the 15th of November 1943 at East Kirkby, a recently opened station on the A155 road some six and nine miles respectively from the bomber stations of Coningsby and Woodhall Spa to the west and six miles from Spilsby to the east. This was Lincolnshire, 5 Group Lancaster territory, and East Kirkby was already home to 57 Squadron, which had moved in as the first resident unit in August, when Scampton closed for the installation of paved runways. 57 Squadron's B Flight, consisting of nine crews under the temporary command of the popular S/L Malcolm Crocker DFC, an American serving in the RAF, was posted across the tarmac as the nucleus of the new unit. F/L "Bill" Kellaway was posted in from 617 Squadron to assume temporary command of B Flight, but it would be sometime in December before S/L Butler arrived to take over A Flight. The trade leaders were F/L Farara DFC DFM, (bombing), F/L Spencer DFC (engineering), F/L Stead (Gunnery), F/L Ehrman DFC (navigation) and P/O Worthington (signals). F/L Frank Cheetham was posted in to fulfil the role of squadron adjutant and was faced with an appalling state of affairs with regard to the administrative office accommodation, which consisted of empty shells devoid of floor coverings, light bulbs, blackout curtains and furniture of any kind, and the fact that the operations record book (ORB) entries were hand-written totally or in part for a considerable time is indicative of the total lack of preparation on behalf of 5 Group for a new squadron expected to hit the floor running and be operational immediately. At the end of his opening comments on the ORB Form 540 on the day of its formation, F/L Cheetham bemoaned the fact that the 15th was a truly miserable day characterised by heavy rain, sleet and high winds.

The squadron was set up as a two-flight unit with a complement of sixteen Lancasters with four in reserve, and aircrew flooded in from the conversion units to supplement the experienced former 57 Squadron crews, while F/L Cheetham borrowed folding chairs and tables and eventually persuaded group to install some of the missing items, including one cupboard and one filing cabinet, along with telephones and electricity, but no typewriter and no stationery. The official establishment allowed for three clerical staff, who arrived five full days after the squadron formed, two of them from overseas and one from a gunnery school and none had squadron experience. There were no toilet facilities within two hundred yards of the offices, and the flight and section offices and crew room were equally unprepared and not fit for purpose. Gradually the squadron achieved some semblance of organisation, each problem dealt with as it arose through a temporary fix, and F/L Cheetham summed it up with the comment, "Domestically – life is extremely uncomfortable", and added that dispersal sites for the Lancasters were by no means ready for occupation. As an essential part of RAF tradition, officers were looked after by a batman in the manner of a manservant, who dealt with all of the "domestic chores" in a ratio of one batman to four officers. In the case of 630 Squadron the ratio was one batman to forty officers, a totally intolerable situation which had to be "cheerfully" endured for as long as it lasted.

630 Squadron was formed during a period of expansion in Lancaster Squadrons, which coincided with the decision by ACM Sir Arthur Harris, the commander-in-chief of Bomber Command, to remove 3 Group's Stirling squadrons from operations over Germany just as the Berlin offensive was about to resume. Harris had never warmed to the Stirling, a type that lacked development potential, was restricted by its design to a lower operating ceiling than its Lancaster and Halifax counterparts and because of its segregated bomb bay was limited to carrying small calibre bombs no larger than a 2,000-pounder. Harris had already taken steps in the late summer of 1942 to limit the proliferation of Stirling units in 3 Group by transferring out 9 and 57 Squadrons to 5 Group and 101 Squadron to 1 Group, just as they were due to swap their Wellingtons for Stirlings. 5 Group was fully equipped with Lancasters and 1 Group was about to begin the process after narrowly dodging the bullet that had intended it to become an all-Halifax group. The problem for Harris was that Stirlings were still in full production, rolling out of the factories in numbers and had to be accommodated, and this was achieved by resurrecting 90 Squadron, posting 199 Squadron in from 1 Group and creating brand-new Stirling units in the summer of 1943 in the form of 513, 620, 622 and 623 Squadrons. 513 Squadron was disbanded before beginning operations, 620 Squadron operated for four months before being transferred from Bomber Command to carry out transport duties and 623 Squadron operated for three months before it too was disbanded. Until 3 Group fully converted to Lancasters, which would not be until September 1944, Stirlings would operate as bombers over the occupied countries and conduct mining operations and eventually supplant Halifaxes as the type to equip the secret 138 and 161 Squadrons operating out of Tempsford on behalf of the Special Operations Executive (SOE) and the Secret Intelligence Service (SIS).

The Berlin offensive had begun with three major operations between the 23rd of August and the 3rd of September and had resulted in a combined loss of 125 Lancasters, Halifaxes and Stirlings in return for moderate success, after which Harris turned his attention elsewhere for the next ten weeks, principally upon Hannover and Kassel in the north, Frankfurt, Stuttgart, Munich and the twin cities of Mannheim and Ludwigshafen in the south and the Ruhr in-between. It was a largely successful period, which caused massive destruction in particular in Hannover, Kassel and Mannheim, and provided Harris with the confidence to resume the assault on Berlin. One innovation to come out of this period was radio counter measures to disrupt enemy night-fighter communications and control. 1 Group's 101 Squadron had been selected to conduct trials with a device called "Jostle", which required an operator who could listen in and pick up German language transmissions, and on hearing them drown them out by broadcasting engine noise. The device was known at 101 Squadron as ABC or Airborne Cigar, and once proved to be effective, 101 Squadron Lancasters would be spread throughout the bomber stream on all major operations, whether or not the rest of 1 Group was involved and they would carry a standard bomb load reduced by 1,000lbs to compensate for the weight of the equipment and its operator. So successful would it prove to be, that a dedicated RCM group, 100 Group, was formed within Bomber Command in November on stations in Norfolk, but 101 Squadron would retain its role for the rest of the war from within 1 Group.

November brought with it the long, dark, cloudy nights that facilitated the deep penetration into north-eastern Germany to target Germany's capital city, the seat and symbol of Nazi power and the key, as far as Harris was concerned, to victory by bombing. The next four months would bring the bloodiest, hardest-fought air battles between Bomber Command and the Luftwaffe Nachtjagd and test the hard-pressed crews to the limit of their endurance. New crews embarking on their first tour with any squadron at this time faced a daunting winter, dominated by Berlin, and characterized by long, dark nights, inhospitable weather conditions, and the Luftwaffe night-fighter force at its most efficient and lethal.

In a minute to Churchill on the 3rd, Harris stated, that with the participation of the American 8th Air Force, he could "wreck Berlin from end to end". He estimated that the campaign would cost the two forces between four and five hundred aircraft, but that it would cost Germany the war. This would remove the need for the kind of bloody, expensive and protracted land campaign, which he had personally witnessed during the Great War, and had prompted him to "get into the air" at the earliest opportunity. It should be remembered that this was the first time in the history of air warfare that the means existed to prove the theory that an enemy could be defeated by bombing alone. It is only in the light of more recent experiences that we have learned of the need, in a conventional conflict at least, to occupy the enemy's territory to secure submission. The Americans, however, were committed to victory on land, where film cameras could capture the glory, and would not accompany Harris to Berlin.

Düsseldorf had been selected to open the month's operational account on that very night, and no doubt, while the Prime Minister was digesting Harris's epistle, a force of 589 Lancasters and Halifaxes was being prepared for action. 5 Group's contribution amounted to 147 Lancasters, of which twenty represented 57 Squadron, and they departed East Kirkby between 16.59 and 17.28 with S/L Crocker, the senior pilot on duty and a number of crews who would be posted to 630 Squadron twelve days hence. The crews of P/Os Piggin and Smith turned back early, each because of an indisposed crew member, while the others joined the bomber stream over the North Sea and set course to approach the south-western Ruhr after flying out over Belgium and passing through the concentration of fifty to sixty searchlights in the Mönchengladbach-Cologne corridor, some fifteen miles from the target. It was at this point that W4822 was attacked by a night-fighter and sustained damage sufficient to persuade 1Lt West to turn back and attempt to make it home. Sadly, the Lancaster crashed at Hechtel in Belgium, killing the pilot and four others and delivering the navigator into enemy hands. The second pilot, F/O Clements RCAF, and bomb-aimer, F/O Elliott, managed to retain their freedom and were spirited away by local civilians.

Meanwhile, the others encountered small patches of cloud and smoke from the early fires drifting across the target at 12,000 feet, despite which, the visibility remained generally good, and the Path Finders *(the Path Finder Force became 8 Group on 8.1.43 and the titles are interchangeable)* employed both sky and ground markers to good effect to identify the aiming-point in the city centre. Bombing by the 57 Squadron crews took place on red and green TIs and skymarkers from an average of 20,000 feet either side of 20.00, and fires were observed to develop on both sides of the Rhine with black smoke rising through 6,000 feet as they turned away. Eighteen aircraft failed to return, and, unusually, eleven were Lancasters and only seven Halifaxes. It was on this night, that 61 Squadron's F/L Bill Reid earned the award of a Victoria Cross for pressing on to bomb the target after his Lancaster was severely damaged, and a number of his crew either killed or wounded. Post-raid reconnaissance revealed that central and southern districts had sustained widespread damage to industry and housing, but no report came out of Düsseldorf to provide detail.

The only serious activity for 57 Squadron, thereafter, until the resumption of the Berlin campaign, came on the 10$^{th}$ as part of a 5 and 8 Group force of 313 Lancasters sent to destroy railway yards at Modane, situated in the foothills of the Alps in south-eastern France. 5 Group supported the operation with 136 Lancasters, of which the fourteen representing 57 Squadron departed East Kirkby between 20.55 and 21.22 with S/L Crocker the senior pilot on duty. Ahead of them lay an outward flight of more than 650 miles, which all from 57 Squadron negotiated to arrive at their destination after around four-and-a-quarter hours to be rewarded by the presence of a full moon shining brightly from a cloudless sky. They established a pinpoint on Lake Bissorte, from where they carried out a time-and-distance run to the target, which they identified visually and by red and green TIs, before bombing from around 15,000 feet either side of 01.00. The attack seemed to be concentrated around the markers, and fires appeared to be taking hold, while a large explosion was observed at 01.13. No aircraft were lost and returning crews had their confidence in the quality of the night's efforts confirmed by two hundred bombing photos, which revealed extensive damage to track and installations within one mile of the aiming-point.

Undaunted by the American response to his invitation to join the Berlin party, Harris would return there alone, and the rocky road to the capital was re-joined by an all-Lancaster heavy force on the night of the 18/19$^{th}$, while a predominantly Halifax and Stirling contingent of 395 aircraft acted as a diversion by raiding Mannheim and Ludwigshafen three hundred miles to the south-west. The Berlin-bound crews would benefit from four Mosquitos dropping dummy fighter flares, while other Mosquitos carried out a spoof raid on Frankfurt to protect the Mannheim force. The two forces would cross the enemy coast simultaneously some 250 miles apart to confuse the enemy night-fighter controllers, and the route chosen for the Berlin brigade was via the Frisian Island of Texel to a point north of Hannover, and thence to the target to pass over its centre on an east-north-easterly heading. After bombing they would return south of Berlin and Cologne, before crossing central Belgium to gain the English Channel via the French coast. An innovation for this operation was a shortening of the bomber stream to reduce the time over the target to sixteen minutes. When the first Thousand Bomber raid had taken place in May 1942, with an unprecedented twelve aircraft per minute crossing the aiming-point, there was considered to be a high risk of collisions. The number had since been increased to sixteen per minute, with large raids lasting up to forty-five minutes, but on this night, twenty-seven aircraft per minute were to pass over the aiming-point.

630 Squadron made ready nine Lancasters for its operational debut as part of a 5 Group force of 182 and dispatched them from East Kirkby between 16.50 and 17.26 with S/L Crocker the senior pilot on duty and a cookie and fourteen small bomb cases (SBCs) of 4lb and 30lb incendiaries in each bomb bay. A "cookie" was a 4,000lb high-capacity bomb, also known as a "blockbuster", the blast from which could demolish buildings, strip tiles from roofs, blow in windows and doors to allow access for the incendiaries dropped simultaneously, and was the staple weapon for city-busting. After climbing out they set course for the North Sea and

undertook the journey to the "Big City" over a blanket of cloud covering the whole of northern Germany. They were grateful for the red spotfire route marker dropped by a Path Finder aircraft north-east of Hannover, which confirmed that they were on track, and described the horizontal visibility as good, despite the absence of a moon. The cloud persisted all the way into north-eastern Germany and at the target the tops were at 6,000 to 10,000 feet and swallowed up the Path Finders' H2S-laid red and green skymarkers as they drifted down to leave a glow over the aiming-point that mingled with that created by the searchlights. The 630 Squadron participants delivered their loads from 20,000 to 23,000 feet either side of 21.00 before returning home, F/Sgt Yates and crew on three engines after losing one to flak over the target. Few had anything of value to pass on to the intelligence section at debriefing, most considering the bombing to have been scattered and probably ineffective, and local sources confirmed that there had been no concentration and that a modest 169 houses and four industrial units had been destroyed, with many more damaged to some extent. The diversion at Mannheim was deemed to have been successful in its purpose, and caused some useful industrial damage, most seriously to the Daimler-Benz motor factory, which suffered a 90% loss of production for an unknown period. In addition to this, more than three hundred buildings were destroyed at a cost of twenty-three aircraft, while the losses from Berlin were encouragingly low at just nine.

The Lancasters stayed at home on the 19th, while 3, 4, 6 and 8 Groups combined to put 170 Halifaxes, eighty-six Stirlings and ten Mosquitos into the air for a raid on the Ruhr city of Leverkusen. They were greeted in the target area by ten-tenths cloud and an absence of marking, which was caused by equipment failure among the Oboe Mosquitos. A few green TIs were spotted some five to ten miles to the north-west of the target during the approach, but the crews were left to establish their positions on the basis of their own H2S, which, over a region as densely built-up as the Ruhr, was a challenge. As a result, the operation was a complete failure, which sprayed bombs over twenty-seven towns in the region, mostly to the north of Leverkusen.

Harris called for a maximum effort on Berlin on the 22nd, and 764 aircraft were made available, of which 166 Lancasters were provided by 5 Group. Ten 630 Squadron crews attended briefing alongside twelve from 57 Squadron, which would be providing two of its Lancasters for use by 630 Squadron crews. They departed East Kirkby between 16.42 and 16.57 with F/L Perrers the senior pilot on duty and a cookie supplemented with fourteen SBCs of 4lb and nine of 30lb incendiaries in each bomb bay. After climbing out over the station, they rendezvoused with the rest of the bomber stream to adopt an outward route similar to that employed by the all-Lancaster force four nights earlier. This took them from Texel to a point north-west of Hannover, where a slight dogleg to port put them on a due-easterly heading directly to the target. Unlike the previous raid, however, rather than the circuitous return south of Cologne and out over the French coast, they would come home via a reciprocal route. This was based on a forecast of low cloud and fog over Germany, which would inhibit the night-fighter effort, while broken, medium-level cloud over Berlin would facilitate ground marking. An additional bonus was the availability to the Path Finders of five new H2S Mk III sets, while a new record of thirty-four aircraft per minute passing over the aiming-point would be achieved by abandoning the long-standing practice of allocating aircraft types to specific waves. On this night, aircraft of all types would be spread through the bomber stream, and this was bad news for the Stirlings, which, by the very nature of their design, would be below the Lancaster and Halifax elements and in danger of being hit by friendly bombs.

There were no early returns among the 630 Squadron element, which arrived at the target to discover that the meteorological forecast had been inaccurate, and that the city was hidden under a blanket of ten-tenths cloud with tops at 10,000 to 12,000 feet, which meant that the planned ground marking would be largely ineffective, and that the least reliable Wanganui (skymarking) method would have to be employed. Crews ran into intense predicted flak and a mass of searchlights as they began their bombing runs, and those from 630 Squadron aimed at red and green TIs and release-point flares from 19,000 to 21,000 feet from around 20.00. The glow of fires was observed beneath the clouds, and a very large explosion lit up the sky at 20.10. The impression was of a successful operation, but an assessment through the clouds was impossible, and it required post-raid reconnaissance and local reports to confirm that this attack on Berlin had been the most effective of the war to date and had caused a swathe of destruction from the city centre through the western residential districts of Tiergarten and Charlottenburg as far as the suburb town of Spandau. A number of firestorm areas were reported, and the catalogue of destruction included three thousand houses and twenty-three industrial premises. Many thousands more sustained varying degrees of damage, costing 175,000 people their homes and an estimated two thousand their lives, and by daylight on the 23rd, the smoke had risen to almost 19,000 feet. Twenty-six aircraft failed to return, eleven Lancasters, ten Halifaxes, and five Stirlings, which amounted to a loss-rate among the types respectively of 2.3%, 4.2% and 10.0%. This provided Harris with the necessary ammunition to banish the Stirling from future operations over Germany in a move that had been decided upon months earlier and compensated for by the proliferation of new Lancaster squadrons, including 550, 576, 625 and 626 Squadrons of 1 Group, which would be entering the fray within days.

A heavy force of 365 Lancasters and ten Halifaxes was made ready with some difficulty on the 23rd for a return to Berlin, back-to-back long-range operations placing a huge strain on those charged with the responsibility of getting the aircraft off the ground. At Ludford Magna, for example, home to 1 Group's 101 Squadron, the armourers were unable to load all nineteen Lancasters with the intended weight of bombs and would have to send them off 2,000lb short. 5 Group detailed 141 Lancasters, of which the ten belonging to 630 Squadron each received a bomb load of a cookie supplemented with thirteen and nine SBCs respectively of 4lb and 30lb incendiaries, before departing East Kirkby between 16.50 and 17.25 with F/L Perrers again the senior pilot on duty. In what became a bad night for the squadron, it lost the services of P/O Don Cheney and crew to W/T failure, despite the wireless operator working for an hour to fix the problem, while the crews of P/Os Piggin and Story were defeated by severe icing that prevented them from climbing to operational height. These were among eighteen "boomerangs" from 5 Group and forty-six from the force as a whole, many of whom might have pressed on in other circumstances had they been fully rested. Another sign of malcontent was the dumping of bombs over the North Sea by crews intending to push on to the target but wanting to gain more height. It involved largely those from 1 Group, who were shedding their cookies in protest at their A-O-C's policy of loading each Lancaster to its maximum all-up weight at the expense of altitude. The slogan "H-E-I-G-H-T spells safety" could be found on the walls of most bomber station briefing rooms at the time.

The target was reached by way of the same route adopted on the previous night and was found to be covered by ten-tenths cloud with tops at between 10,000 and 15,000 feet. Guided by the glow of fires still burning beneath the clouds from the night before, and the presence of red and green TIs, the remaining 630 Squadron crews carried out their attacks from 16,500 to 20,000 feet from around 20.00 and contributed to another stunning blow. Returning crews described a column of smoke reaching 20,000 feet, and the glow of fires on the horizon visible again from the Hannover area some 150 miles from the target. It was on this night that fake broadcasts from England caused annoyance to the night-fighter force by ordering them to land because of fog over their bases, despite which, they still had a major hand in the bringing-down of twenty Lancasters, five of them from 5 Group. Two empty dispersal pans at East Kirkby were evidence that the squadron had suffered its first casualties and the crews of F/L Perrers RNZAF, and P/O Howe were duly posted missing. The former in JB246 had crashed onto a bombing range near Fassberg, located some fifty miles north of Hannover, killing the pilot and four others and delivering the wireless operator and rear gunner into enemy hands, while the latter, JB135, was lost without trace, presumably in the sea. Both were experienced crews, F/L Perrers on his twentieth sortie and P/O Howe on his fifteenth, and they would be missed by the East Kirkby community. Post-raid reconnaissance and local reports confirmed that this operation had added greatly to the previous night's damage and had destroyed a further two thousand buildings and killed around fifteen hundred people.

While 1, 3 and 5 Groups enjoyed a night off on the 25th, 216 Halifaxes of 4 and 6 Groups and forty-six 8 Group Halifaxes and Lancasters carried out an operation against Frankfurt, where the blind markers established a firm H2S fix and delivered yellow TIs and red flares with green stars to coincide with the e.t.a. of the main force crews. Local reports described a modest amount of housing damage and 3,500 people bombed out of their homes, in return for which eleven Halifaxes and a single Lancaster failed to return.

After a three-night rest for most of the Lancaster crews, 443 of them were briefed on the 26th for a return to the "Big City" for the fourth attack on it since the resumption of the campaign. 5 Group detailed 161 Lancasters, ten of them made ready by 630 Squadron, which departed East Kirkby between 17.09 and 17.32 with F/L Patterson the senior pilot on duty and a cookie and eleven and seven SBCs respectively of 4lb and 30lb incendiaries in each bomb bay. A diversionary raid on Stuttgart by a predominantly Halifax force followed the same route as those bound for Berlin, which involved an outward leg across the French coast and Belgium to a point north of Frankfurt, where they separated. An indication of the beneficial effects of the three-day lay-off was a 44% reduction in early returns by 5 Group crews compared with the previous Berlin raid, and all from 630 Squadron pressed on to find Berlin under clear skies. Despite such favourable conditions, the Path Finders overshot the city centre aiming-point by six or seven miles, and marked an area well to the north-west, which happened to contain many war-industry factories. The 5 Group squadrons bombed on red and green TIs those from 630 Squadron from 20,000 to 22,000 feet sometime between 21.15 and 21.30 and left a mass of fires in their wake and thick smoke rising to 15,000 feet. The bomber stream became scattered as it withdrew from the target area, and night-fighters were able to pick up individual Lancasters during the return flight, contributing to the loss of twenty-eight of them, while a further fourteen were written off in crashes in England.

At debriefing, a number of crews commented on a chaotic situation over Beachy Head on the way out, where some sections of the bomber stream were orbiting to shed time, while others were arriving to begin the next leg, all at the same altitude. 57 Squadron posted missing one crew, but 630 Squadron came through unscathed, although all were diverted on return to stations in Yorkshire and F/Sgt Edwards wrote off JB597 when undershooting the runway at Holme-on-Spalding-Moor. Post-raid reconnaissance and local sources confirmed that thirty-eight war-industry factories had been destroyed in Berlin and many others damaged, and the zoo was also hit, killing most of the animals that had not already been evacuated and releasing some of a dangerous nature to roam the streets.

These last three operations against Berlin undoubtedly represented the best phase of the entire campaign, and according to local reports, the total death toll on the ground resulting from them amounted to 4,330 people, while the destruction of 8,700 apartment buildings containing more than 104,500 flats and damage to several times that number robbed 450,000 residents of their homes for varying lengths of time. However, Berlin was not Hamburg, where narrow streets had aided the spread of fire. Berlin was a modern city of concrete and steel with wide thoroughfares and open spaces to create natural firebreaks, and each building destroyed added to these, so that the campaign would become a bitter struggle of ever decreasing returns.

During the course of the month, the squadron took part in four operations and dispatched thirty-nine sorties for the loss of three Lancasters and two crews.

# December 1943

Berlin would continue to be the dominant theme during December, and, as November had ended, so December began. A heavy force of 443 aircraft stood ready to take off in the late afternoon of the 2nd, all but fifteen of them Lancasters, after the main Halifax element had been withdrawn because of fog over their Yorkshire stations. 5 Group contributed 145 Lancasters, of which thirteen represented 630 Squadron, and they departed East Kirkby between 16.12 and 16.43 with F/L Paterson the senior pilot on duty and a cookie and SBCs containing 1,200 x 4lb and 64 x 30lb incendiaries in each bomb bay. After climbing out, they headed for the Lincolnshire coast to rendezvous over the North Sea with the rest of the force for a straight-out-straight-in route across Holland and northern Germany with no feints or diversions. First, however, the crews had to negotiate a towering front of ice-bearing cloud over the North Sea, which would contribute to a 10% rate of early returns, nine of them involving 5 Group crews, including those of 630 Squadron's Sgt Drinkall because of intercom failure, F/Sgt Whyte after losing flying instruments, F/Sgt Homewood for an undisclosed reason and P/O Syme because of excessive fuel consumption after first bombing a flak position at Den Helder. The rest pushed through the challenging conditions to then contend with large numbers of enemy night-fighters that would harass sections of the bomber stream all the way to the target, after the controller had been able correctly to predict it. When the Path Finder spearhead arrived, the blind marker crews' navigators realised that they were mostly south of track after variable winds had thrown them off course and dispersed the bomber stream. They were employing H2S to establish their position at Stendal, but had strayed some fifteen miles south of track and mistakenly used the town of Genthin as their reference for the run-in. The 630 Squadron crews found good visibility and were drawn by release-point flares to the aiming-point, where they encountered a thin layer of two to three-tenths cloud at around 5,000 feet, but up to nine-tenths between 10,000 and 12,000 feet, which the searchlights were unable to pierce. They bombed on skymarkers and red and green TIs, and where possible, ground detail like burning streets, from 20,000 to 21,000 feet either side of 20.30. They reported light flak hosing up to 14,000 feet and observed scattered fires and a number of large explosions, some claiming the glow from the burning city to be visible from 120 miles into the homeward leg.

It was a bad night for the bomber force, which lost forty aircraft, mostly in the target area and on the way home, and for the East Kirkby community, who would mourn the loss of three crews, 630 Squadron's ED777 coming down at Gross Schulzendorf, some twenty miles south of Berlin city centre with no survivors from the crew of P/O Clark. On each station a Committee of Adjustment team would sweep through the affected billets and remove all personal belongings to leave no trace of their former occupants and prepare the accommodation for the arrival of new ones later in the day. The bombing photographs suggested that the raid had been only partially successful, causing useful damage in industrial districts in the west and east, but scattering the main weight of bombs over the southern districts and outlying communities to the south.

Having been spared by the weather from experiencing an effective visitation from the Command in October and exploiting the enemy's expectation that Berlin would be the target again, Leipzig found itself at the end of the red tape on briefing-room wall-maps from County Durham to Cambridgeshire on the 3rd. A force of 527 aircraft was made ready, which included 103 Lancasters of 5 Group, ten of them belonging to 630 Squadron, which departed East Kirkby between 00.11 and 00.38 with no senior pilot on duty. The crews of P/O Cartwright and Sgt Johnson turned back within the first ninety minutes, the former after the failure of the port-outer engine and consequent loss of power to the rear turret, and the latter because of an issue with instruments and rear guns, and they were among seven 5 Group "boomerangs". The rest of the bomber stream headed for Berlin as a feint, passing north of Hannover and Braunschweig with ten-tenths cloud beneath them and an hour's journey to Leipzig still ahead of them. Then, as they turned towards the south-east near Stendal, the Mosquito element continued on to carry out a diversion at the capital, and although night-fighters had already infiltrated the stream at the Dutch coast, the feint was largely effective. However, some combats did take place during this stage of the operation and one involving 630 Squadron's ED920 culminated with a crash on the approach to Stendal with fatal consequences for P/O Syme RAAF and all but the wireless operator, who fell into enemy hands. Shortly afterwards, F/Sgt White's JB561 was engaged by a number of night-fighters, which severely damaged a starboard engine, the hydraulics system, the intercom, the rear turret and both main tyres. The mid-upper gunner claimed a Me210 as probably destroyed, and he and the other members of the crew would be commended in the post-raid report for "putting up a good show". However, the report is ambiguous and cites Berlin as the target, where they may have released their bomb load as an alternative, from 15,000 feet, before turning for home. Unaccountably, having lost intercom contact with the rear turret, which appeared to be swinging naturally as if under control, no crew member checked on the state of its occupant, and it was only after landing that F/Sgt Rossiter was found to be dead. For his airmanship and determination to bring his aircraft and crew home, F/Sgt White would be awarded a coveted DFM and promotion to warrant officer rank.

Meanwhile, the others encountered two layers of ten-tenths cloud in the target area with tops at around 7,000 and 15,000 feet, prompting the Path Finders to mark by H2S with green skymarkers. The remaining six 630 Squadron crews bombed from 19,500 to 21,000 feet, some two thousand feet above the barrage of bursting heavy flak shells, shortly after 04.00, observing explosions and a strong glow beneath the clouds. The emergence through the cloud tops of black smoke suggested that an accurate and concentrated attack had taken place and the smoke and glow remained visible for more than two hundred miles into the return journey south-west towards the French frontier. Had many aircraft not then strayed into the Frankfurt defence zone, the losses may have been fewer, but twenty-four aircraft failed to return, fifteen of them Halifaxes. Local reports confirmed this as a highly successful operation, which had hit residential and industrial areas and was the most destructive raid visited upon this eastern city during the war. Sadly, for the Command, it would take its revenge in time.

Thereafter, minor operations carried the Command through to mid-month, and it was left to Path Finder Mosquitos to maintain the pressure on Germany, by nightly raiding one or more of the Ruhr towns and cities. On the 8th, a WAAF clerk who could type was sent to East Kirkby on attachment from 5 Group to ease the pressure on the beleaguered adjutant, F/L Cheetham. Meanwhile, great demands were being heaped upon 3 Group's highly secret "Moon" squadrons, 138 and 161, which operated out of Tempsford on behalf of the Special Operations Executive (SOE) and the Secret Intelligence Service (SIS) to deliver and collect agents from the Continent and maintain a supply of arms and equipment to the resistance organisations. Harris had little time for SOE matters, which, in his view, drew resources away from the bombing of Germany, and he absolutely would not allow precious Lancasters to be diverted to the cause. However, the resident squadrons now needed to supplement their numbers by importing aircraft and crews from less busy units, which at the moment meant 5 Group's now famous 617 Squadron and the Stirlings of 3 Group, that had been removed from the front line. Somewhat surprisingly, Harris allowed three of the Dams-configured Type 464 Provisioning Lancasters to be lent to Tempsford and on the night of the 10/11th, the former 57 Squadron crew of W/O "Chuffy" Bull and F/O Weeden RCAF and crew were sent on supply drops to France, the former in Bill Townsend's Dams Lancaster, ED886, and the latter in Joe McCarthy's ED825, which had attacked the Sorpe Dam. Harris's worst fears were realized when both fell victim to flak, nine men died, one evaded and four were taken into captivity.

Earlier on the 10th, a new office gadget had been delivered to F/L Cheetham and his growing team in the form of a rotary duplicator, which would have a great impact on efficiency. With a visit by the A-O-C, AVM Sir Ralph Cochrane, due on the 11th, S/L Crocker inspected the No 6 living site and found both the NCO living quarters and officers' ablutions to be most unsatisfactory. Having worked all day at their assigned jobs, two humble aircraft hand/general duties "erks" (ACH/GD) worked through the night to ensure that all was in order by the time that Cochrane arrived for an inspection and lunch. On the 12th, S/L Crocker relinquished command of the squadron and in time would be rewarded for his efforts with a Bar to the

DFC he had earned during his service with 57 Squadron. He was succeeded by W/C John Rollinson, who had served with 614 Squadron in 1938/39, and also as a flight commander and later commanding officer of 38 Squadron on Malta in 1941, and had fifty-two sorties to his credit. He brought with him navigator, S/L Butler DFC** (*=Bar), who was appointed A Flight commander, while S/L Kenneth Vare AFC succeeded F/L Kellaway as B Flight commander, although the latter appointment would be short-lived.

On the 16th, the Lancaster stations were roused and instructed to prepare 483 of the type for that night's operation to Berlin for the sixth time since the resumption of the campaign. 5 Group put up 165 aircraft, eleven of them representing 630 Squadron, which departed East Kirkby between 16.34 and 16.57 with S/L Crocker the senior pilot on duty, accompanied as second pilot by W/C Rollinson, who would only recently have undergone a conversion course on Lancasters. Each Lancaster had been loaded with a cookie and twelve and six SBCs respectively of 4lb and 30lb incendiaries, including a hundred of the X-type 4-pounders, and climbed out over the station, eventually to rendezvous with the rest of the group and ultimately the bomber stream over the North Sea. Sadly, for W/C Rollison, a starboard-outer engine issue ended his interest in proceedings very early into the sortie, and as S/L Crocker turned for home, the others continued on to cross the Dutch coast in the region of Castricum-aan-Zee, and then head due east all the way to the target with no deviations. A three-quarter moon would rise during the long return leg over the Baltic and Denmark, but it was hoped that the very early take-off and the expectation of fog over enemy night-fighter stations would reduce the risk of interception. Night-fighters were sent to meet the bomber stream at the Dutch coast, but no contact was made with 630 Squadron aircraft, which arrived in the target area to find Berlin obscured by ten-tenths cloud with tops at around 5,000 feet, but still identifiable by red and green skymarkers, which were bombed from 18,000 to 21,000 feet sometime after 20.00. *(The 630 Squadron ORB does not record bombing times during this period.)*

The return over Denmark passed largely without major incident, but the greatest difficulties awaited the 1, 6 and 8 Group crews as they arrived in home airspace to find their stations shrouded in a blanket of impenetrable fog, and few, if any, had sufficient reserves of fuel to divert to other areas. The minutes between midnight and 02.00 were filled with frantic searches by exhausted crews to find somewhere to land, and many aircraft came to grief as they stumbled around in the murk. Some flew into the ground, while others collided with obstacles or other aircraft and a few crews opted to take to their parachutes as their fuel ran out. These were generally the fortunate ones as twenty-nine Lancasters and a mine-laying Stirling were lost in these cruelest of circumstances, and around 150 airmen lost their lives when so close to home and safety. To this number was added the twenty-five Lancasters failing to return from the raid, many of which were accounted for by night-fighters while outbound. Returning crews reported the glow of fires, while others saw nothing through the cloud and it was a local report that confirmed a moderately effective raid, which had fallen principally onto central and eastern districts, where housing suffered most.

This was not the only operation to take place during the evening, and one of those of a more minor nature was to have great significance for the future of the Command, 5 Group and the Path Finder Force. Two flying bomb sites in the Pas-de-Calais, at Tilley-le-Haut and

Flixecourt, were attacked by small forces, the former by 3 Group Stirlings, and the latter by nine Lancasters of 617 Squadron under the command of W/C Leonard Cheshire. The marking was carried out by Oboe Mosquitos at both locations, although it was by just a single aircraft at the latter. Neither operation was a success, after the markers missed the aiming points by a few hundred yards, and this demonstrated the shortcomings of the Oboe system. Whilst it was ideal for marking an urban target, where there was a large margin for error, it was too imprecise for use against a small target like a flying bomb site or an individual building. This was precisely the kind of target to which 617 Squadron was to be assigned for the remainder of the war, and it was frustrating for Cheshire and his crews to have plastered the markers, only for the target to escape damage. A similar disappointment would take place at the end of the month at the same flying bomb site, and this set minds working at 617 Squadron.

A three-day stand-down allowed the crews to recover from the Berlin operation and it was the 20th when all stations were notified of an operation that night to Frankfurt, for which a force of 390 Lancasters and 257 Halifaxes was assembled. While the main operation was in progress, forty-four Lancasters and ten Mosquitos of 1 and 8 Groups were to carry out a diversion at Mannheim, some forty miles to the south. 5 Group made ready 168 Lancasters and at East Kirkby the fifteen belonging to 630 Squadron were each loaded with the requisite amount of fuel and a cookie and SBCs of 4lb and 30lb incendiaries before taking off between 16.45 and 17.25 with S/L Crocker the senior pilot on duty, accompanied again by W/C Rollinson as second pilot. F/L Kellaway and crew abandoned their sortie during the climb-out because of an unserviceable rear turret, while the others set course for Southwold and the North Sea-crossing to the Scheldt estuary, before passing north of Antwerp and flying the length of Belgium to the German frontier north of Luxembourg. P/O Cartwright and crew progressed as far as the mouth of the Scheldt with an underperforming port-outer engine, before deciding that it was folly to press on at a lowly 16,500 feet, below the protection of the bomber stream. The German night-fighter controller had picked up transmissions from the bomber stream as soon as it left the English coast and was able to track it all the way to the target and through the "Sahme Sau" Tame Boar running commentary system, vector his fighters into position. Many combats took place during the outward flight and the diversion failed to draw fighters away from the main action.

The problems continued at the primary target, where the forecast clear skies failed to materialise, and the crews were greeted by four to nine-tenths cloud at between 5,000 and 10,000 feet. This allowed some of them to pick out ground features, while others fixed their positions by H2S, if so equipped, and the main force Lancaster crews simply waited for TIs on e.t.a. The Path Finders had prepared a ground-marking plan in expectation of good vertical visibility, and dropped red, green and yellow TIs, while the Germans lit a decoy fire-site five miles to the south-east of the city. Some crews described the marking as late and erratic, and a number from 630 Squadron as sparce as they bombed on red and green TIs from 19,000 to 21,000 feet either side of 19.45. A large explosion was observed in the north-east of the city at 19.47 and black smoke was mushrooming through the cloud tops as they turned away, despite which most crews thought the attack to be scattered in the early stages, becoming more concentrated as it progressed, and many commented on the new cookies detonating with a brighter flash than the old ones. On return, P/O Mackintosh and crew reported two attacks by enemy night-fighters and claimed one of them as damaged.

An analysis concluded that the operation had been moderately successful, and at least one crew reported the glow of fires remaining visible for 150 miles into the return journey. There were also many comments that the diversionary raid on Mannheim appeared to be successful. Any success at Frankfurt was achieved largely as the result of the creep-back from the decoy site, which fell across the suburbs of Offenbach and Sachsenhausen, situated on the southern bank of the River Main. 466 houses were destroyed and more than nineteen hundred seriously damaged, despite which, the operation fell well short of its aims and the loss of forty-one aircraft was a high price to pay. The Halifaxes suffered heavily, losing twenty-seven of their number, a loss-rate of 10.5% compared with the Lancasters' 3.6%.

The Canadian Liaison Officer for the area called in at East Kirkby on the 23rd bearing gifts in the form of Christmas stockings stuffed with packs of cigarettes for RCAF personnel. Just two more operations remained before the year ended and both were to be directed against Germany's capital city, the first posted on that day and involving an all-Lancaster heavy force with seven Halifaxes among the Path Finder element and eight Mosquitos to provide a diversion. The 130 Lancasters of 5 Group included a dozen representing 630 Squadron, each of which was loaded with a cookie and ten and six SBCs respectively of 4lb and 30lb incendiaries before departing East Kirkby between 23.57 and 00.36 with F/L Patterson the senior pilot on duty. The route to the target was somewhat circuitous and took the bomber stream in a south-easterly direction to the Scheldt estuary, before hugging the Belgian/Dutch frontier to cross into Germany south of Aachen, as if threatening Frankfurt. When a point was reached south of Leipzig, the route turned sharply towards the north and Berlin, while the Mosquito feint threatened Leipzig. The vanguard of the bomber stream reached the target to find it enveloped in up to eight-tenths cloud at between 5,000 and 10,000 feet, which might not have been critical had the Path Finders not suffered an unusually high failure rate of their H2S equipment, resulting in scattered and sparse sky-marking. The 630 Squadron crews found red and green skymarker flares at which to aim their bombs, but no details of bombing heights were recorded in the ORB, possibly because F/L Cheetham had gone on leave and Section Officer Vickers had been parachuted in from station HQ to fill the breech, probably without a great deal of training in adjutant duties. The other 5 Group squadrons bombed within a general range of 19,000 to 23,000 feet between 04.00 and 04.15 and observed well-concentrated fires and at least four large explosions, one described as orange and red and lasting for thirty seconds. A relatively modest sixteen Lancasters failed to return, and all but one 57 Squadron Lancaster returned to East Kirkby to observe the fifth wartime Christmas in traditional style. A local report named the south-eastern suburbs of Köpenick and Treptow as the ones to sustain the most damage, with 287 houses and other buildings suffering complete destruction.

Christmas Day dawned foggy and cold, but the conditions could not dampen the high spirits of the NCO aircrew, who relished receiving their festive lunch at the hands of their officer colleagues, and that evening were entertained by them at a dance and cabaret in No 2 dining hall that proved to be a great success.

Festivities over, the "Big City" was posted as the target again on the 29th, for what, for the Lancaster operators, would be the first of three raids upon it in five nights spanning the turn of the year. A force of 712 aircraft included 163 Lancasters of 5 Group, of which fifteen represented 630 Squadron and departed East Kirkby between 16.49 and 17.19 with W/C Rollinson undertaking his first sortie and each crew sitting on a cookie and seven deep SBCs containing 150 x 4lb incendiaries each and seven standard SBCs of the 30lb denomination. It was from this juncture that the intolerable strain on the crews of successive long-range flights in difficult weather conditions began to manifest in some squadrons through the rate of early returns, which on this night reached forty-five or 6.3%. The bomber stream was routed out over the Dutch Frisian islands pointing directly for Leipzig and having reached a point just to the north of that city, was to turn to the north towards Berlin, while Mosquitos carried out spoof raids on Leipzig and Magdeburg. F/Sgt Homewood and crew headed directly for the jettison area after a broken oil pipe rendered the rear turret unserviceable, leaving the rest of the squadron to continue on and reach the target area to find ten-tenths cloud with tops at anywhere between 7,000 and 18,000 feet and heavy flak bursting at up to a lofty 25,000 feet. Red and green Path Finder release-point flares could be seen hanging over the city, at which the 630 Squadron participants aimed their bombs from 19,000 to 22,000 feet shortly after 20.00. At debriefing, crews reported a considerable red glow beneath the clouds, which remained visible for a hundred miles and gave the impression of a concentrated and successful assault. This was not entirely borne out by local reports, which revealed that the main weight of the raid had fallen onto southern and south-eastern districts and also into outlying communities to the east, destroying 388 buildings, although none of significance, and ten thousand people were bombed out of their homes. Eleven Lancasters and nine Halifaxes failed to return, a loss-rate of 2.4% for the former and 3.5% for the latter.

During the course of the month the squadron participated in six operations and dispatched seventy-six sorties for the loss of two Lancasters and their crews and a rear gunner. It had been a testing end to a year which had brought major successes and advances in tactics, but it had also been a year of high losses, particularly among the Stirling and Halifax squadrons. While the introduction of "window" during Operation Gomorrah in July had been an instant success in disrupting enemy night-fighter communications, it had also caused the Luftwaffe to rethink and reorganize, with the result that the night-fighter force emerging from the ruins of the old system was a leaner, more efficient and altogether more lethal beast than that of before. As far as the crews of Bomber Command were concerned, the New Year offered the same fare as the old one, which few would view with relish and the next three months would see morale at its lowest ebb as the winter campaign ground on.

## January 1944

The change of year was not destined to effect a change in the emphasis of operations, and this was, no doubt, a disappointment not only to the hard-pressed crews of Bomber Command but also to the beleaguered residents of Germany's capital city. Proud of their status as Berliners first and Germans second, they were a hardy breed and just like their counterparts in London during the Blitz of 1940, would bear their trials with fortitude and humour and would not buckle under the constant assault from above. "You may break our walls", proclaimed banners in the streets, "but not out hearts", and the most popular song of the day, "Nach jedem Dezember kommt immer ein Mai", "After every December there's always a May", was played endlessly over the airwaves, its sentiments hinting at a change in fortunes with the onset of spring. Harris allowed the Berliners little time to enjoy New Year, and as New Year's Day dawned, plans were already in hand to continue the onslaught. Before it ended, the first of 421 Lancasters, 161 representing 5 Group, would be taking off and heading eastwards to arrive over the city as the clock showed 03.00 hours on the 2nd.

Take-off had actually been delayed because of doubts over the weather, and this meant that insufficient hours of daylight remained to allow the planned outward route over Denmark and the Baltic. Instead, the bomber stream would adopt the previously used almost direct route across Holland and northern Germany, but return as originally planned more circuitously, passing east of Leipzig, before racing across Germany between the Ruhr and Frankfurt and traversing Belgium to reach the Channel near the French port of Boulogne. 630 Squadron's fourteen participants departed East Kirkby between 23.49 and 00.38 with F/Ls English, Macdonald and Paterson the senior pilots on duty and each bomb bay filled with a cookie and ten and six SBCs respectively of 4lb and 30lb incendiaries. Flying as second pilot to F/L Macdonald was the new B Flight commander, S/L Vare. P/O Hegarty and crew had to contend with an engine fire during the climb-out and proceeded directly to the jettison area, while their colleagues pressed on to join the bomber stream, which was gradually depleted by twenty-eight other early returns. The bomber stream had covered the four-hundred-mile leg from the Dutch coast to Berlin in under two hours without once catching a glimpse of the ground through the dense cloud, and it was no different at the target, which was completely obscured by a layer of ten-tenths cloud with tops in places as high as 19,000 feet. The Path Finders had to employ skymarking (Wanganui), which was somewhat scattered, and the 630 Squadron crews aimed for these parachute flares from 20,000 to 21,000 feet from around 03.00. They observed the glow of fires and smoke rising through the cloud tops and a huge explosion was witnessed at 03.07, which lit up the clouds for three seconds, but it was impossible to assess what was happening on the ground. It was established, ultimately, that the operation had been a failure, which had scattered bombs across the southern fringes of the city causing only minor damage, while the main weight of the attack had fallen beyond the city boundaries into wooded and open country. The disappointment was compounded by the loss of twenty-eight Lancasters, a dozen of them belonging to 5 Group, among which was 630 Squadron's JB532, which was hit by flak while homebound and had an engine knocked out of its mounting. The Lancaster dived steeply and crashed some twenty miles south-south-west of Berlin city centre, killing F/L Macdonald DFC RCAF, S/L Vare AFC and the other six occupants.

F/L Kellaway took temporary command of B Flight on the 2nd, and during the course of the day a heavy force of 362 Lancasters and nine of the new Mk III Hercules-powered Halifaxes was made ready for a return to Berlin that night. There was snow on the ground, and many of the crews called to briefing were still tired from being late to bed following the almost-eight-hour round trip the night before, which left a few in a mutinous frame of mind at being on the order of battle again so soon. 5 Group cancelled twenty-five of its intended contribution, leaving 119 to take part, the eleven-strong 630 Squadron element departing East Kirkby between 23.14 and 00.06 with F/Ls English and Paterson the senior pilots on duty and each bomb bay containing the same bomb load as for the previous operation. The outward route crossed the Dutch coast near Castricum and took the bomber stream to a point south-east of Bremen, followed by a dogleg to the north-west and, finally, a ninety degree change of course to the south-east in the Parchim area to leave a ninety-mile run to the target. A massive sixty aircraft returned early, 15.7% of those dispatched, and three of them were from the ranks of 630 Squadron. F/O Probert and crew were defeated by a malfunctioning supercharger that prevented JB710 from climbing beyond 12,000 feet and compelled them to turn back from a position some twenty-five miles east of Lowestoft. At around the same time Sgt Rodbourn and crew abandoned their sortie after losing their starboard-inner engine, while P/O Johnson and crew were among a number to run into an electrical storm and severe icing conditions over Holland. Having lost control of ED758 when some five miles from the German frontier, P/O Johnson ordered the bombs to be jettisoned in order for him to drag the Lancaster out of a steep dive. Others abandoned their sorties because of minor problems that might have seen them carry on had they been fully rested.

The route changes worked well to throw off the night-fighters, but they would congregate in the target area after the controller correctly identified Berlin as the target forty minutes before zero hour. Ten-tenths cloud with tops at 16,000 feet forced the bombing to take place on red skymarkers with green stars or on the glow of fires, the 630 Squadron crews carrying out their attacks from 20,000 to 21,600 feet between 02.45 and 02.59. They reported smoke rising to 20,000 feet as they turned away, but it was not possible to make an accurate assessment of the outcome and the impression was of an effective attack, when in fact, it had been another failure. Bombs had been scattered across the city and destroyed just eighty-two houses for the loss of twenty-seven Lancasters, most of which had fallen victim to night-fighters in the target area.

After three trips to the "Big City" in five nights, it would now be left to the Mosquitos of 8 Group's Mosquito squadrons to disrupt the residents' sleep with cookies until the final third of the month, allowing Harris to turn his attention on the 5$^{th}$ upon the Baltic port-city of Stettin, which had not been attacked in numbers since the previous April and was home among other war-supporting industrial concerns to the Oderwerke A G U-Boot construction yard. It was to be another predominantly Lancaster affair involving 348 of the type accompanied by ten Halifaxes, 5 Group putting up 120 aircraft and 630 Squadron thirteen, each of which received an unusual bomb load of three 1,000-pounders, a single 500-pounder and ten and six SBCs respectively of 4lb and 30lb incendiaries. They departed East Kirkby between 23.39 and 00.29 with F/L Kellaway the senior pilot on duty, and in contrast to the seventeen early returns by 5 Group crews during the last Berlin operation, only one came home early on this night. The bomber stream found itself in thick cloud at cruising altitude, some crews struggling to find a clear lane even when as high as 23,000 feet, but on the plus side, they all benefitted from a Mosquito diversion at Berlin, which kept the night-fighters off the scent. Stettin was found to be partially visible through five-tenths thin cloud with tops at around 10,000 feet, and crews were able to identify some ground features before focusing on H2S-laid flares and green TIs, which the 630 Squadron crews bombed from 19,000 to 22,500 feet shortly before 04.00. They returned home to provide the intelligence section with accounts of a highly accurate and concentrated attack, which seemed to leave the entire city on fire. Fourteen Lancasters and two Halifaxes failed to return, in exchange for which, post-raid reconnaissance and local reports confirmed heavy damage in central and western districts, where 504 houses and twenty industrial buildings had been destroyed, a further 1,148 houses and twenty-nine industrial buildings seriously damaged and eight ships sunk in the harbour.

Following this operation, the crews of the heavy squadrons were rested until mid-month, while the Halifax units would spend three weeks in virtual hibernation apart from isolated mining forays. When briefings finally took place on the 14th, there was doubtless some relief to see the red tape on the wall maps terminate some way short of Berlin. It led, in fact, to Braunschweig (Brunswick), the historic and culturally significant city situated some thirty-five miles to the east of Hannover. It had not been attacked by the Command in numbers before, and on this night, would face a force, which at take-off numbered 496 Lancasters and two Halifaxes. 5 Group supported the operation with 153 Lancasters, of which fifteen represented 630 Squadron and departed East Kirkby between 16.35 and 17.10 with F/Ls English and Kellaway the senior pilots on duty and a cookie and mix of 4lb and 30lb incendiaries in each bomb bay. After climbing out they headed towards Germany's north-western coast, losing P/O Johnson and crew to a hydraulics leak on the way, and were soon met by part of the enemy night-fighter response, which would harass the bomber stream all the way to the target and back. Complete cloud cover at the target, in places up to around 15,000 feet, dictated the use of red skymarkers with green stars, at which the 630 Squadron crews aimed their cookies and incendiaries from 20,000 to 21,000 feet. The enemy fighters scored consistently and accounted for the majority of the thirty-eight missing Lancasters, many of which came down in the Hannover defence zone. The attack almost entirely missed the city, falling mostly onto outlying communities to the south and was reported locally as a light raid. This would be a continuing theme in future attacks up to the autumn, as Braunschweig enjoyed something of a charmed life, leading to a belief among the populace of the surrounding villages that they were being targeted intentionally in an attempt to drive them into the city, before a major operation destroyed it with them in it!

The Path Finders, in particular, had been taking a beating since the turn of the year, with 156 Squadron alone losing fourteen Lancasters and crews in just three operations, four and five on Berlin, and five again on Braunschweig. This was creating something of a crisis in Path Finder manpower, particularly with regard to experienced crews, and a number of sideways postings took place between the squadrons to ensure a leavening of experience in each one. One of the solutions was to take the cream from among the crews emerging from the training units, rather than wait for them to gain experience at a main force squadron.

During another lull in operations, a signal on the 19th confirmed that S/L Crocker, who had now completed his tour, was to be awarded a Bar to his DFC, and that the Danish navigator in F/L Macdonald's crew, F/O Neils Westergaard, was to receive a DFC. At the time, it had not been confirmed by the Red Cross that he and the rest of the crew had lost their lives. It was the 20th when orders were received to prepare for a maximum effort for the next round of the Berlin offensive, and the Halifax squadrons, which had remained largely dormant since late December, were roused from their slumber to allow 264 of them to join 495 Lancasters, while two small Mosquito elements carried out spoof raids on Kiel and Hannover. 5 Group weighed in with 155 Lancasters, fourteen of them made ready by 630 Squadron, and they took off between 16.10 and 17.02 with F/Ls Kellaway and Paterson the senior pilots on duty and a cookie and four and seven SBCs respectively of 4lb and 30lb incendiaries in each bomb bay.

It was a rare pleasure for them to be taking off in daylight, and they circled as they climbed out above East Kirkby before setting course, while observing the dozens of Lancasters rising up into the dusk to join them from the neighbouring stations. They turned their snouts towards the west coast of Schleswig-Holstein at a point opposite Kiel, rendezvousing with the other groups over the North Sea and all the time shedding individual aircraft as a hefty seventy-five crews abandoned their sorties and turned back. The others made landfall over the Nordfriesland coast, before turning to the south-east on a more-or-less direct course for Berlin and soon found themselves being hounded by night-fighters.

The enemy controller had fed a proportion of his resources into the bomber stream east of Hamburg, and they would remain in contact until a point between Leipzig and Hannover on the way home, although, curiously, the 5 Group brigade saw nothing of this. The two Mosquito diversions had been completely ignored by the Luftwaffe controller, who knew well in advance that Berlin was to be the target. The Path Finders arrived over the Müritzsee to the north of Berlin with a sixty-mile run-in to the aiming point, and they found this to be concealed beneath the same ten-tenths cloud that had accompanied them for the entire outward leg. The tops of the cloud lay beneath the bombers at up to 15,000 feet as the main force crews carried out their attacks on red skymarkers with green stars, those from 630 Squadron from 19,500 to 21,200 feet sometime between 19.35 and 19.51. On return, the crews commented on the lack of flak activity over Berlin and reported the glow of large fires under the cloud and smoke rising through the tops. Thirty-five aircraft failed to return, twenty-two of them Halifaxes, which represented an 8.3% casualty rate compared with 2.6% for the Lancasters. 57 Squadron posted missing one crew, but there were no absentees from the 630 Squadron side of East Kirkby, although, tragically, W/O Davies, the mid-upper gunner in the crew of P/O Piggin, was found to be unconscious as a result of oxygen starvation and despite the efforts of other members of the crew, he could not be resuscitated. It took a little time for an assessment of the operation to be made because of continuing cloud over north-eastern Germany, by which time four further raids had been carried out. It seems from local reports that the eastern districts had received the heaviest weight of bombs in an eight-mile stretch from Weissesee in the north to Neukölln in the south, although no details of destruction emerged.

On the following day, the city of Magdeburg was posted to host its first major attack of the war. The city had, in fact, been a regular destination for small forces as far back as the summer of 1940, when the Command targeted a ship lift at the eastern end of the Mittelland Canal at its junction with the River Elbe and the important Bergius-process Braunkohle A G synthetic oil refinery (hydrogenation plant), both located in the same Rothensee district to the north of Magdeburg city centre. Situated some fifty miles from Braunschweig and slightly to the south of east, it was on an increasingly familiar route as far as the enemy night-fighter controllers were concerned, and within easy striking distance of the night-fighter assembly beacons. In an attempt to deceive the enemy, a small-scale diversion was planned eighty miles to the east at Berlin involving twenty-two Lancaster of 5 Group and twelve Mosquitos of 8 Group, and it was for this "spoof" operation that the 630 Squadron crews of F/O Ames and F/Sgt Homewood were briefed, while out on their dispersal pans their Lancasters were being loaded with a cookie and four 1,000-pounders. 5 Group contributed 122 Lancasters to the main event, thirteen of them made ready by 630 Squadron, and they each received a bomb load of a cookie and SBCs of 4lb and 30lb incendiaries, before both elements departed East Kirkby between 19.14 and 20.21 with F/Ls English, Kellaway and Paterson the senior pilots on duty. P/O Hughes lost his artificial horizon during the climb-out and he and his crew took no further part in the operation, leaving the others to fly out over the North Sea to a point some one hundred miles off the west coast of Schleswig-Holstein, before turning to the south-east to pass between Hamburg and Hannover.

Enemy radar was able to detect H2S transmissions during night-flying tests and equipment checks, and the night-fighter controller was, thereby, always aware of an imminent heavy raid. On this night, the night-fighters were able to infiltrate the bomber stream even before the German coast was crossed and the recently introduced "Tame Boar" night-fighter system provided a running commentary on the bomber stream's progress, enabling the fighters to latch onto it and remain in contact. The final turning-point was twenty-five miles north-east of the target, and this was identified both by Path Finder markers and the bombing of twenty-seven main force aircraft. These had been driven by stronger-than-forecast winds to arrive ahead of schedule and contained crews anxious to get the job done and get out of the target area as soon as possible. They bombed using their own H2S without waiting for the TIs to go down, and together with dummy fires, would be blamed by the Path Finders as the reason for their failure to produce concentrated marking.

The conditions over Magdeburg varied according to the time of arrival, the early birds encountering seven to nine-tenths thin cloud at around 6,000 feet, while those turning up towards the end of the raid found the northern half of the city completely clear with cloud over the southern half only. The 630 Squadron crews reported three to nine-tenths cloud, and in the face of fairly modest opposition, bombed on green TIs from 20,000 to 21,000 feet from around 23.00, all gaining the impression that the attack was concentrated around the markers. Returning crews from other groups reported explosions and fires or their glow, and smoke beginning to rise as they turned away. A number reported a flash some twelve minutes after the bombing that lit up the clouds for seven seconds, and two large explosions were witnessed at 23.15. Fires that initially seemed to be scattered, appeared to become more concentrated as the crews headed for home and the impression was of a successful operation. P/O Johnson's DR compass was found to be 7° off, and when a built-up area was spotted beneath them, which the navigator identified by H2S as Erfurt, the bombs were dropped.

While all of this was in progress, the diversionary force arrived at Berlin, some seventy miles away to the north-east, where they encountered a layer of eight to ten-tenths cloud. On return, F/O Ames and crew would report that they had been unable to gain sufficient height and speed to keep up with the Berlin-bound force and had joined in at Magdeburg instead. F/Sgt Homewood and crew failed to return from Berlin in JB294, having crashed in the Berlin defence zone as the sole loss from the "spoof" raid and only the bomb-aimer survived to fall into enemy hands. The 5 Group ORB expressed the opinion that the diversion had succeeded in the early stages in reducing the impact of the Nachtjagd, although this was not borne out by the figures. In the absence of post-raid reconnaissance and a local report, the outcome at Magdeburg was not confirmed and it is generally believed now that most of the bombing fell outside of the city boundaries. A record fifty-seven aircraft failed to return, thirty-five of them Halifaxes, and this provided another alarming statistic of a 15.6% loss-rate compared with 5.2% for Lancasters.

It was a tough time for new crews to embark on a first tour of operations, and among those joining the squadron in January was that of P/O Len Barnes, who arrived from The end of the month would bring the final concerted effort to destroy Berlin and involve three trips to the capital in the space of an unprecedented four nights, a hectic round of operations beginning on the 27th, after five nights of rest since the bruising experience of Magdeburg. It involved an all-Lancaster heavy force of 515 aircraft, of which a record 172 were provided by 5 Group, thirteen of them belonging to 630 Squadron, which took off from East Kirkby into a glorious sunset between 17.34 and 18.00 with the recently arrived and new B Flight commander, S/L Calvert, the senior pilot on duty. Among them was the crew of P/O Barnes undertaking their maiden sortie, and like the others, they were sitting on a bomb load of a cookie and ten and six SBCs respectively of 4lb and 30lb incendiaries. After climbing out and rendezvousing with the rest of the group, they set course on a complex route that would take the bomber stream towards the north German coast, before swinging to the south-east to enter enemy territory over the Frisians and northern Holland. Having then feinted towards central Germany, suggesting Leipzig as the target, the force was to turn north-east to a point west of Berlin, from where the final run-in would commence. The long return route passed to the west of Leipzig before turning due east to miss Frankfurt on its northern side and traverse Belgium to gain the Channel south of Boulogne. F/O Weller and crew turned back within the first hour for an undisclosed reason, leaving the others to press on towards the target, while a mining diversion off Heligoland and the dispensing of dummy fighter flares and route-markers partially succeeded in reducing the numbers of enemy night-fighters making contact.

It was, therefore, a relatively intact bomber force that approached the target over ten-tenths cloud with tops at 15,000 feet, the Path Finders employing sky-marking in the form of red Wanganui flares with green stars, which were driven by a strong tail wind across the city along the line of approach. They drew on the 630 Squadron crews to the aiming point, where they bombed from 19,500 to 21,000 feet from around 20.30, and later, at debriefing, reported the glow of fires and the appearance of a successful raid, but no detailed assessment. Of course, not all would make it back to tell their stories at debriefing, and thirty-three Lancaster dispersal pans stood empty in dawn's early light, one of them belonging to 57 Squadron. Reports from Berlin described bombs falling over a wide area, more so in the south than the north, and damage to fifty industrial premises, a number of them engaged in important war work, while twenty thousand people were bombed out of their homes. A feature of the campaign was the number of outlying communities suffering collateral damage, and on this night sixty-one such hamlets recorded bombs falling.

The early time-on-target had allowed crews to get a full night in bed and they were, hopefully, fully rested by the time that news came through on the 28th that many of them would be returning to the "Big City" that night. A heavy force of 673 aircraft was assembled, of which 432 were Lancasters and 241 Halifaxes, 155 of the former provided by 5 Group, eleven of them by 630 Squadron. They departed East Kirkby between 23.45 and 00.45 with W/C Rollinson the senior pilot on duty and a cookie and the usual mix of 4lb and 30lb incendiaries in each bomb bay. After climbing out they adopted a route out over southern Denmark before turning south-east on a direct course for the target, with an almost reciprocal return and various diversionary measures to distract the night-fighter controller. Among the diversions was a raid on Berlin by six Mosquitos four hours before the main attack, a round trip of less than four hours for the "Wooden Wonder", and at least one 627 Squadron crew was back at Oakington in time to wish his heavy-weight 7 Squadron counterparts a good flight. Sixty-six crews turned back early, suggesting some adverse reaction to the back-to-back operations, and those reaching the target area encountered ten-tenths cloud and a mixture of sky and ground-marking to aim at. The 630 Squadron crews delivered their bombs on red and green release-point flares from 20,000 to 21,500 feet from around 03.10, while F/L Kellaway and crew bombed nine minutes after the attack was due to finish, by which time the markers had long-since burned out and the bombs were aimed at huge fires after an H2S-fix. Some crews reported huge explosions at 03.15, 03.18 and 03.25, the second-mentioned one described by a 10 Squadron crew as lighting up the sky over a radius of fifty miles. Forty-six aircraft failed to return, twenty-six of them Halifaxes as the defenders fought back to exact another heavy toll of bombers, and there were three empty dispersal pans at East Kirkby. Two should have been occupied by 630 Squadron aircraft, one of them, JB666, having been brought down in the target area with no survivors from the crew of W/C Rollinson, who was on his fifty-seventh sortie, while JB654 disappeared without trace with the crew of P/O Story RAAF. The impression gained from returning crews at debriefing was of a concentrated and effective attack, and this was partly borne-out by local reports of heavy damage in western and southern districts, where 180,000 people were bombed out of their homes. However, as had been the pattern throughout the campaign against Berlin, seventy-seven outlying communities had also been afflicted.

After a night's rest a force of 534 aircraft was made ready on the 30th for the final operation of this concerted effort against Berlin. 5 Group offered 156 Lancasters, of which nine belonged to 630 squadron and departed East Kirkby between 17.02 and 17.47 with F/Ls Armour, English, Paterson, Probert and Roberts the senior pilots on duty and a cookie and twelve-and-a-third SBCs of 4lb incendiaries and eight of 30lbs in each bomb bay. This was sortie number two for the Barnes crew, and after they had climbed out over the station, they joined with the rest of the squadron and group, before rendezvousing with the bomber stream to follow a route similar to that adopted two nights earlier. Some ninety minutes into the flight, the navigator in P/O Hughes' crew, F/O Brake, realised that they were lurching on and off track, and unable to obtain a coherent response from the pilot, alerted the flight engineer, who changed the oxygen supply. The pilot complained of feeling unwell and F/O Brake took it upon himself to have the bomb load jettisoned and to return to base. The bomber stream remained relatively free of harassment and on reaching the target the main force element was greeted by ten-tenths cloud at around 8,000 feet and the sight of Path Finder skymarking in progress. The 630 Squadron crews bombed on these from 19,500 to 21,000 feet either side of 20.30, and all commented on the smoke rising through 12,000 feet and the glow of fires beneath the cloud, which, according to some, was still visible from a hundred miles into the return flight. Thirty-two Lancasters and a single Halifax failed to make it home, among them eleven belonging to 5 Group. In return for these significant losses and according to local sources, central and south-western districts suffered heavy damage with serious areas of fire, while other parts of the city were also hit, many bomb loads were again scattered liberally onto outlying communities and at least a thousand people lost their lives. As a result of these three operations at the end of January, 112 heavy bombers and their crews had been lost to the Command and with the introduction of the enemy's highly efficient Tame Boar night-fighter system based on running commentaries, the advantage had swung back in the defenders' favour.

Two further heavy raids would be directed at Berlin before the end of the winter offensive, one in February and the other in March, but they would be almost in isolation. There is no question that Germany's capital had been sorely afflicted by the three latest operations, but it remained a functioning city and showed no signs of imminent collapse. During the course of the month, the squadron took part in ten operations and dispatched 115 sorties for the loss of four aircraft and crews and a gunner, a casualty rate of 3.5%.

# February 1944

A signal was received at East Kirkby on the 1st announcing that twenty-nine-year-old South African, W/C William "Bill" Deas DFC*, would be arriving soon to assume command of the squadron. Bill Deas had sailed to England shortly after the outbreak of war and was commissioned in the RAF in October 1939. After training he completed two tours with 61 Squadron, the first on Hampdens in 1941 and the second on Lancasters and was a highly respected and popular officer.

Bad weather and the start of the "moon" period during the first two weeks of February prevented Harris from mounting further attacks on Berlin and allowed the crews to draw breath and the squadrons to replenish. This meant that the time would be filled by endless lectures, training when the conditions allowed and minor and mining operations for a few, the former by 8 Group Mosquitos roaming far and wide from the Ruhr to Berlin. Aircrew detested long lay-offs and welcomed the distraction of a concert given by the Woodhall Spa Concert Party on the 5th, the day on which W/C Deas arrived at East Kirkby. A full parade was held on the 8th, which involved the Hoisting of the Colours, otherwise it was a round of lectures in the mornings, P/T and flying training in the afternoons and occasional evasion exercises at night. There was a flurry of excitement on the 13th when a briefing was held, only for hopes to be dashed when the operation was scrubbed forty-five minutes before take-off.

During the lull, on the night of the 8/9th, 617 Squadron carried out an operation of great significance against the Gnome & Rhone aero-engine factory at Limoges in west-central France. The marking was carried out by W/C Cheshire in a Lancaster at very low level, after making a number of passes across the site to warn the workers. Eleven other Lancasters from the squadron then bombed the target with great accuracy from medium level, and the operation was an outstanding success that demonstrated the potential of the low-level visual marking method, and ultimately, would secure virtual independence for 5 Group.

When the Path Finder and main force squadrons next took to the air, finally, it would be for a record-breaking effort to Berlin on the 15th and would also be the penultimate operation of the campaign, and indeed of the war, by Bomber Command's heavy brigade against Germany's capital city. The force of 891 aircraft represented the largest non-1,000 force to date, and, therefore, the greatest-ever to be sent against the "Big City", and it would be the first time that more than five hundred Lancasters and three hundred Halifaxes had operated together. 5 Group surpassed its previous best effort by fifty Lancasters when putting 226 of them into the air, twenty-one of them representing 630 Squadron. In the event, 630 Squadron had only nineteen crews available and drafted in one each from 61 and 619 Squadrons to facilitate a maximum effort. The bomb bays of this huge armada would convey to Berlin the greatest-ever tonnage of bombs to any target to date, and 630 Squadron's contribution would be a cookie and ten and six SBCs respectively of 4lb and 30lb incendiaries in each bomb bay. They departed East Kirkby between 16.50 and 17.40 with W/C Deas the senior pilot on duty, and displaying excellent leadership by putting himself on the order of battle at the earliest opportunity for a challenging operation. The Barnes crew, on operation number three, tucked themselves into the East Kirkby contingent and after joining up with the rest of the 5 Group squadrons, set course for the western coast of Denmark, before crossing southern Jutland and entering Germany via the Baltic coast between Rostock and Stralsund on a direct heading for the target. The return route would require the bombers to pass south of Hannover and Bremen and cross Holland to the North Sea via Castricum, and it was hoped that the extensive diversionary measures, including a mining operation in Kiel Bay ahead of the arrival of the bombers, a raid on Frankfurt-an-Oder to the east of Berlin by a small force of 8 Group Lancasters and Oboe Mosquitos attacking five night-fighter airfields in Holland, might persuade the enemy night-fighter force to become thinly-spread.

The force was depleted by seventy-five early returns during the outward flight and among those turning back was 630 Squadron's F/L Probert and crew, who lost the intercom connection to the rear turret early on and proceeded to the jettison area. The night-fighter controller observed the progress of the bomber stream but held his response back until it crossed Denmark's Baltic coast a little north of Flensburg, prompting the now familiar running battle, thereafter, all the way to the target, and around twenty aircraft in the rear half of the stream were brought down. The H2S ground-mapping radar, which had been the preserve of Path Finder heavy aircraft, was now being rolled out across the main force, and 630 Squadron was among those equipped with the device, which enabled its crews to "see" through the ten-tenths cloud greeting them at around 10,000 feet over the target and confirm their positions, while the others relied on the Path Finders' red release-point flares with green stars and red and green TIs on the ground. The 630 Squadron crews carried out their attacks from 20,000 to 23,800 feet, and on return reported the markers to be highly effective and well-concentrated. The burgeoning glow beneath the clouds convinced them that they had taken part in a successful operation, which they learned later had been gained at a cost of forty-three aircraft, made up of twenty-six Lancasters (4.6%) and seventeen Halifaxes (5.4%). Perhaps slightly disturbing was the fact that eight of the missing Halifaxes were Mk IIIs, only one fewer than the nine now obsolete Mk II/Vs.

Three Lancasters failed to return to East Kirkby, one belonging to 57 Squadron and another, 630 Squadron's JB665, having crashed near Güstrow, some thirty miles south of the Baltic coast at Rostock, with fatal consequences for F/L English and the other seven occupants. The other 630 Squadron casualty was ED655, which was attempting to land in the hands of P/O Roberts RAAF of 619 Squadron when it was wrecked in a crash near Old Bolingbroke, three miles from Spilsby, fortunately without fatalities among the occupants. Post-raid reconnaissance and local sources confirmed that the 2,642 tons of bombs dropped in the Berlin area had caused extensive damage in central and south-western districts, destroying a thousand houses and more than five hundred temporary wooden barracks, but had also spilled out into surrounding communities. In addition, the important Siemens & Halske and Siemens-Schuckert electronics factories in the Siemensstadt district sustained damaged, as did possibly, the nearby sub-camp of the infamous Sachsenhausen concentration camp, which was occupied largely by Hungarian Jews.

Briefings took place on the 16th, 17th and 18th and preparations were at the advanced stage when scrubs came through on each occasion, a frustrating experience for all involved after the effort expended and the pre-operational tensions created. Further orders were received on stations across the Command on the 19th to prepare for another major assault that night, this time on Leipzig, where four Messerschmitt aircraft factories were the principal targets. The heavy squadrons were able offer 816 aircraft, 561 Lancasters and 255 Halifaxes, 5 Group contributing 209 of the Lancasters and 630 Squadron seventeen, which was actually nineteen at start-up, only for one to become bogged down while taxying and obstruct the path of another. They departed East Kirkby between 23.29 and 00.26 with W/C Deas the senior pilot on duty, bomb loads of a cookie, 950 x 4lb incendiaries, 100 x Type X 4lb incendiaries and six deep SBCs of 30lb incendiaries and the Barnes crew undertaking sortie number four. After climbing out over the station, they joined up with the others heading for the Dutch coast near Groningen, where a proportion of the Luftwaffe Nachtjagd was waiting for them, while others had been drawn away by a mining diversion off Kiel. P/O Barnes and crew were around an hour out over the North Sea when the air-speed-indicator (a.s.i) failed, forcing them to turn back along a number of others from 5 Group, a crew from 49 Squadron describing a chaotic scene over the North Sea, with aircraft flying in every direction, the wiser crews with their navigation lights on, but most without and three aircraft were seen to explode, possibly as a result of collision. The bomber stream continued on to pass south of Bremen and north of Hannover on a south-easterly course, parts of it to become embroiled in a running battle with night-fighters all the way into eastern Germany.

Inaccurately forecast winds caused some aircraft to reach the target early, forcing them to orbit while they waited for the Path Finders to arrive, and the local flak batteries accounted for around twenty of these, while four others were lost through collisions. The 630 Squadron crews arrived to find ten-tenths cloud with tops at around 10,000 feet and bombed on green Wanganui flares and red and green TIs from 21,000 to 23,000 feet either side of 04.00. It seems that there was a brief period during the attack when skymarking stopped and led to some scattering of bombs, but the marker-flares were soon replenished with the arrival of more backers-up and a considerable glow beneath the cloud remained visible for some fifty minutes into the return journey, giving the impression of a successful assault. When all of those aircraft returning home had been accounted for, there was a massive shortfall of seventy-eight, a record loss by a clear twenty-one aircraft. Forty-four Lancasters and thirty-four Halifaxes had failed to return, with a loss-rate of 7.8% and 13.3% respectively, and of the three absentees from East Kirkby, two belonged to 630 Squadron. JB710 was lost without trace with the experienced crew of F/L Armour, while P/O Yates DFC and four of his crew found final resting places in the Berlin War Cemetery, suggesting that ND532 was probably brought down during the outward flight, delivering the flight engineer and bomb-aimer into enemy hands as the only survivors. The losses prompted Harris immediately to withdraw the Merlin-powered Mk II and V Halifaxes from further operations over Germany, which at a stroke, removed a proportion of 4 and 6 Groups' fire-power from the front line until they could be re-equipped with the Mk III. In the meantime, the Mk II and V operators would focus their energies for the remainder of the month on gardening duties.

Despite this depletion of available numbers, a force of 598 aircraft was made ready on the 20th for an operation that night against Stuttgart, which would be the first of three against the city over a three-week period. 5 Group contributed 176 Lancasters, the fourteen belonging to 630 Squadron lining up at East Kirkby with five pilots of flight lieutenant rank leading the way, B Flight commander, S/L Butler navigating for P/O Hughes and each Lancaster carrying the same bomb load as for the previous operation. ND563 was the first to roll with the debutant crew of P/O Murray on board and was observed by flying control to have covered three-quarters of the length of the main runway before appearing to swing out of control to port, and a second witness suggested that it had actually left the ground. The Lancaster crashed through the boundary fence, crossed the Stickney Road, ripping off its undercarriage, and the bomb load went up, killing all but the rear gunner, who escaped with just minor injuries after his turret became detached. As P/O Rogers climbed through 600 feet his port-outer engine burst into flames, always a challenging situation for any pilot with a fully loaded Lancaster straining for flying speed, but he made it to the North Sea to dump the bombs before landing safely. The others were all safely airborne by 00.25, before rendezvousing with the Bomber stream as it headed south to cross the Channel and make landfall over the French coast, from where the cloud would remain at ten-tenths with tops at 8,000 feet all the way into southern Germany. A North Sea sweep and a diversionary raid on Munich two hours ahead of the main activity had caused the Luftwaffe to deploy its forces early, and this allowed the bomber stream to push on unmolested to the target, where the cloud had thinned to five to eight-tenths at around 6,000 feet and the excellent visibility enabled the crews to draw a bead on the Path Finder red and green sky-markers and similar-coloured TIs on the ground. The 630 Squadron crews confirmed their positions by H2S and carried out their attacks on red TIs and red and green skymarkers from 21,000 to 23,000 feet either side of 04.00, and on return reported many large fires and the glow from the burning city visible on the horizon from 250 miles into the return flight. Despite some scattering of bombs, local reports described central districts and those in a quadrant from north-west to north-east suffering extensive damage, and a Bosch factory was one of the important war industry concerns to be hard-hit. In contrast to twenty-four hours earlier, a modest nine aircraft failed to return, but among them was 630 Squadron's ND338, which crashed some fifteen miles south-west of Karlsruhe and within sight of the French frontier. There was just one survivor from the crew of P/O Mackintosh RAAF, the wireless operator, Sgt Newson, who was taken into captivity.

An official enquiry into the loss of ND563 and the crew of P/O Murray was convened on the 23rd under the presidency of W/C Bowes, the 44 (Rhodesia) Squadron commanding officer. The panel was told that remarkably little peripheral damage had occurred at the scene of the crash, but that glass had been broken as far away as Skegness and Boston. Funerals were held in cemeteries at Cambridge and Harrogate on the 24th and attended by representatives of the squadron.

In an attempt to reduce the prohibitive losses of recent weeks, a new tactic was introduced for the next two operations. A force of 734 aircraft was assembled later on the 24th for an operation to the centre of Germany's ball-bearing production, Schweinfurt, situated some sixty miles to the east of Frankfurt in south-central Germany. The largest of its four factories was Kugelfischer-Georg-Schäfer and together with the others, Fichtel & Sachs, Vereinigte Kugellagerfabriken A G and Deutsche Star GmbH, were responsible for 50% of Germany's total ball-bearing output. The Americans had attacked it famously in daylight in mid-August 1943 and suffered catastrophic casualties on the same day that Bomber Command went to Peenemünde, and when they returned in October they lost equally heavily. They caused significant damage on both occasions, but the loss of production was temporary and further attacks were required. The 5 Group A-O-C, AVM Cochrane attended the East Kirkby briefing at which crews were informed that 392 aircraft would depart their stations between 18.00 and 19.00, to be followed into the air two hours later by 342 others in the hope of catching the night-fighters on the ground refuelling and re-arming as the second wave passed through. While this operation was in progress, extensive diversionary measures were to be carried out involving more than three hundred other aircraft, including 179 from the training units conducting a North Sea sweep and 110 Halifaxes and Stirlings mining in northern waters.

5 Group contributed 204 Lancasters, of which sixteen were made ready by 630 Squadron, all assigned to the second phase. According to the 57 Squadron ORB, its Lancasters were flown over to Dunholme Lodge for bombing up, leaving the 630 Squadron element to depart East Kirkby between 20.12 and 20.45 with S/L Calvert the senior pilot on duty and S/L Butler navigating for P/O Hughes. Ten of the Lancasters were carrying a cookie and ten and seven SBCs respectively of 4lb and 30lb incendiaries, while six other bomb bays contained four 2,000-pounders and one 1,000-pounder, but not all would reach the target as four crews turned back early. F/L Weller and crew were passing over Beachy Head when the rear gunner was struck down by suspected appendicitis, and they were the first to land at base at 23.13. P/O Allen's wireless operator was unable to pick up any 5 Group broadcasts and they were back at home by 23.52, to be followed fifteen minutes later by F/L Roberts and crew, who lost their starboard-inner engine at the French coast. Finally, P/O Kilgour and crew completed the "boomerangs" at 01.04, also after the failure of their starboard-inner engine. The first phase bombers reached the target to find between zero and three-tenths cloud at 3,000 to 4,000 feet, with haze spoiling the vertical visibility to an extent, but identified the aiming point by red and green TIs and already established fires towards the south-western edge of the town. Two columns of black smoke were observed to be rising through 5,000 feet as they turned away, and the consensus was of an effective, if, somewhat scattered attack.

Meanwhile, the second phase crews were well on their way and picked up the glow of fires from the earlier raid at a distance of two hundred miles. The visibility in the target area remained good, despite the rising smoke, and bombing by the 630 Squadron crews took place out of almost cloudless skies onto red and green TIs from 20,000 to 23,000 feet from around 01.00. All indications suggested an effective raid, but a post-raid analysis revealed that both phases of the operation had suffered from undershooting after some Path Finder backers-up had failed to press on to the aiming point. In that regard, it was a disappointing night, but an interesting feature was the loss of 50% fewer aircraft from the second wave in comparison with the first in an overall casualty figure of thirty-three, and this suggested some merit in the tactic. Since the turn of the year, a wind-finder system had been in use, which employed selected crews to monitor wind speed and direction and pass their findings back to HQ, where the figures were collated and any changes from the briefed conditions re-broadcast to the bomber stream. This had been found to be extremely useful, but as would be discovered in the ensuing weeks, the system had its limitations.

The main operation on the following night was directed at the beautiful and culturally significant southern city of Augsburg, situated around thirty miles north-west of Munich, which was home to a major Maschinenfabrik Augsburg Nuremberg (M.A.N) factory, which was the largest producer of diesel engines for U-Boots and had been the target for an epic low-level daylight raid by 44 and 97 Squadrons in April 1942. It was also the site of the Messerschmitt aircraft company HQ and a factory drawing slave labour from a nearby sub-camp of the Dachau concentration camp, and large barracks accommodated three Wehrmacht regiments, including one armoured unit. On this night, 594 aircraft were divided into two waves, and among them were 164 Lancasters of 5 Group, including fourteen representing 630 Squadron, thirteen of them assigned to the first phase and just one to the second. They departed East Kirkby between 17.58 and 18.38 with F/Ls Ames, Probert, Roberts and Weller the senior pilots on duty, and the standard cookie and incendiary mix in each bomb bay, and for the second operation running, F/L Weller and crew were forced to turn back early after a hydraulics pipe burst in the rear turret and saturated the occupant. An attempt was made to rectify the problem so that they could take part in phase two, along with P/O Hill and crew, who took off at 21.59, but unaccountably no replacement clothing could be located for the rear gunner and their participation was scrubbed. P/O Johnson and crew returned after two hours, also because of rear turret issues, and F/L Roberts and crew bombed the docks at Dieppe as a last resort target after the starboard-inner engine surged and cut intermittently and caused severe vibration.

The first wave bomber stream flew out over Belgium with ten-tenths cloud beneath them, but that had dissipated by the time the target drew near, and on arrival it was possible for crews to gain a visual reference, particularly on the confluence of the Rivers Lech and Wertach. The Path Finders' red and green TIs were in the bomb sights as the 630 Squadron crews carried out their attacks from 20,000 to 21,000 feet roughly between 22.40 and 22.50, and fires were beginning to take hold as they turned away. The second wave crews were drawn on by the glow in the sky from a hundred miles away and arrived to find visibility still good despite copious amounts of smoke rising through 10,000 feet. P/O Hill and crew carried out their attack from 20,000 feet at around 01.15 aiming at existing fires and red and green Wanganui flares and TIs, and landed back at East Kirkby after three minutes short of seven hours in the air. The loss of twenty-one aircraft seemed to confirm the benefits of splitting the forces, and this tactic would remain an important part of Bomber Command planning for the remainder of the war. It had been a devastatingly destructive operation, in which all facets of the plan had come together in near perfect harmony, spelling disaster for this lightly defended historical treasure trove. Its heart was torn out by blast and fire that destroyed almost three thousand houses, some 25% of the city's living accommodation, along with buildings of outstanding historical significance, and centuries of irreplaceable culture was lost forever. There was also some industrial damage, and around ninety-thousand people were bombed out of their homes.

During the course of the month the squadron took part in five operations and dispatched eighty-two sorties for the loss of six Lancasters, four complete crews and six members of another.

# March 1944

March would bring an end to the winter campaign, but a long and bitter month would have to be endured first before any respite came from long-range forays into northern, eastern and southern Germany. Despite the existence of a typewriter, the 630 Squadron Form 540 was still handwritten, while the 541 was typed, and one wonders if two scribes were involved, one typewriter literate and the other not. The crews had enjoyed a few nights off when the second raid of the series on Stuttgart was posted on the 1st, for which a force of 557 aircraft was made ready. This number included 178 Lancasters representing 5 Group, fourteen of which were provided by 630 Squadron and dispatched from East Kirkby without incident between 23.36 and 23.34 with W/C Deas and S/L Calvert the senior pilots on duty. The bomb loads were divided equally between a cookie and mix of incendiaries and four 2,000-pounders supplemented with a 1,000-pounder and one of 500lbs. They flew out over ten-tenths cloud with tops at between 12,000 and 17,000 feet and must have run into icing conditions, as P/O Allen and crew returned after three hours blaming a frozen a.s.i for curtailment of their sortie. The others encountered similar conditions in the target area, where the Path Finders employed a combination of sky and ground-marking, which became scattered and caused the bombing to be directed between two main concentrations, the 630 Squadron crews carrying out their attacks on Wanganui red markers with green stars from 20,000 to 23,000 feet between 03.00 and 03.20. It was not possible to assess the accuracy of the attack, although a column of smoke had reached 25,000 feet by the end of the raid and large fires were evident from the glow in the sky visible on the horizon from up to 150 miles away. The presence of thick cloud all the way there and back made conditions difficult for enemy night-fighters and a remarkably modest four aircraft failed to return. Among three missing Lancasters was 630 Squadron's ND561, which crashed in southern Germany with no survivors from the crew of P/O Piggin. They had been part of 57 Squadron's B Flight that became the nucleus of 630 Squadron, and before the move, had actually been posted to 617 Squadron on the 3rd of October 1943, only to be sent back ten days later. It was eventually established that the raid had been an outstanding success, which caused extensive damage in central, western and northern districts, where a number of important war-industry factories, including those belonging to Bosch and Daimler-Benz, had sustained damage.

At the end of the first week, the Halifax brigade, particularly those withdrawn from operations over Germany, fired the opening salvoes of the pre-invasion campaign, the purpose of which was to dismantle by bombing thirty-seven railway centres in France, Belgium and western Germany. It began on the night of the 6/7th at Trappes marshalling yards, situated some ten miles west-south-west of Paris and continued at Le Mans in north-western France on the following night. For most of the heavy crews, however, there was no employment following Stuttgart, until a return there in mid-month, but in the meantime, matters were afoot at 5 Group, and had been ever since the frustrating series of operations against flying bomb launching sites conducted by 617 Squadron since December had failed to achieve the desired results. The problem had been an inability to put markers right on the aiming point, which was vital to destroy small, precision targets, and Oboe was just not precise enough. W/C Cheshire and S/L Martin experimented with a dive-bombing technique, which had proved to be successful but impracticable in a Lancaster and Cheshire had borrowed a Mosquito for further trials. These were so promising, that the 5 Group A-O-C, AVM Cochrane, authorized a number of operations by the squadron against factory targets in France, before taking the idea to Harris. Harris approved, paving the way for 5 Group to become effectively independent of the main bomber force and begin larger-scale trials.

Orders were received on the 53 Base stations at Bardney, Skellingthorpe and Waddington on the 9th to prepare eleven Lancasters each for a 5 Group attack that night against the Lioré et Olivier aircraft factory at Marignane, situated a few miles to the north of Marseilles in southern France. The area had been the main pre-war hub for commercial flying boat operations, particularly for the Pan American Clipper Class flights, and the factory had been engaged in the manufacture of the LeO 45 twin-engine medium bomber for the French Air Force. They took off in mid-evening with a round-trip ahead of them of some 1,350 miles if they flew direct, and arrived in the target area under clear skies and bright moonlight, which facilitated an easy identification of the factory buildings marked by red spotfires. The bombing was carried out from medium level either side of 01.30, and the high-explosives were seen to fall among the buildings, while the incendiaries appeared to be a little scattered. A large explosion was witnessed at 01.24 and a huge pall of smoke was rising through 6,000 feet as the force turned away. All arrived home safely, most having spent more than nine hours aloft.

5 Group's 54 Base, consisting of the stations at Coningsby, Woodhall Spa and Metheringham, and Base East Kirkby, which on the 15th of April would add Spilsby and later Strubby to become 55 Base, received orders on the 10th to prepare 102 Lancasters to form four small forces, each to attack a specific factory in France that night. The targets were the Michelin tyre factory at Clermont-Ferrand, the Bloch aircraft factory at Châteauroux, which was the first to be set up by the famed designer, Marcel Dassault, in 1935, the Morane Saulnier aircraft plant at Ossun, just north of the Pyrenese and the Ricamerie needle-bearing works at St-Etienne, the last-mentioned, the objective for sixteen Lancasters from 617 Squadron. Thirty-three Lancasters from 57, 207 and 630 Squadrons were assigned to the Michelin factory, 630 Squadron briefing eleven of its most experienced crews including W/C Deas and S/L Calvert and the former was appointed raid leader and Master Bomber with the experienced S/L Butler providing the navigation. His Lancaster's payload consisted of a red spotfire, three bundles of 4.5 reconnaissance flares and 168 x 30lb incendiaries, while the others were carrying either a cookie and seven 1,000-pounders or eleven 1,000-pounders as they departed East Kirkby between 19.32 and 20.12 and joined up with the other squadrons as they headed south to begin the Channel crossing over the Dorset coast. They arrived in the target area to find patches of cloud with a base at around 10,000 feet, through which bright moonlight filtered, and aimed at the red spotfires, which had landed a hundred and four hundred yards to the south-west of the aiming point. The spotfires were plastered by the main force crews, those from 630 Squadron attacking from 6,000 (S/L Calvert) to 11,000 feet between 23.15 and 23.30 in accordance with the Master Bomber's instructions and observing many explosions among buildings. The factory complex was defended by a small amount of light flak, and it was this that accounted for the only casualty from the four raids, 207 Squadron's S/L Pike MiD and his seven-man crew, who all lost their lives. At the East Kirkby and Spilsby debriefings the consensus was that if the Spotfires had been accurate, then the

factory had been obliterated, and this appears to have been the case, as it was at the other locations.

A second attack by 4 and 6 Groups on the Le Mans yards took place on the night of the 13/14th, and this time fifteen locomotives and eight hundred wagons were destroyed, while collateral damage was inflicted upon two nearby factories. The moon period began at this time, and the wet misty conditions proved to be ideal for tidying up and the planting of garden areas around the crew rooms and offices.

Liberation from horticultural toil came with a tannoy call to briefing on the 15th, when the details for the third and final raid of the series on Stuttgart were presented to the assembled throng. Now that the Mk III Halifax was becoming available in larger numbers, the Command was quickly returning to full strength, which enabled a force of 863 aircraft to be assembled, among them 206 Lancasters provided by 5 Group. The twenty representing 630 Squadron departed East Kirkby between 18.57 and 19.33 with S/L Calvert the senior pilot on duty and a bomb load in each Lancaster of either two 1,000-pounders and the usual mix of 4lb, 4lb X-Type and 30lb incendiaries or a cookie and incendiaries. They rendezvoused with the rest of the force as they passed over Reading on their way to the south coast, and an elongated bomber stream crossed the French coast at 20,000 feet over broken cloud with clear conditions above. It maintained a course parallel with the frontiers of Belgium, Luxembourg and Germany as if heading for Switzerland, and it is believed that 630 Squadron's ND583 was lost at this point, crashing and exploding with great force some fifteen miles north-west of Soissons in the Aisne region of north-eastern France with no survivors from the crew of P/O Rodbourn.

The bomber stream crossed the German border between Strasbourg and Freiburg, before turning towards the north-east for the run-in to the target and it was during this final leg that the night-fighters managed to infiltrate a section of the stream in numbers and score heavily. Adverse winds were responsible for the Path Finders arriving up to six minutes late to open the attack, when they employed both sky and ground-markers in the face of seven to ten-tenths cloud at between 8,000 and 15,000 feet. The Wanganui flares drifted in the wind, marking an area to the north-east of the River Neckar, while the TIs landed far apart in the north and south of the city, the 630 Squadron crews bombing on whatever markers presented themselves, mostly red TIs, from 20,000 to 23,000 feet either side of 23.15. They observed a spread of fires, including two large ones ten miles apart and smoke rising to bombing altitude, which suggested a partially successful raid at least. It would be established later that some of the early bombing had been accurate, but that most of the loads had undershot and fallen into open country, a disappointment compounded by the loss, mostly to night-fighters, of thirty-seven aircraft. In some small compensation for the heavy losses, the rear gunner in the crew of F/L Ames claimed a BF109 as destroyed.

ND530 was homebound over the Marne region to the west of Reims when intercepted and engaged by a Ju88, which killed both gunners and left P/O Barnes and the rest of the crew with no option but to take to their parachutes. P/O Barnes was the last to leave and as he arrived at the forward escape hatch, the Lancaster lurched, throwing him against something solid, which rendered him unconscious. He came to as he fell through the air with his scarf flapping in his face, and because of the altitude of the encounter, probably at between 18,000 and 20,000 feet he had time to deploy his chute and drift down into the welcoming arms of members of the Comete Resistance line, who spirited him and the flight engineer away, while the three remaining crew members soon found themselves in captivity. P/O Barnes spent some six weeks hidden by a brave French family, until, in May, he was moved further down the line to Paris where he met a group of other airmen, one RAF and three USAAF, with whom he would undertake the final part of the journey. They travelled by train to Bayonne and were then taken by Basque guides over the Pyrenees, just as the D-Day landings were taking place further north on the Normandy beaches. Once in Spain he felt suspicious and uncomfortable about being held in a Spanish farmhouse rather than travelling on to the coast, his instinct prompting him to take his chance and leave under his own steam, accompanied by the other airmen. They were picked up by Spanish police and ultimately returned to England. Many years later, P/O Barnes learned that the intention had been to hand them back to the Germans for a sack of corn for each airman.

Many operations had been mounted against Frankfurt during the preceding two years, only a small number of which had been really effective. This state of affairs was about to be rectified, however, and the first of two raids against this south-central powerhouse of industry was posted on the 18th, for which a force of 846 aircraft was made ready. 5 Group supported the operation with 212 Lancasters, eighteen of which belonged to 630 Squadron, and they were each loaded at East Kirkby with a cookie and incendiaries, before taking off between 19.06 and 19.39 with W/C Deas and S/L Calvert the senior pilots on duty. They benefitted from favourable weather conditions as they pressed on across France and entered Germany, where they encountered a layer of haze 20,000 feet thick over the target, and according to most, no more than three-tenths cloud. This allowed the Path Finders to employ the Newhaven ground marking technique (blind marking by H2S, followed by visual backing-up), which the 630 Squadron crews exploited when carrying out their attacks on red and green TIs from 19,000 to 23,000 feet either side of 22.00. A large explosion was witnessed at 22.05, and the participants in the raid flew home confident that their efforts had been worthwhile. They had, indeed, contributed to an outstandingly successful raid, during which 5 Group alone dropped more than one thousand tons of bombs for the first time at a single target. Twenty-two aircraft failed to return, five of them belonging to 5 Group, and among them was 630 Squadron's ND686, which crashed within sight of the Channel coast on the Belgian side of the frontier with France and there were no survivors from the rookie crew of P/O Orchiston RNZAF. Local sources in Frankfurt calculated that six thousand buildings had been destroyed or seriously damaged in predominantly eastern, central and western districts, and there would be little time for the residents to recover before they found themselves in the firing line again.

Frankfurt was named again on the 22nd as the target for that night, and 217 crews of 5 Group learned that they were to be part of another huge force of 816 aircraft, of which the fifteen Lancasters provided by 630 Squadron each received a bomb load of either a cookie and mix of incendiaries, or a 2,000-pounder and ten 1,000-pounders. They departed East Kirkby between 18.34 to 19.11 with W/C Deas and S/L Calvert the senior pilots on duty and after climbing out above the station and rendezvousing with the bomber stream, adopted an unusual route for a target south of the Ruhr, crossing the enemy coast over Vlieland and Terschelling, before passing to the east of Osnabrück on a direct course due south for the target. P/O Kilgour and crew were back home before three hours had passed for an undisclosed reason, leaving the others to arrive at the target and find five to six-tenths thin, low cloud at around 4,000 feet and Paramatta marking (blind marking by H2S) in progress. The 630 Squadron crews focused their attention on the release-point flares and red and green TIs marking out the aiming point, before bombing from 20,000 to 22,500 feet either side of 22.00, and observed a massive rectangular area of unbroken fire across the centre of the city, the glow from which could be seen for at least a hundred miles into the return flight. Returning crews reported numerous searchlights lighting up the cloud, and moderate to intense flak that reached up to the bombers' flight level. At debriefing W/O White and crew reported an encounter with a Ju88 twenty miles from the target, which left both aircraft damaged, the Lancaster to the extent that the bomb-aimer was unable to release the bombs over the target and the whole load had to be brought home.

Local reports confirmed the enormity of the devastation, which was particularly severe in western districts and left this half of the city without electricity, gas and water for an extended period. More than nine hundred people lost their lives and a further 120,000 were bombed out of their homes as the old Frankfurt, which had developed from the Middle Ages, was obliterated. The success was gained at a cost to the Command of twenty-six Lancasters and seven Halifaxes, a loss-rate of 4.2% and 3.8% respectively. It was a bad night for senior officers, 207 and 7 Squadrons losing their commanding officers, while Bardney's station commander, G/C Norman Pleasance, failed to return in a 9 Squadron Lancaster. What was about to happen over the next week and a half, however, would overshadow anything that had gone before and would certainly not fall within what might be considered acceptable.

It was more than five weeks since the main force had last visited the "Big City", Berlin, and 811 aircraft were made ready on the 24th for what would be the final raid of the war upon it by RAF heavy bombers, after which it would be left to the USAAF and the Mosquitos of 8 Group's Light Night Striking Force to harass right up to the moment that Russian troops arrived in the suburbs. 5 Group put up 193 Lancasters, of which fifteen were provided by 630 Squadron and loaded with a cookie and incendiaries each, the latter made up of 850 of the 4lb denomination, 50 of the X-Type 4-pounders and 80 x 30lbs, before departing East Kirkby between 18.29 and 19.04 with S/L Calvert the senior pilot on duty. Six second pilots were also flying to gain operational experience, and accompanying F/L Weller and crew was F/Sgt "Blue" Rackley, an Australian who was to survive an eventful tour with the squadron. They had a long flight ahead of them, which would take them across the North Sea to the Danish coast near Ringkøbing and then to a point on the German Baltic coast near Rostock. When north-east of Berlin they were to adopt a south-westerly course for the bombing run, and once clear of the defence zone homebound, dogleg to the west and then north-west to pass around Hannover on its southern and western sides, before heading for Holland and an exit via the Castricum coast.

The extended outward leg provided a time-on-target of around 22.30, but an unexpected difficulty was encountered, which rendered void all of the meticulous planning. The existence of what we now know as "Jetstream" winds was unknown at the time, and the one blowing from the north with unprecedented strength on this night pushed the bomber stream south of its intended track. Navigators, who were expecting to see the northern tip of Sylt on their H2S screens, were horrified to find the southern end, which meant that they were thirty miles south of track and about to fly over Germany rather than Jutland. The previously mentioned "wind-finder" system had been set up for precisely this eventuality, but the problem on this night was that the wind-finders refused to believe what their instruments were telling them. Winds in excess of one hundred m.p.h had never been encountered before, and fearing that they would be disbelieved, many modified the figures downward. The same thing happened at raid control, where the figures were modified again, so that the information rebroadcast to the bomber stream bore no resemblance to the reality of the situation.

There were no early returns among the 630 Squadron contingent, and by the time that they had reached Westerhever on the west coast of Schleswig-Holstein, most realized that they were some distance south of track and set course for the north to try to regain the planned route and avoid the defences that would be met if they turned east over Germany. Many commented on the inaccurate wind information received during the outward journey, and some crews were so far off course with no possibility of reaching the primary target within the allotted window, that they bombed last resort targets, P/O Johnson and crew selecting a built-up area south-west of Leipzig, and they were not alone. Having arrived in the target area, some of the others were convinced that the Path Finders were up to ten minutes late in opening the raid, a fact confirmed to some by the voice of the Master Bomber exhorting them to hurry up. Crews reported a variety of cloud conditions from three to ten-tenths at between 6,000 and 15,000 feet, but most were able to pick out the red and green TIs on the ground, and if not, found red Wanganui flares with green stars to guide them to the aiming point. The 630 Squadron crews confirmed their positions by H2S before bombing from 20,000 to 22,250 feet sometime after 22.30 and observed what appeared to be a scattered attack in the early stages, until fires began to become more concentrated in three distinct areas and large explosions were witnessed at 22.42 and 22.54. The defences were very active with moderate flak bursting at up to 24,000 feet and light flak attempting to shoot out the skymarkers, but night-fighter activity was described by the 5 Group ORB as unusually quiet.

There was a shock awaiting the Command as the returning aircraft landed to leave a shortfall of seventy-two, and it would be established later that two-thirds of them had fallen victim to the Ruhr flak batteries after being driven into that region's defence zone by the wind on the way home. 630 Squadron's P/O Kilgour and crew reported being hit by flak as they traversed the Ruhr, but were fortunate and survived, while three others from the squadron and two from 57 Squadron failed to return among eleven posted missing by 5 Group. LL886 fell to the Ruhr flak, and W/O White DFM lost his life, while the other seven occupants of the Lancaster parachuted into the arms of their captors. ND657 and ND788 were shot down over the Münsterland to the north of the Ruhr, with just one survivor from the crew of P/O Allen in the former, who was joined in captivity by F/Sgt Perry RAAF and five members of his crew, the flight engineer managing to evade a similar fate, presumably by walking the relatively short distance across farmland to cross into Holland and make contact with the local Resistance. Post-raid analysis revealed that the wind had also played havoc with the marking and bombing and had pushed the attack towards the south-western districts of the capital, where most of the damage occurred, while 126 outlying communities also received bombs.

It had been an exhausting campaign against Berlin for all concerned, and 630 Squadron had been present on each of the sixteen main raids on Berlin from the November resumption and the diversion there on the night of the Magdeburg debacle in January. Eleven 630 Squadron Lancasters had failed to return from 201 sorties, a loss rate of 5.5%, one crashed, sixty-two men had lost their lives and an unusually high number of eighteen were in captivity, with one other on the run and on his way home. (The Berlin Raids. Martin Middlebrook).

Twenty 5 Group Lancasters from 53 Base were invited to take part in an attack on the extensive railway yards at Aulnoye in north-eastern France to be carried out on the evening of the 25th, while twenty-two 617 Squadron Lancasters returned to the Sigma aero-engine factory at Lyons. The former found clear skies at the target and ground haze, through which a bend in the river Sambre provided a useful pinpoint, although the aiming-point had been clearly marked by concentrated red and green TIs. They bombed from 7,000 to 8,400 feet between 22.01 and 22.23 and observed fires and a large explosion at 22.03.

Although Berlin had now been consigned to the past, the winter campaign still had a week to run, and two more major operations for the crews to negotiate. The first of these was posted on the 26th and would bring a return to the old enemy of Essen that night, for which a force of 705 aircraft was assembled. Essen was home to the Krupp empire, and it is a name that conjures up a vision of a massive factory, but this is far from what actually existed. The Krupp organisation had been the largest manufacturer of weapons in Europe since before the Great War and had a hand in all aspects of German war production from tanks to artillery and ship and U-Boot construction having been given a controlling share in all major heavy engineering companies in Germany and the occupied countries. It also built manufacturing sites in other parts of Germany, many situated close to concentration camps, and employed vast numbers of forced workers in all of its factories. Once known as "Die Waffenschmiede des Reichs", the weapons-forge of the realm, its manufacturing sites in Essen included among others the Friedrich Krupp steelworks, the Friedrich Krupp locomotive and general engineering works, six coal mines and ten coke-oven plants, the Altenberg zinc works, the Presswerk plastics factory and the Goldschmidt non-ferrous metals smelting plant, all situated either within or close to the four Borbeck districts in a segment radiating out from near the city centre to the Rhine-Herne Canal on the north-western boundary on the banks of the Emscher River. The steel and engineering works alone employed in the region of eighty thousand workers, and the company's sites covered an area of more than two thousand acres, of which three hundred acres were occupied by factories and workshops. All of that required massive rail and canal access in the form of marshalling yards and its own harbour, and energy from at least four nearby power stations. Harris had been at war with Essen from within days of his enthronement as command-in-chief, and it was a war he eventually won, but at great cost and not before experiencing seven months of failure and frustration between March and September 1942.

5 Group contributed 172 of the 476 Lancasters, fourteen of them belonging to 630 Squadron, which each received a bomb load of a cookie, ten deep SBCs of 4lb incendiaries and ten standard SBCs containing the 30lb denomination. They departed East Kirkby between 19.16 and 19.45 with S/L Calvert the senior pilot on duty and climbed out over the station before setting course for the Dutch coast to pass north of Haarlem and Amsterdam, and then swing to

the south-east on a direct run to the target. P/O Bailey and crew were back in the circuit within two hours for an undisclosed reason, while the others reached the target to find it covered by eight to ten-tenths cloud with tops in places as high as 14,000 feet. Oboe performed well, however, and enabled the Path Finders to mark the aiming point with red and green TIs and Wanganui flares, upon which the 630 Squadron bomb-aimers focused their attention to deliver their payloads from 19,000 to 22,250 feet from around 22.00. They had been unable to assess the results of their efforts, but the impression was of a successful raid, and this was based on a considerable glow beneath the clouds as they withdrew. Post-raid reconnaissance soon confirmed another outstandingly destructive operation against this once elusive target, thus continuing the remarkable run of successes here since the introduction of Oboe to main force operations a year earlier. Over seventeen hundred houses were destroyed in the attack, with dozens of war industry factories sustaining serious damage, and on a night when the night-fighter controllers were caught off guard by the switch to the Ruhr, the success was gained for the modest loss of nine aircraft.

The period known as the Battle of Berlin, but which was better referred to as the winter campaign, was to be brought to an end on the night of the 30/31$^{st}$ with a standard maximum-effort raid on Nuremberg in southern Germany. The plan of operation departed from normal practice in only one important respect, and this was to prove critical. It had become standard practice for 8 Group to plan operations and to employ diversions and feints to confuse the enemy night-fighter controllers. Sometimes they were successful and sometimes not, but with the night-fighter force having clearly gained the upper hand with its "Tame Boar" running commentary system, all possible means had to be adopted to protect the bomber stream. During a conference held early on the 30$^{th}$, the Lancaster Group A-O-Cs expressed a preference for a 5 Group-inspired route, which would require the bomber stream to fly a long straight leg across Belgium and Germany to a point about fifty miles north of Nuremberg, from where the final run-in would commence. The Halifax A-O-Cs were less convinced of the benefits, and AVM Bennett, the Path Finder chief, was positively overcome by the potential dangers and predicted a disaster, only to be overruled. A force of 795 aircraft was made ready, of which 201 Lancasters were to be provided by 5 Group, sixteen of them representing 630 Squadron, and the crews attended briefings to be told of the route, wind conditions and the belief that a layer of cloud would conceal them from enemy night-fighters. Before take-off, a 1409 Meteorological Flight Mosquito crew radioed in to cast doubts upon the weather conditions, which they could see differed markedly from those that had been forecast. This also went unheeded, and from around 21.45 for the next hour or so, the crews took off for the rendezvous area, and headed into a conspiracy of circumstances, which would inflict upon Bomber Command its heaviest defeat of the war.

At East Kirkby the armourers winched a cookie and ten and eight-and-a-half SBCs respectively of 4lb and 30lb incendiaries into each bomb bay, before waving them off between 21.46 and 22.27 with S/L Calvert the senior pilot on duty. It was not long into the flight before they and the rest of the force began to notice some unusual features in the conditions, which included uncommonly bright moonlight and a crystal clarity of visibility that allowed them the rare sight of other aircraft in the stream. On most nights, crews would feel themselves to be completely alone in the sky all the way to the target, until bang on schedule, TIs would be seen to fall, and other aircraft would make their presence felt by the turbulence of their slipstreams as they funnelled towards the aiming point. Once at cruising altitude on this night, however, they were alarmed to note that the forecast cloud was conspicuous by its absence, and instead lay beneath them as a white tablecloth, against which they were silhouetted like flies. Condensation trails began to form in the cold, clear air to further advertise their presence to the enemy and the Jetstream winds, which had so adversely affected the Berlin raid a week earlier, were also present, only this time blowing from the south. As then, the wind-finder system failed to cope, and this would have a serious impact on the outcome of the operation. The final insult on this sad night was the route's close proximity to two night-fighter beacons, which the enemy aircraft were orbiting while they awaited their instructions, unaware initially that they were about to have the cream of Bomber Command handed to them on a plate.

The crews of F/Sgt Rackley and F/O Nail turned back with oxygen and intercom issues before the carnage began over Charleroi in Belgium, and from there to the target, the route was sign-posted by the burning wreckage on the ground of eighty Bomber Command aircraft. ND337 was the nineteenth to go down and crashed at Bickenbach, some fifteen miles south of Koblenz, killing all but the bomb-aimer in the debutant crew of F/Sgt Clark RAAF. Another rookie crew, that of F/O Langlands, who were on just their third operation together, were the sixty-third to be shot down, after being intercepted at 20,000 feet while approaching the final turning point at the end of the long, straight leg. ME664 crashed near Ruhla, some one hundred miles north of the target, with the wireless operator and both gunners still on board and the rest of the crew drifting down into the hands of their captors. The experienced crew of P/O Johnson, who was a native of Nassau in the Bahamas, were on their sixteenth operation and were heading south in JB288 on the final leg to the target when becoming the seventy-eighth to be shot down. The Lancaster crashed near Eggolsheim, some ten miles south-east of Bamberg and within about twenty miles of the target, killing the pilot and three others and delivering the three survivors into the hands of the enemy, where they would meet up with the five other survivors from the squadron. (The Nuremberg Raid. Martin Middlebrook.)

The wind-finder system broke down again, and those crews who either failed to detect the strength of the wind, or simply refused to believe the evidence, were driven up to fifty miles north of their intended track, and as a result turned towards Nuremberg from a false position. This led to more than a hundred aircraft bombing at Schweinfurt in error, which combined with the massive losses sustained before the target was reached to reduce considerably the numbers arriving at the primary target. As the remaining 630 Squadron crews approached Nuremberg, they encountered eight to nine-tenths cloud with tops as high as 16,000 feet and bombed from 19,000 to 22,500 feet from around 01.00, aiming at red and green TIs and sky-markers after confirming their positions by H2S. Many fires were observed, the glow from which, according to some reports, remained visible for 120 miles into the return journey. Ninety-five aircraft failed to return home, twenty-one of them from 5 Group, and many others were written off in landing crashes or with battle damage too severe to repair. The shock and disappointment were compounded by the fact that the strong wind had driven the marking beyond the city to the east, and Nuremberg had, consequently, escaped serious damage.

During the course of the month, the squadron participated in eight operations, which generated 123 sorties for the loss of ten Lancasters and their crews.

# April 1944

The winter campaign had brought the Command to its low point of the war and was the only time when the morale of the crews was in question. What now lay before the hard-pressed men of Bomber Command was in marked contrast to that which had been endured over the seemingly interminable winter months. In place of the long slog to Germany on dark, often dirty nights, shorter range hops to France and Belgium in improving weather conditions would become the order of the day. However, these operations would be equally demanding in their way, and require of the crews a greater commitment to accuracy to avoid casualties among friendly civilians. Despite this, a decree from on high insisted that such operations were worthy of counting as just one third of a sortie towards the completion of a tour, a policy that gave rise to a sense of injustice. In fact, the number of sorties to complete a tour would fluctuate up and down between this point and the end of hostilities. Despite the horrendous losses of the winter campaign, the Command was in remarkably fine fettle to face its new challenge, with 3 Group gradually changing to Lancasters and the much-improved Hercules powered Halifaxes equipping 4 Group and most of 6 Group. Harris was now in the enviable position of being able to achieve what had eluded his predecessor, namely, to attack multiple targets simultaneously with enough strength to be effective. Such was the hitting-power now at his disposal, that he could assign targets to individual groups, to groups in tandem or to the Command as a whole, as dictated by operational requirements. Although invasion considerations would come first, while Harris was at the helm his favoured policy of city-busting would never entirely be shelved.

5 Group returned to operations on the 5th, with an undertaking involving 144 Lancasters and a Mosquito flown by W/C Cheshire of 617 Squadron. The target was the former Dewoitine aircraft factory located on the Montaudran aerodrome at Toulouse in south-western France, which, under a nationalization plan in 1936 involving six aircraft companies, including Lioré et Olivier and Potez, was now operating under the name SNCASE, or Sud Est for short. Cheshire was to mark it with spotfires from low level, using the system that he was instrumental in developing, and one which would become an integral part of 5 Group operations, with refinements, from this point on. This would be Cheshire's first operational flight in a Mosquito and the first time that he marked a target for 5 Group rather than just 617 Squadron. Much depended upon its success if Harris were to become sold on the idea of the low-level visual marking technique and give it his backing. At East Kirkby, 630 Squadron loaded eight of its Lancasters with a cookie, ten 500lb incendiary cluster bombs and thirty-six 30lb incendiaries and the one to be flown by F/L Ames in the role of second deputy leader six fewer 500-pounders in favour of thirty-six 4.5 reconnaissance flares. They took off between 19.48 and 20.17 with S/L Calvert the senior pilot on duty and S/L Butler navigating for P/O Hill. The Master Bomber for the occasion was Wing Commander Operations, W/C James "Willie" Tait, a veteran of operations with 4 Group, former commanding officer of 51 and 10 Squadrons, future commanding officer of 617 Squadron and now a member of the 5 Group Master Bomber fraternity at 54 Base, Coningsby. He would be flying from Waddington in a 467 Squadron RAAF Lancaster with a borrowed crew, and it is believed that his Deputy was W/C Adams, the commanding officer of 49 Squadron. Ahead of them lay an outward flight of more than four hours, which all of the 630 Squadron crews negotiated and arrived in time to watch Cheshire lob two red spotfires onto the roof of the factory at 00.17 during his third

pass. So accurate were they, that the two 617 Squadron Lancaster backers-up were not required, and bombing took place in bright moonlight, sadly the 630 Squadron ORB providing no details of bombing heights and times. We can assume from the ORBs of other squadrons that it was from somewhere between 8,000 to 17,000 feet either side of 00.15 and large fires were observed, which sent smoke rising through 7,000 feet. One 207 Squadron Lancaster was hit by flak over the target at 00.30 and exploded, killing all on board, and this was the only loss from an outstandingly successful operation, made more impressive by the fact that the 5 Group main force crews were from squadrons of the line, with no special training. It was the defining moment of the war for 5 Group, which had always considered itself to be the elite of the Command. Within hours, Harris gave the go ahead for 5 Group to take on its own target marking force, and become, in effect, an independent entity.

It would be almost two weeks before the necessary moves took place, and in the meantime, the pre-invasion campaign got into full swing with the posting of two operations on the 9th. The Lille-Delivrance goods station in north-eastern France was assigned to 239 aircraft from 3, 4, 6 and 8 Groups, while the marshalling yards at Villeneuve-St-Georges, on the southern outskirts of Paris, were to be targeted by 225 aircraft drawn from all groups. The weather conditions were excellent, and clear skies greeted the latter force as it crossed the French coast at around 14,000 feet. The target could be identified visually, but crews aimed for the red and green TIs that had been accurately placed by the Path Finders, delivering their hardware from between 13,000 and 14,500 feet in the face of little opposition. Many bomb bursts were observed along with orange explosions, and to those high above, the raid appeared to be highly successful. In fact, many bomb loads had fallen into adjacent residential districts, where four hundred houses had been destroyed or seriously damaged, and ninety-three people killed. This was far fewer than had died in the simultaneous operation at Lille, many miles to the north-east, where over two thousand items of rolling stock had been destroyed and buildings and installations seriously damaged, but at a collateral cost of 456 French civilian lives. Civilian casualties would prove to be an unavoidable by-product of operations over the occupied countries.

While the above operations were in progress, 103 Lancasters of 1 and 5 Groups were engaged in mining activities off the Baltic ports of Danzig, now Gdansk in Poland, Gdynia and Pillau, the last-mentioned now Baltiysk in Russia, which involved a round-trip of some seventeen hundred miles and was the most distant of all mining regions visited by the Command. The mining of enemy sea lanes had been pioneered by 5 Group back on the night of the 13/14th of April 1940 in what was the initial tentative step in an entirely new departure for Bomber Command operations, which would prove to be hugely successful, and by war's end, would have sunk or damaged more enemy vessels than the Royal Navy. The laying of parachute mines by air was given the code-name "gardening" and the entire enemy-held coastline from the Pyrenees in the south-west to the Baltic port of Königsberg in the north-east, and even the northern Italian coast, was split up into gardens, each with a horticultural or marine biological name. The process of delivery was known as planting and the mines themselves were referred to as vegetables, and it was not long afterwards that the other groups joined in to maintain a spiders' web of mines in chains across all of the sea-lanes employed by the enemy. Within ten months of the start of the campaign, in the Baltic alone, it was known that seventeen ships had been sunk in the Great and Little Belts and eighteen damaged. Eighteen more had probably been sunk and as the campaign progressed, it was considered safe to estimate that for every ship known to have been sunk or damaged, another had been sunk or damaged without news of it reaching England. Among the vessels known to have sunk was a troop ship, and out of three thousand men on board, fewer than 350 had been saved.

Until the advent of H2S, mining had been conducted predominantly from low-level, based on establishing a visual pinpoint from which to carry out a timed run to the release point, with a low cloud base and poor visibility providing the main challenges, and shore and shipboard light flak the greatest danger. That said, gardening was generally less dangerous than bombing and became a useful means of blooding freshman crews at the start of their tour. H2S allowed mines to be delivered from high level, typically 15,000 feet, which removed the risk from light flak but exposed crews to heavy flak and night-fighters. 630 Squadron briefed ten crews for its maiden mining operation, for which the crews were assigned to the Tangerine garden off Pillau, the extreme range probably restricting the payload in each Lancaster to some 6,000lbs, which was four standard 1,500lb parachute mines, although various types of different weights were available and the ORB does not enlighten us with the necessary details. They departed East Kirkby between 21.17 and 21.34 with S/L Calvert the senior pilot on duty supported by four pilots of flight lieutenant rank and lost the services of F/L Probert and crew to an engine issue when some distance out over the North Sea. The others arrived at their destination under clear skies and bright moonlight and visually established pinpoints with ease, confirming them by H2S, before conducting timed runs to the release points. The squadron ORB is once more short on detail, but a few miles to the west other 5 Group crews were planting their vegetables from around 15,000 feet between 01.40 and 01.50, and one must assume that 630 Squadron followed suit. They returned safely after nine hours aloft and reported mostly uneventful sorties, although a number commented on a response from shore and shipboard flak. Nine Lancasters failed to return, having been intercepted by night-fighters on the route home over the western coast of Denmark, and it was a reminder, that this most productive of enterprises could occasionally be as dangerous as operating over a city.

On the following day, Monday the 10$^{th}$, a further five railway yards, four in France and one in Belgium, were posted as the targets for that night and assigned to individual groups. 5 Group was handed those at Tours in the Loire region of western France, for which a force of 180 Lancasters was assembled, the seventeen belonging to 630 Squadron each receiving a bomb load of thirteen 1,000-pounders, all but one with a six-hour delayed-action fuse. They departed East Kirkby between 22.02 and 22.39 with W/C Deas the senior pilot on duty and set course for England's south coast and the Channel crossing. There were no early returns, and all arrived at the target to find bright moonlight and red spotfires marking the aiming point. Master Bombers were on hand to direct the two phases of the attack, the first against the western side of the yards and the second its eastern counterpart. The squadron ORB is devoid of detail, but it is likely that it and 57 Squadron had been assigned to aiming point A, where matters proceeded according to plan with bombing taking place from 8,000 to 10,000 feet either side of 02.00, crews describing the yards as an avenue of fire. However, the scene soon became confused as smoke began to spread across the site and billow into the air, rising through 8,000 feet in the later stages. This affected to an extent the second phase bombing, which was carried out from around 5,500 to 10,000 feet either side of 02.30. The main force had been called upon to approach the aiming-point in a left-hand orbit from the east, during which the Master Bomber called a temporary halt as he reassessed the changing visibility, before reinstating the bombing order, until the smoke forced him to end the attack at 02.48 and send home any crews with bombs still on board. There were mixed opinions as to the effectiveness of the operation, some gaining the impression that the eastern half of the yards had not been touched, while others claimed the attack to have been accurate and concentrated within the yards. Two large fires were observed, and P/O Bailey and crew reported a mighty explosion that "rippled the earth" and rocked the Lancaster. Post-raid reconnaissance confirmed the success of the operation, but the Germans routinely rounded up local civilians and pressganged them into repairing the damage to get the yards working again before long.

Aachen was a major railway centre with marshalling yards at both the western and eastern ends, Aachen-West and Rothe Erde, but the size of the force assembled for the attack planned for the night of the 11/12$^{th}$ was clearly designed to cause as much damage as possible within what was Germany's most westerly city. The force of 341 heavy aircraft was drawn from 1, 3, 5 and 8 Groups with six of the Lancasters provided by 630 Squadron, their bomb bays loaded with a dozen 1,000-pounders each and two deep SBCs containing a total of 300 x 4lb incendiaries. They departed East Kirkby between 20.29 and 20.42 with F/L Roberts the senior pilot on duty and joined the bomber stream as it climbed to between 18,000 and 20,000 feet by the time it reached the Belgian coast at 3° East. That altitude was maintained all the way to the target, where six to ten-tenths thin cloud was encountered at between 7,000 and 8,000 feet, through which the red and green TIs could be seen marking out the aiming point. The 57 and 630 Squadron ORBs are disappointingly short on detail during this period, and it is necessary to rely on accounts from other 5 Group squadrons to paint a picture of events. It seems that the 5 Group bombing was carried out from an average of 18,000 feet and many bomb bursts and fires were observed, which suggested that the attack had been accurate. The bombers maintained height on the way home until fifty miles from the coast, at which position they began a gentle descent to exit enemy territory at 15,000 feet or above. Nine Lancasters failed to return, five belonging to 5 Group, three Path Finders and one from 3 Group, and at debriefing, P/O Nash and crew reported that they had almost become a statistic themselves after an encounter with an enemy night-fighter left ND797 severely damaged by cannon fire. No casualties were sustained, and they arrived home safely after a round trip of a little over four hours. Reports coming out of Aachen revealed this to be the city's worst experience of the war to date, with extensive damage in central and southern districts, disruption of its transport infrastructure and a death toll of 1,525 people. However, post-raid reconnaissance revealed that the railway yards had not been destroyed and would require further attention.

On the 14$^{th}$, the Command became officially subject to the orders coming from the Supreme Headquarters of the Allied Expeditionary Force (SHAEF), under General Dwight D Eisenhower, and would remain thus shackled until the Allied armies were sweeping towards the German frontier at the end of the summer. On the 15$^{th}$, 83 and 97 Squadrons were loaned to 5 Group from the Path Finders, on what amounted to a permanent detachment, and took up residence on the 54 Base main station at Coningsby, while 627 Squadron and its Mosquitos joined 617 Squadron on the satellite station at Woodhall Spa. 54 Base had been formed on the 1$^{st}$ of January 1944 and included the nearby station of Metheringham, home to 106 Squadron. Also on this day, East Kirkby became 55 Base with responsibility for Spilsby, where 207 Squadron was the resident unit. The base system allowed groups an efficient way of standing down a part of the force as required, and in the case of 55 Base, it would mean 630, 57 and

207 Squadrons, and eventually 44 (Rhodesia) Squadron when it moved to Spilsby later in the year, generally operating as a unit. 83 and 97 Squadrons were to become the 5 Group heavy marker force, while the Mosquitos would eventually take over the low-level marking role currently performed by 617 Squadron.

This was a major coup for AVM Cochrane and 5 Group and a bitter blow to AVM Bennett, the Path Finder Force chief, and the relationship between them, which had never been cordial, plunged to a greater depth. Both were brilliant men, Bennett, an Australian, a man of the greatest intellect, who had unparalleled pre-war experience as a pilot and master navigator, had been entrusted with setting up the Atlantic Ferry organisation to bring much needed aircraft from America, and possessed valid operational experience through his command of 77 and 10 Squadrons in 1942, which included an evasion after being shot down over Norway. Despite his total lack of humour, and the fact that his brain operated on a higher level than most, which made him despise fools, he commanded the deepest respect, loyalty and even affection from his men. Cochrane enjoyed a closer relationship with Harris, having served as a flight commander under him in Mesopotamia between the wars and having been chosen by Harris as 5 Group A-O-C, a post held by Harris himself from the start of the war to November 1940. Bennett and Cochrane possessed vastly different opinions on the subject of target marking, Bennett believing that a low-level method exposed the crews to unnecessary danger, while Cochrane insisted that the risks in a fast-flying Mosquito were negligible and would produce greater accuracy. Though 83 and 97 Squadrons were formerly of the "elite" 5 Group and drew fresh crews from it, 8 Group was now viewed by its aircrew as the pinnacle and they were upset at being removed from what they considered to be an elevated status. They were fiercely proud, once qualified, to wear the Path Finder badge and enjoyed the enhanced benefits of their status, although, happily for them, as the squadrons were only officially on loan to 5 Group, they would retain these privileges.

The manner of their arrival and welcome at Coningsby was unfortunate in the extreme and did nothing to cement relations between 5 Group and the new crews, who were already unhappy at being posted on loan to 5 Group. As they disembarked their transports from the dispersals, the crews were summoned to the briefing room, where the 54 Base commander, Air Commodore A C H "Bobby" Sharp, had prepared a lecture. Rather than welcoming these battle-hardened, highly professional men as brothers-in-arms, he proceeded to harangue them over their "bad" 8 Group habits and told them to knuckle down to learning 5 Group ways. This was an insult to crews used to marking procedures far more complex than those required for 5 Group operations, and it would be a long time before the damage was repaired and a grudging loyalty to 5 Group developed. There are favourable accounts of A/C Sharp's courage under fire and his frequent operational flights in both RAF and USAAF aircraft as a passenger, but there are others, by the likes of Joe Northrop, a highly respected and experienced flight commander at 83 Squadron at the time, that paint an entirely different picture of a self-important, pompous and vain officer. Of course, as far as 5 Group was concerned, the new arrivals should have viewed the move from 8 Group as a promotion. From this moment on, 5 Group would be referred to in 8 Group circles somewhat disparagingly as "The Independent Air Force", or "The Lincolnshire Poachers".

The 5 Group target on the 18th was the marshalling yards at Juvisy, situated on the West Bank of the Seine south of Paris, which was one of four similar targets for the night. The intention had been for the new arrivals to participate, but the disgruntled commanding officers, G/C Laurence Deane of 83 Squadron and W/C Jimmy Carter of 97 (Straits Settlement) Squadron, announced that they were not yet ready, and the operation would have to go ahead without them. 202 Lancasters and four Mosquitos were made ready, the latter belonging to 617 Squadron, and 8 Group would provide three Oboe Mosquitos to deliver the initial marking. 630 Squadron loaded a dozen 1,000-pounders into each of its seventeen participating Lancasters and sent them on their way from East Kirkby between 20.37 and 21.22, with F/Ls Ames, Probert, Roberts and Weller the senior pilots on duty and S/L Butler occupying his usual seat at P/O Hill's navigator's table. The latter time was that of P/O Jackson and crew, who took off nineteen minutes late after an undisclosed delay. All reached the target to find clear skies and ideal bombing conditions and watched as W/C Cheshire released red spotfires, which were backed up by green TIs. Despite black smoke drifting across the aiming-point and upwards from the destruction of a fuel dump at 23.32, the crews were able to hit the markers from an average of 10,000 feet entirely unopposed from the ground, and on their return were enthusiastic about the success of the operation. This was confirmed by post-raid reconnaissance and prompted the crews to make the valid comment that to count this operation as just one-third of a sortie was undervaluing it, and this was a sentiment shared by all whose job involved putting their lives on the line.

Briefings on 5 Group stations on the 20th informed crews of their part in the first operation to include the three newly transferred squadrons, a two-phase attack on railway yards at La Chapelle, situated just to the north of Paris. Meanwhile, the night's main event was to be conducted by a force of 357 Lancasters and twenty-two Mosquitos drawn from 1, 3, 6 and 8 Groups against Cologne. A meticulous plan had been prepared for 5 Group, in which the heavy force of 247 Lancasters was to be split into two phases an hour apart, each with its own specific aiming-point, 54 and 55 bases taking the early shift with 83 Squadron's W/C Deane as the Master Bomber and S/L Sparks his deputy, and 53 Base following up with 54 Base's 97 Squadron's as the heavy marker force and W/C Tait acting as Master Bomber from his position in a Lancaster borrowed from 463 Squadron RAAF. The plan called for the involvement of twenty-two 5 and 8 Group Mosquitos, the latter to drop cascading flares by Oboe to provide an initial reference, and for a Mosquito element from 627 Squadron to lay a "window" screen ahead of the main force Lancasters. Once the target had been identified, the first members of the 83 Squadron flare force were to provide illumination for the low-level marker Mosquitos of 617 Squadron, which would mark the first aiming-point with red spot fires for the main force element to aim at, before the whole procedure was repeated an hour later at the second aiming point. At Coningsby, W/C Deane conducted the briefing, and at its conclusion, wished the assembled throng good luck, before dismissing them, whereupon a voice from the back declared that the briefing wasn't over, and that the base and station commanders, A/C Sharp and G/C "Tiny" Evans-Evans wanted their say. This had not been standard practice in 8 Group, and left Deane mystified and a little humiliated. The senior officers had only waffle to offer, but it made them feel important, while confirming the first impressions of A/C Sharp.

The two East Kirkby squadrons each contributed sixteen Lancasters, those belonging to 630 Squadron receiving a bomb load of thirteen 1,000-pounders before taking to the air between 21.50 and 22.08 with S/L Calvert the senior pilot on duty. F/L Weller and crew were back home within ninety minutes because of intercom and W/T failure, leaving the others to arrive at the target to find largely clear skies, good visibility and only some ground haze to mar the vertical view. Zero hour for the opening phase had been set for 00.05, but the Oboe Mosquitos were two minutes late, and some communications problems had to be ironed out before matters began to run smoothly. A large orange explosion at 00.28 sent a column of black smoke skyward, which impaired visibility to some extent, but those attacking afterwards were able to identify a red spotfire and bomb it, observing large explosions and fires that were visible to the second phase crews as they approached.

The second phase attack took place either side of 01.30, and crews had the glow of the burning target visible behind them for a hundred miles into the return flight. At debriefing, confidence was expressed in the effectiveness of the operation, and post-raid reconnaissance confirmed the success of both phases, which had left the yards severely damaged for the loss of six Lancasters, one belonging to 57 Squadron. Another, while attempting to land at Croydon airport, overshot the runway and crashed into three houses bordering the airfield in the village of Wallington. The pilot, flight engineer and navigator died in the wreckage and the wireless operator succumbed to his injuries while being treated in Croydon hospital. A congratulatory message from A-O-C Cochrane was received on all participating stations on the following day.

The real test for the 5 Group low-level marking system would come at a heavily defended German target, for which Braunschweig was selected on the 22nd, while the rest of the Command targeted the Ruhr city of Düsseldorf. 5 Group put together a force of 238 Lancasters and seventeen Mosquitos, with ten ABC Lancasters of 1 Group's 101 Squadron to provide radio countermeasures (RCM). Braunschweig was a major centre of arms production with the huge Hermann Göring steelworks dominating the town of Salzgitter to the south-west and the Hermann Göring benzol plant in nearby Hallendorf, while to the north-east was the largest car plant in the world, the KdF-Wagens at Wolfsburg, and the city itself was home to the Büssing bus and truck works, and a Volkswagen plant. 630 Squadron loaded each of its fifteen Lancasters with a 2,000-pounder, twelve 500-pounders and J-Type 30lb incendiaries before sending them on their way from East Kirkby between 22.59 and 23.32 with S/L Calvert the senior pilot on duty. There were no early returns from among the East Kirkby squadrons, and they were guided on their way across northern Germany by Path Finder route-markers to arrive in the target area and encounter six to eight-tenths thin cloud at between 8,000 and 10,000 feet. The main force crews benefitted from accurate marking by the 617 Squadron Mosquito element, and the first clear bombing instruction from the Master Bomber were heard at 01.56 calling for crews to aim for the red spotfires and then later, at 02.04, to bomb a second spotfire indicated by green TIs. Despite the guidance, the main force crews were unable to properly identify the target, a situation again compounded by communications problems between various controllers caused by the failure of VHF and the consequent need to pass on instructions instead by W/T. This led to confusion, and many crews were forced to orbit for up to fifteen minutes before bombing. In the absence of information in the 57 and 630 Squadrons' ORBs, we can assume that the crews carried out their attacks on green TIs and red spotfires from an average of 17,000 feet at around 02.00, before returning safely to report what appeared to be a successful operation, while also complaining about the dangers of orbiting a target with aircraft heading in a variety of directions. Although some bombs did fall in the city centre, most were directed at reserve H2S-laid TIs to the south of the city, and damage was less severe than it might otherwise have been.

A major mining effort in five Baltic regions on the 23rd involved the 630 Squadron crews of P/O Nash and F/L Weller, who departed East Kirkby at 21.08 and 21.30 respectively bound for the Geranium garden located in the Baltic off the port of Swinemünde in the Bay of Pomerania. Apparently, pinpoints were established with ease in favourable conditions and the vegetables planted according to brief during sorties of around seven hours duration.

When Munich was posted across 5 Group as the target on the 24th for another live test of the low-level visual marking method, it might have been seen as somewhat ambitious to select such a major city, that was protected by two hundred flak guns. The main operation on this night was to be conducted by a force of 637 aircraft against Karlsruhe, 150 miles to the north-west, which, it was hoped, would help to distract the night-fighters. 234 Lancasters were made ready by 5 Group and supplemented by ten of the ABC variety from 101 Squadron, while four Mosquitos of 617 Squadron were loaded with spotfires to carry out the marking and twelve of 627 Squadron with "window" to dispense during the final approach to the target. 630 Squadron's sixteen Lancasters received a variety of bomb loads including six 500lb J-Type incendiary cluster bombs and 136 x 30lb incendiaries, a cookie and 132 x 30lb incendiaries or 2,010 x 4lb incendiaries, before departing East Kirkby between 20.40 and 21.14 with S/L Calvert the senior pilot on duty and S/L Butler navigating for P/O Hill. P/O Bailey's port-inner engine burst into flames immediately after take-off, and unable to gain height, the pilot set off to complete a circuit before landing, only to be thwarted when the port-outer engine cut and condemned JB556 to a crash-landing on the perimeter track on the edge of the aerodrome. The wreck caught fire, but the station commander G/C Taaafe and medical officer, S/L Elliott, raced to the scene with F/L Nelson of the crash rescue team, and all of the crew were helped clear, the flight engineer with a fractured ankle as the only casualty. Sadly, it would prove to be only a temporary reprieve for five of the crew.

Unaware of the drama, the others headed for the south coast for the Channel crossing and once on the other side set course across France towards the south-east, feinting towards Italy, while the 617 and 627 Squadron Mosquitos remained on the ground for a further three hours before they took off in pursuit and because the target was at the limit of their range, adopted a direct route, the latter laying a "window" screen from high level six minutes from the target to mask the arrival of the flare force which would be providing seven minutes of illumination for the 617 marker Mosquitos. The force arrived at the target under clear skies and in good visibility, and in the light of illuminating flares W/C Cheshire dived onto the aiming-point in the face of murderous light flak, before racing away across the rooftops to safety. The main force followed hard on his heels, the 630 Squadron crews bombing on the red spotfires and green TIs from an average of 18,000 feet either side of 02.00 in the face of intense searchlight and flak activity. Many fires were seen to take hold, and as the bombers pointed their snouts back towards France to eventually pass to the north of Paris, Karlsruhe could be seen burning over to starboard. P/O "Blue" Rackley and crew were leaving the target area when attacked by a night-fighter, which set the port-inner engine on fire, and although it was brought under control, they were unlikely to reach England and decided to make for Swiss airspace in order to bale out. However, with insufficient power to cross the Alps, Corsica presented itself as a better option and they were approaching the airfield at Borgo when the port-outer engine cut at the last moment, precipitating a heavy landing, during which ME717 swung out of control and its rear turret struck a parked aircraft. The rear gunner, F/Sgt Dunbar RAAF, had been ordered to emergency stations for the landing, but had remained in his turret and was killed. JA872 had been caught in the intense flak barrage on the run-up to bomb release and flew home with severely damaged mid-upper and rear turrets for a landing at Thorney Island, which P/O Hooper accomplished safely and was awarded an immediate DFC. Post-raid reconnaissance and local sources confirmed the success of the raid, which left 1,104 buildings in ruins and a further thirteen hundred severely damaged. Some among the experienced crews described the attack as the best they had seen, and it was probably this operation that sealed the award to Cheshire of the Victoria Cross at the conclusion of his operational career in July, after completing one hundred sorties.

At briefing on the 26th, fifteen 630 Squadron crews were told that Schweinfurt was to be their target that night, after the failure of the RAF to destroy it in February and the American 8th Air Force just two weeks ago. The tone was very much, "leave it to RAF Bomber Command", and with the satisfaction of Munich still fresh in the mind, and the natural rivalry existing between the two forces, such attitudes were to be expected. They learned that, for this operation, 627 Squadron would act as the low-level marker force for the first time and for a main force of 215 Lancasters, including nine from 101 Squadron to provide RCM protection. This was just one of three major operations taking place, with the main event at Essen, while the railway yards at Villeneuve-St-Georges were being attended to by a predominantly Halifax main force. Ten of the 630 Squadron Lancasters had 1,860 x 4lb incendiaries in their bomb bays and the rest a cookie and 136 x 30lb incendiaries as they departed East Kirkby between 21.13 and 21.38 with S/L Calvert the senior pilot on duty. They set course for the French coast and once in enemy airspace, met stronger-than-forecast head winds, which delayed the arrival in the target area of the heavy brigade. The 627 Squadron crews failed to exploit the generally clear skies and good visibility as their debut marking effort proved to be inaccurate. The 83 Squadron crews remarked on the lack of illumination, and those carrying hooded flares were called in a number of times to back-up, while bombing instructions generally were transmitted by W/T. The East Kirkby crews bombed from an average of 19,000 feet, aiming at red spotfires and green TIs, some following the instructions of the Master Bomber to overshoot by a thousand yards. A large white explosion was witnessed at 02.29, and many fires were reported, but once again at this target, most of the hardware fell outside of the target area, leaving ball-bearing production more or less unaffected.

Night-fighters had got amongst the outbound heavy force at the French coast and remained in contact all the way to the target, shooting down twenty-one Lancasters, a hefty 9.3%. 630 Squadron's ND789 was a night-fighter victim and crashed at Mühlhausen, some seventy miles north of the target with no survivors from the crew of P/O Kilgour. Also failing to return were two 57 Squadron Lancasters, one of which contained the crew of a long-established flight commander, who was among those losing their lives after colliding in the air with a 44 (Rhodesia) Squadron aircraft. It was during this operation, that Sgt Jackson of 106 Squadron earned the Victoria Cross for climbing out onto the wing of his Lancaster to attempt to quell a fire in a fuel tank. Other members of the crew held on to his parachute rigging, but when the force of the slipstream whipped the fire extinguisher from his hand, and flames began to lick around him and his chute, they allowed him to slip off the trailing edge to provide him with the slimmest of chances to survive. Despite a smouldering parachute, he survived his fall to earth, but suffered serious burns and a broken ankle and spent many months in a German hospital. It was only after the war, when he and his crew mates returned from captivity, that his outstanding courage was recognised.

5 Group made preparations on the 28th to send a force of eighty-eight Lancasters and four Mosquitos to attack the Alfred Nobel Dynamit A G explosives works at St-Médard-en-Jalles, situated in a wood on the north-western outskirts of Bordeaux in south-western France. A further fifty-one Lancasters and four Mosquitos would head in the opposite direction to target an aircraft maintenance facility at the Kjeller Flyfabrikk, some ten miles north-east of Oslo, which had been occupied by the Germans since April 1940 and was used by Junkers, Daimler-Benz and BMW. Clear skies prevailed over south-western France, but some flares had landed in a nearby wood, causing volumes of smoke to drift across the factory and obscure it from view. A few bomb loads went down before a signal was picked up from the Master Bomber instructing crews to withhold their bombs and orbit while he assessed the situation, and he eventually called a halt to proceedings at 03.30 and sent the rest of the force home with their bombs. Meanwhile, more than eleven hundred miles to the north, the crews had found clear skies and excellent visibility, and had identified the target by H2S, confirmed by yellow TIs at the start of the bombing run and flares and red spotfires supposedly on the aiming-point. In the event, a two-thousand-yard correction was broadcast to compensate for a poor marking performance, which resulted in explosions on the airfield and runway and among barrack buildings and some of the sheds, and an ammunition dump went up at 01.40.

55 Base sat out the above operations and was called into action on the following night when the operation against the dynamite works was rescheduled and the Michelin tyre factory at Clermont-Ferrand was added to the target list. Sixty-eight Lancasters were assigned to the explosives works and fifty-four, including the 630 Squadron element of twelve, to the tyre factory, with five 627 Squadron Mosquitos at each to provide the low-level marking. The 630 Squadron Lancasters each received a bomb load of a cookie and 216 x 30lb incendiaries before departing East Kirkby between 22.09 and 22.20 with S/L Calvert the senior pilot on duty and S/L Butler navigating for P/O Hill. P/O Wilson and crew turned back early after losing their intercom, leaving the others to reach the target area, where they identified the aiming-point both visually and by red spotfires and red and green TIs, which could be seen burning between factory buildings. They attacked from around 6,000 feet, before returning home filled with enthusiasm at the explosions that had ripped the site apart, some from other squadrons commenting that it was the most destructive attack they had taken part in. On the way home across the Channel, F/L Weller and crew found themselves in a running battle with a FW190, which the mid-upper gunner, F/L Neison, shot down to earn for himself the immediate award of a DFC. Post-raid reconnaissance confirmed that both targets had been severely damaged with a massive loss of production.

During the course of the month the squadron participated in eleven operations and dispatched 135 sorties for the loss of three Lancasters, one crew and a rear gunner.

*F/O Winston Herbert Kellaway DSO*

*F/Sgt C W Walker Rear Gunner in F/O Dave Roberts Crew*

*630 Squadron Lancaster LE-S East Kirkby*

*Crew of Lancaster ME717*

*L-R: 2 unidentified ground crew, F/Sgt Max Dunbar (RG), P/O L N Rackley (Blue) (Pilot), F/Sgt Doug Morgan (BA), F/Sgt Stan Jones, P/O Ian Gow (Nav), Sgt Jack Watt (W.Op) F/Sgt Jack Jones (MUG). Photo taken immediately prior to take off on Juvisy (Paris) railway yards on the 18$^{th}$ April 1944. F/Sgt Max Dunbar was killed just one week later on the 25$^{th}$ April 1944 during a crash on landing on Borgo airfield, Corsica following severe damage to ME717 over Munich. The aircraft was totally destroyed in the crash.*

*P/O L N Rackley RAAF*  *Sgt Max Dunbar RAAF (KIA)*

*Sgt Stan Jones and pilot P/O Blue Rackley. Photo taken shortly after crash in Corsica.*

*Corsica, France. May 1944. The shattered remains of Lancaster ME717 which, with two engines shot up over Munich, crossed the Alps, Italy and the Mediterranean on the other two engines to land on Corsica. The Lancaster coded LE-E took off from RAF East Kirkby, Lincolnshire, at 8.51pm to bomb Munich. Upon crash landing at 5.25am at Borgo airfield, Corsica, the aircraft's tail hit a parked aircraft killing Sgt Maxwell Dunbar the rear gunner. The rest of the crew were uninjured.*

*Left - Sgt Maurice Henley rear gunner. Lancaster LL949 LE-E was lost on the 23rd November 1944 on a raid to Trondheim. The crew were killed when the Lancaster crashed on a sandbank near the north bank of the Humber on Sunk Island. Sgt Woodward died from injuries on the 1st December. Crew: F/O G R Flood (Pilot), Sgt L T Woodward, F/Sgt C Agnew F/Sgt K J Aspell, F/Sgt W R Ingram, Sgt F Hughes Sgt M B Henley.*

*Three of the crew of Lancaster ME739 having a briefing with the pilot before a raid on Juvisy on 18th April 1944. The aircraft was shot down over Leipzig 11th April 1945. While the crew were taken prisoner or evaded, Sgt J R Dicken was killed when his parachute caught fire and he fell to his death.*

*Top: F/O Bill Goodwin (BA), Sgt Eric Darton (MUG), F/O Tom Scrivener (Nav). Below: Sgt 'Gem' Jewell (W/Op), S/L Roy Millichap (Pilot), F/Sgt Dave Schwab (RG).*

*Sgt Jack Warwick (Nav), Sgt Leslie Meace (FE), F/Sgt C Roy Griffin (BA), P/O Douglas Hawker (Pilot), Sgt Alfred Dawson (BA), Sgt Ron Adams (MUG), Sgt John Miller (RG). The location and identity of the Stirling are unknown. Below: Three of the Hawker Crew.*

*F/Sgt Leslie Meace (FE)*  *Three of 630 Squadron Crew*

*Remains of an unidentified crashed Lancaster*

*Photographs from Sgt Les Meace, Flight Engineer in P/O Hawker's crew*

*630 Lancaster T for Tare September 1944*
*F/O W A Sparks (Pilot), Sgt W G Armour (Nav), F/O Barker (BA), Sgt Wilfred Shillito (W.Op), Sgt Rye (RG), F/O Cullington (FE), P/O Harvey (MUG)*

*Lancaster LE-P on dispersal August 1944.*

*F/O F H A Watts*

*630 Squadron East Kirkby - Lancaster LE-C*
*Back L-R: Sgt Dennis Cooper (W.Op/AG), Sgt Harry Louk (F/E), Sgt Melvyn Mackay DFC (BA), Sgt George Matthews (RG). Front: F/Sgt Charles Housden DFC, Sgt Robbert Heggie (MUG), P/O F H A Watts DFC.*

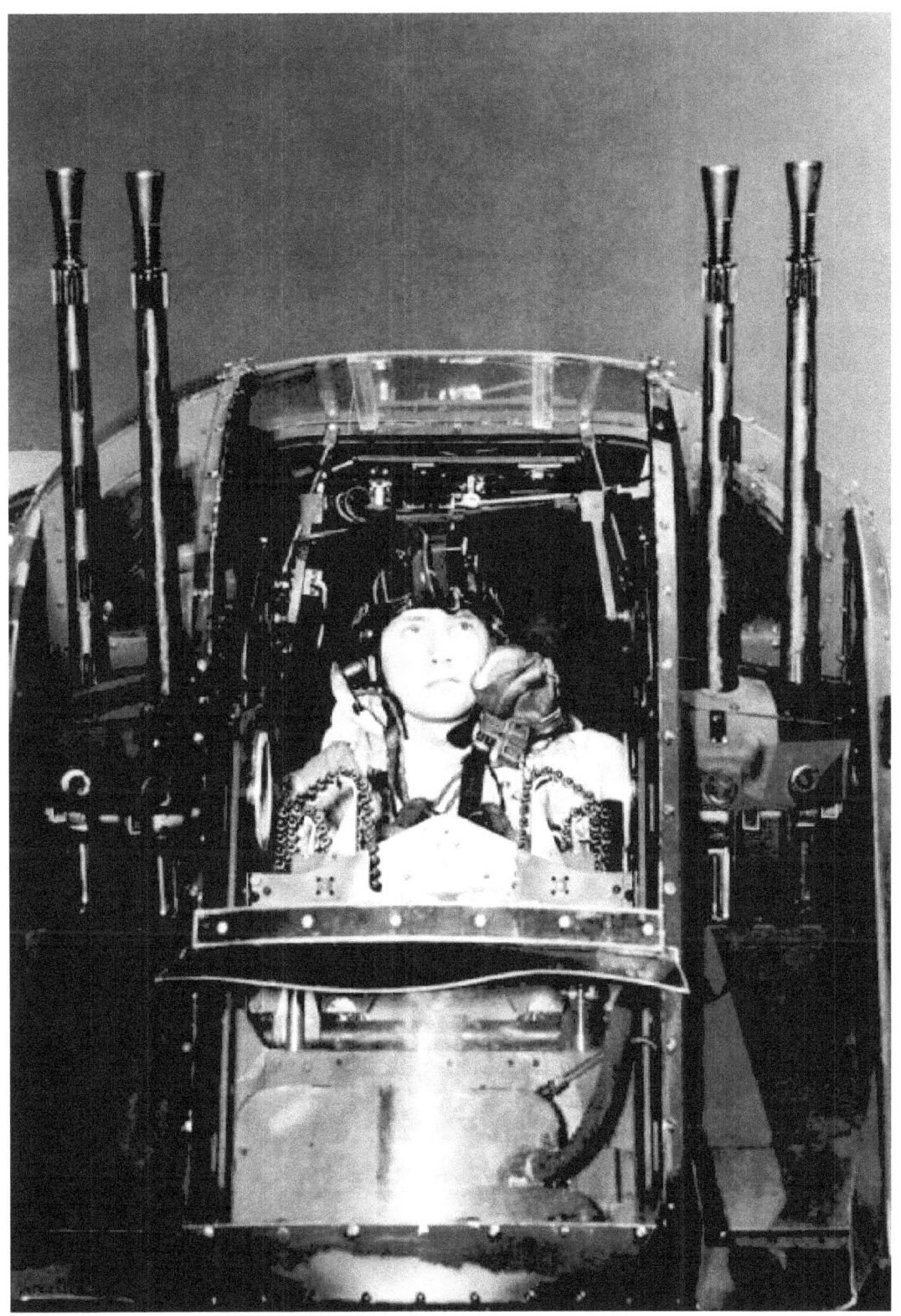
*F/Sgt J Morgan, the rear gunner of a 630 Squadron Lancaster at RAF East Kirkby, checks his guns before taking off on a night raid on the marshalling yards at Juvisy-sur-Orge, France.*

*Crew of Lancaster ME650*
*All lost when their Lancaster crashed at South Grene Denmark, 27th August 1944. Back: Sgt Guy Stott (FE), Sgt Alan Langridge (RG), W/O William Carrier, Sgt Leslie Thompson (W.Op). Front: F/O Burton McLauchlin (BA), F/L Evelyn Bowers (Pilot), P/O Wilfred Fingland.*

*S/L Kenneth Frederick Vare AFC*
*A New Zealander, S/L Vare joined the RAF prior to the outbreak of war. He was a flight commander in 630 Squadron but killed in action on a Berlin operation 2nd January 1944.*

*'Siemensstadt' on the Elmowerk, framed by the SSW logo (left) and the S&H logo (right), 1936.*

*Housing built for Siemensstadt workers.*

*Anti-aircraft searchlight, 1940*

*The Wernerwerk M production facility in Siemensstadt in Berlin, 1944*
*(All Siemens photographs by kind permission of Siemens Historical Institute. The copyrights remain with Siemens AG, Munich/Berlin).*

*Attacks on Dortmund Ems Canal*

*The vitally important steelworks (Reichswerke Hermann Göring) at Salzgitter were an obvious RAF target that warranted as much protection as possible. (Photo by kind permission of Malcom Brooke Military Histories)*

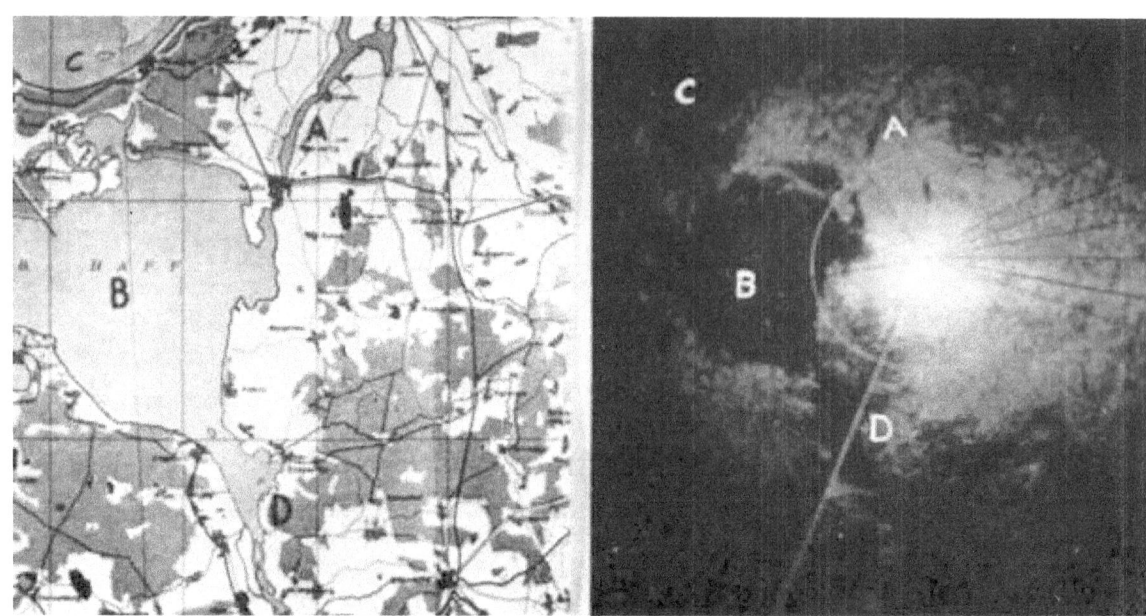

*A H2S radar image of a lagoon near the Baltic coast. The radar return from the water is much darker and the features of the lagoon are clearly visible. (Malcolm Brooke)*

*Target indicators falling over Berlin during a raid on the city*

*Pilot P/O Alfred Jackson (with mother and wife). Killed with all his crew when homeward-bound, the aircraft was shot down on a Bourg-Leopold Military Camp raid on the 12th May 1944. Crew: Sgt Harold Edgar Frank Owen (FE), F/Sgt Denis Walter Muddiman (Nav), F/O Joseph Feldman RCAF (BA), Sgt Richard Matthew Cartlidge (W.Op), Sgt Arthur William Seago (MUG), Sgt Ernest Albert Louis (RG).*

*Sgt Eric Day (W.Op), Sgt William Goodyear (FE), Sgt George Tyler (RG), Sgt Fred Hard (MUG), Sgt Harold Bradley (Nav), P/O Ralph Taft (Pilot), Sgt Frank Hartley (BA). All lost on a St Leu operation on 5th July 1944.*

*F/O John Stanley Cross. (BA)*
*Lost without trace on a Leipzig operation. 20$^{th}$ February 1944.*

*P/O Harold Kidd*
*Lost without trace 22$^{nd}$ February 1944.*

Sgt Wallace Jenkins (RG), F/Sgt Eric Doram (Nav), F/Sgt John Davison (B/A), Sgt Max White, Sgt Steve Dougan (W.Op), P/O Joe Kilgour (Pilot). Flight Engineer is probably Sgt H Owen. On the night of the 27$^{th}$ April 1944, he was replaced by Sgt R Middleton. All lost when shot down on a Schweinfurt raid.

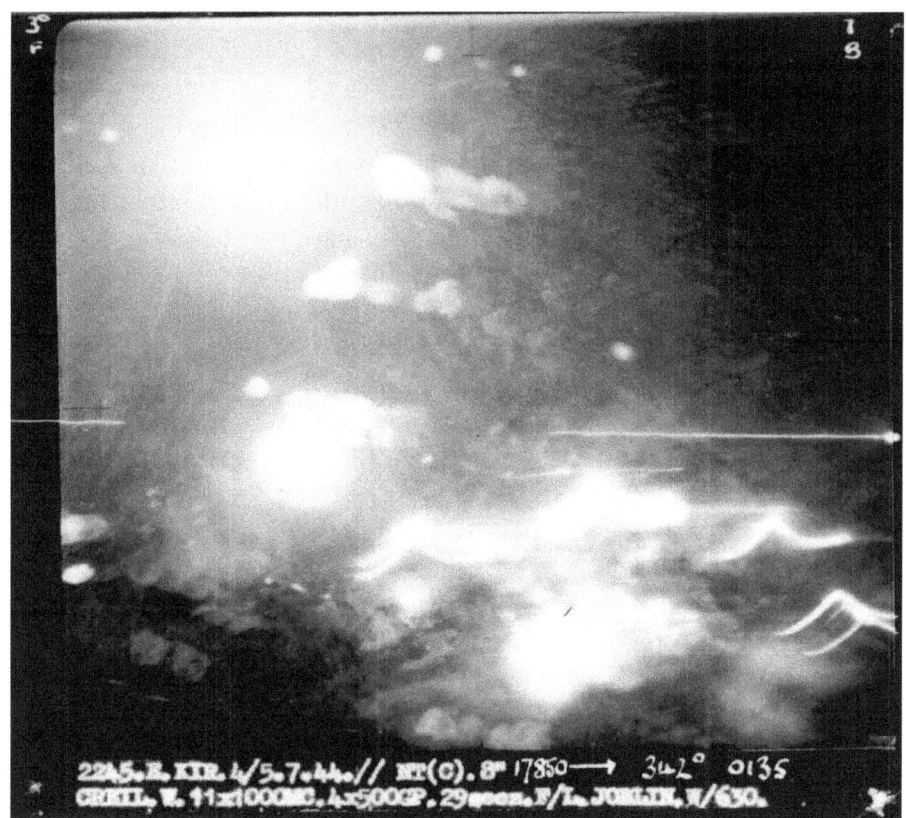

*Target Photograph of Creil, France – a flying-bomb site.*

*F/Sgt Arthur McGill (KIA), Sgt William France (KIA), F/Sgt G Withey, F/Sgt William Pearson, (PoW), F/Sgt Ernest Farnell (KIA), P/O Alan Johnson (Pilot) (KIA), Sgt G E Watts (PoW). Their Lancaster JB288 was shot down on the outward flight to attack Nuremburg on the 30/31$^{st}$ March 1944. F/Sgt G Withey was the crew's usual bomb aimer. However, he was sick and had been replaced by F/L Headlam who became a PoW.*

# May 1944

Fifteen 630 Squadron crews joined a dozen from 57 Squadron in the briefing room at East Kirkby on the 1st to learn that their target for that night as part of a force of forty-six Lancasters from 55 Base and four 627 Squadron Mosquitos was an aircraft repair workshop at Tours in western France. This was one of three 5 Group operations for the night, the others involving a total of 131 Lancasters and eight Mosquitos against a SNCASE aircraft assembly factory at Saint-Martin-du-Touch, a western suburb of Toulouse, and the Poudrerie explosives works in the same city. The 630 Squadron element took off between 22.02 and 22.12 with F/Ls Hill, Probert and Weller the senior pilots on duty, the first mentioned, with S/L Butler again occupying the navigation cubicle, having been recently promoted. Each Lancaster lifted thirteen 1,000-pounders into the air, all of which reached the intended destination, where moonlight shone from largely clear skies and the excellent visibility facilitated a visual identification of the factory buildings. Yellow TIs identified a datum point and red spotfires the aiming-point, but the deplorable state of the squadron ORB for April and May, with no daily summary at all provided on Form 540, denies us detail of the squadron's involvement. The comments against each crew for this operation on Form 541 is limited in most cases to "Night bombing attack on Paris", and even that is incorrect. We know from other more detailed ORBs that they carried out their attacks from 6,000 to 9,000 feet, and miraculously from the squadron ORB for the first time, that the bombing took place between 00.38 and 01.07 in accordance with the instructions of the Master Bomber. We are further informed that bomb bursts appeared to be concentrated around the spotfires.

Meanwhile, at Toulouse, the attacks were clearly focused on the respective aiming-points, and the main assembly shop and boiler house at the SNCASE site were observed to be hit, although there was a degree of disappointment that fire was less extensive than anticipated as the force withdrew to the north. All crews returned to their respective stations confident of a successful outcome, and post-raid reconnaissance revealed all three factories to have been heavily damaged.

Briefings took place on 1 and 5 Group stations on the 3rd, for what would become a highly contentious operation that night against a Panzer training camp and transport depot at Mailly-le-Camp, situated some seventy-five miles east of Paris in north-eastern France. The units based there posed a potential threat to Allied forces as the invasion unfolded and needed to be eliminated. The events of the operation proved to be so controversial that recriminations abound to this day concerning the 5 Group leadership provided by W/Cs Cheshire and Deane. Although the grudges by 1 Group aircrew against them can be understood in the light of what happened, they are unjust, and based on emotion and incorrect information and it is worthwhile to examine the conduct of the operation in some detail. W/C Cheshire was appointed as marker leader, and was piloting one of four 617 Squadron Mosquitos, while 83 Squadron's commanding officer, W/C Laurence Deane, was overall raid controller with S/L Sparks his Deputy. Deane and Cheshire attended separate briefings, and neither seemed aware of the complete plan, particularly the role of the 1 Group Special Duties Flight from Binbrook, which was assigned to its own specific aiming point to mark for an element of the 1 Group force.

The thirteen 630 Squadron Lancasters each received a bomb load of a cookie and fifteen 500-pounders before departing East Kirkby between 21.50 and 22.04 with S/L Calvert the senior pilot on duty and S/L Butler navigating for F/L Hill. All reached the target area to find clear skies, moonlight and excellent bombing conditions, but confusion already beginning to influence events. 617 Squadron's W/C Cheshire and S/L Shannon were in position before midnight, and as the first flares from the 83 and 97 Squadron Lancasters illuminated the target below, Cheshire released his two red spot fires onto the first aiming point at 00.00½ from 1,500 feet. Shannon backed them up from 400 feet five and a half minutes later, and as far as Cheshire was concerned, the operation was bang on schedule at this stage. A 97 Squadron Lancaster also laid markers accurately to ensure a constant focal point, and Cheshire passed instructions to Deane to call the bombers in. It was at this stage of the operation that matters began to go awry, when a commercial radio station, believed to be an American forces network, jammed the VHF frequencies in use. Deane called in the 5 Group element, elated that everything was proceeding according to plan, but nothing happened. He checked with his wireless operator that the instructions had been transmitted and called up S/L Sparks, who was also mystified by the lack of bombing.

Post raid reports are contradictory, and it is impossible to establish an accurate course of events, particularly when Deane and Cheshire's understanding of the exact time of zero hour differed by five minutes. Remarkably, it also seems, that Deane was unaware that there were two marking points, or three, if one includes 1 Group's Special Duties Flight. Cheshire, initially at least, appeared happy with the early stages of the attack and described the bombing as concentrated and accurate. It seems certain, however, that many minutes had passed between the dropping of Cheshire's markers and the first main force bombs falling, during which period, Deane was coming to terms with the fact that his instructions were not getting through. A plausible scenario is, that in the absence of instructions, and with red spot fires clearly visible in the target, some 5 Group crews from 53 and 55 Base squadrons opted to bomb, and others followed suit, and it was at this point that W/C Deane attempted to control the operation by W/T, which also failed. Some 630 Squadron crews were among those bombing early from 00.07, one must assume at altitudes ranging from around 6,000 to 8,000 feet, while others joined in later between 00.25 and 00.30 when predominantly 1 Group Lancasters were over the target. The consensus appeared to be that the aiming points were well-marked and the air above them was ridiculously congested.

Now a new problem was arising as smoke from these first salvoes threatened to obscure the target area, and Cheshire had to decide whether or not to send in Fawke and Kearns to mark the second aiming point. His feeling and that of Deane, as it later transpired, was that it was unnecessary as the volume of bombs still to fall into the relatively compact area of the target would ensure destruction of the entire site. However, by 00.16, the first phase of bombing should have been completed, leaving a clear run for Fawke and Kearns across the target, but the majority of 5 Group crews were still on their bombing run, and Cheshire asked Deane for a pause in the bombing while the two Mosquitos went in. As far as Cheshire was concerned, there was no response from Deane, who would anyway have been confused by mention of a second aiming point. In the event, Deane's deputy, S/L Sparks, eventually found a channel free of interference, and did, in fact, transmit an instruction to halt the bombing both by W/T and R/T, and some crews reported hearing something. While utter chaos reigned, Kearns and Fawke dived in among the falling cookies at 00.23 and 00.25 respectively to mark the second aiming point on the western edge of the camp. At 2,000 feet, they were lucky to survive the turbulence created by the exploding 4,000 pounders, when 4,000 feet was considered to be a minimum safe height. They were not entirely happy with their work, but F/O Edwards of 97 Squadron dropped a stick of markers precisely on the mark, and S/L Sparks was then able to call the 1 Group main force in along with any from 5 Group with bombs still on board. Meanwhile, the night-fighters continued to create havoc among the Lancasters as they milled around in the target area, and as burning aircraft were seen to fall all around, some of 1 Group's Australian crews succumbed to their anxiety and frustration and in a rare breakdown of R/T discipline, let fly with comments of an uncomplimentary nature, many of which were intended for, and, indeed, heard by Deane.

Despite the problems, the operation was a major success, which destroyed 80% of the camp's buildings and 102 vehicles, of which thirty-seven were tanks, while over two hundred men were killed. Forty-two Lancasters failed to return, however, two thirds of them from 1 Group, and 50 Squadron was 5 Group's most afflicted unit with four Lancasters and crews unaccounted for. 55 Base lost three aircraft, one from 57 Squadron and two from 207 Squadron, but 630 Squadron somehow avoided the carnage, and welcomed back all thirteen of its participants. At debriefing, the always outspoken and future commanding officer of 630 Squadron, S/L Blome-Jones of 207 Squadron, described the situation as a complete shambles and chaos, the controller as inefficient and the discipline of some crews as bad. Others returned to the theme that this was a trip worthy of counting more than one-third of a sortie. On the following day, an inquest into the conduct of the raid revealed that the wireless transmitter in Deane's Lancaster had been sufficiently off frequency to allow the interference from the American network to mask the transmission of instructions and prevent the call to bomb from reaching the main force crews. The 1 Group A-O-C, AVM Rice, decided he would not participate in further operations organised by 5 Group, which was probably not a blow to Cochrane, who was confident that his group did not need back-up.

On the 6th, 1 and 5 Groups were invited to send a modest force each to attack ammunition dumps in France, 5 Group detailing sixty-four Lancasters and four Mosquitos from 52 and 54 Bases for a site at Louailles, situated some four miles south-east of the town of Sable-sur-Sarthe, south-west of Le-Mans. Clear skies and excellent visibility provided ideal conditions, and a Master Bomber was on hand to direct the attack, which resulted in numerous bomb flashes that lit up the long storage sheds and two enormous explosions were each followed by a large mushroom of smoke rising through 3,000 feet as the force withdrew.

On the following day, 5 Group was invited to participate in two of five small-scale operations to be mounted against airfields, ammunition dumps and a coastal battery in support of the coming invasion. Its targets were the airfield at Tours and an ammunition dump at Salbris, some sixty miles to the east, for which forces of fifty-three and fifty-eight Lancasters were assembled. It was for the former that 630 Squadron loaded each of its thirteen Lancasters with a cookie and sixteen 500-pounders, before sending them on their way from East Kirkby between 00.15 and 00.35 with W/C Deas and S/L Calvert the senior pilots on duty and S/L Butler navigating for F/L Hill. Also operating as a guest to hone his operational skills before being installed as the commanding officer of 61 Squadron was the twenty-eight-year-old Rhodesian W/C "Reg" Stidolph, who had spent the early war years in the Middle-Eastern theatre before serving in Burma in 1943. The bomber stream formed up as it headed south to pass by Reading en-route to Selsey Bill for the Channel crossing with a view to making landfall on the French coast at Cabourg. It turned out to be another night of perfect conditions, with Gee functioning faultlessly all the way out, and with twenty miles horizontal visibility under bright moonlight, the red spotfires were observed well in advance of arrival at the two aiming points, one among the main buildings complex and the other on the hangars on the south side of the aerodrome. The Master Bomber was W/C Tait, who was piloting a 467 Squadron RAAF Lancaster with two photographers on board, but unfortunately, an electrical fault in the bomb-aimer's compartment caused a fire that rendered the nose camera inoperable. He controlled the attack by R/T backed up by W/T and announced the markers to be "bang-on" before giving the order to proceed. At the end of a two-and-a-quarter-hour outward flight, the 630 Squadron crews carried out their attacks from around 6,000 to 8,000 feet between 02.54 and 03.13 in accordance with Tait's instructions, Tait himself delivering his attack in the middle of the raid from 6,000 feet at 02.59. Cookies and 500-pounders were observed to detonate across the airfield on the runways, hangars and other buildings, causing thick smoke to drift over the area as the force turned away. This made it difficult to assess the outcome, but post-raid reconnaissance would reveal heavy damage and there was a similarly successful outcome at 5 Group's other target at Salbris.

Another small-scale operation was mounted by the group on the 8th against the airfield and seaplane base at Lanveoc-Poulmic, located on the northern side of the peninsular forming the southern boundary of the L'Elorn estuary opposite Brest. A force of fifty-eight Lancasters from 53 Base and six Mosquitos easily identified the target after pinpointing on the coastline, and bombing was carried out from low to medium level either side of midnight. Hangars and other buildings were seen to be on fire and enveloped in smoke at the conclusion of the attack, from which all but one Lancaster returned safely.

55 Base was called into action on the 9th to participate in an attack by thirty-nine Lancasters and four Mosquitos on a small ball-bearing factory at Annecy, situated in south-eastern France close to the frontiers with Switzerland and Italy. While this was in progress, more than four hundred aircraft were to target seven coastal batteries in the Pas-de-Calais to confirm in the mind of the enemy the false belief that the Allied invasion forces would land at Calais, and right up to D-Day itself, the coastal region between Gravelines to the east of the port and Berck-sur-Mer to the south-west would be subjected to frequent bombardments. A second 5 Group operation on this night involving fifty-six Lancasters and eight Mosquitos was to be directed at two factories, the Gnome & Rhône aero-engine works and the Goodrich tyre factory at Gennevilliers in northern Paris. 630 Squadron briefed ten crews for Annecy, while out on the dispersals the armourers were loading each of their Lancasters with two 1,000 and thirteen 500-pounders, before they departed East Kirkby between 21.00 and 21.35 with F/Ls Hill and Weller the senior pilots on duty. Ahead of them was an outward flight of four-and-a-half hours, which all of the 630 Squadron crews completed without incident, but two of the Mosquitos had to turn back. On arrival in the target area they found a green TI on the datum point and generally clear conditions with some haze to contend with. The aiming-point was identified by red spotfires, but it was not long before the early bombing caused smoke to

obscure ground detail, and there appeared to be a degree of overshooting. A very large yellowy-orange explosion occurred at 02.02, from which point, smoke became a problem, and some crews reported the bombing falling to starboard of the spotfires. Concentration was achieved later, and many explosions and fires were observed, although the large clouds of smoke rendered an accurate assessment difficult. It would require post-raid reconnaissance to confirm that a successful operation had taken place.

Meanwhile, moonlight and clear skies had enabled the Paris-bound crews to map read after Gee was jammed at the French coast, and H2S proved useful as they closed on the target. Yellow TIs and red spotfires identified the aiming-point, and detonations appeared to be focused as intended in the centre of the marked area. Local sources confirmed damage to the target, but also collateral damage that killed twenty-seven French civilians and injured more than a hundred.

Five railway targets were selected for attention on the night of the 10/11th, among them the marshalling yards at Lille, situated close to the Belgian frontier in north-eastern France, which was the target for a 5 Group main force from 53 Base, with 97 (Straits Settlement) Squadron from 54 Base providing the illumination and back-up marking. W/C Tait was guesting again in a 467 Squadron RAAF Lancaster with two photographers on board to record the outcome, and they found the target area to be under clear skies with the aiming-point slightly obscured by ground haze, a situation easily negated by red spotfires and green TIs. Whether or not flak or night-fighters were responsible is unclear, but three 467 Squadron RAAF Lancasters and another from 463 Squadron RAAF exploded with great force over the target as they orbited awaiting instructions from the Master Bomber, and two others from 463 Squadron fell to night-fighters less spectacularly, but with equally devastating consequences for the occupants. The attacks were delivered in the light of flares from 7,000 to 10,000 feet and bomb bursts were observed across the tracks and resulted in two large explosions that confirmed a successful assault on this important hub linking north-eastern France with Belgium. There was shock at Waddington when six of its crews failed to return, and deep sadness at the loss, in particular, of two highly popular flight commanders, one reputedly on the last sortie of his tour.

5 Group put together a force of 190 Lancasters and eight Mosquitos on the 11th, to target a military camp at Bourg-Leopold in north-eastern Belgium, for which 630 Squadron made ready nineteen Lancasters, loading each with a cookie and sixteen 500-pounders. They departed East Kirkby between 22.16 and 22.32 with pilots of flight lieutenant rank leading the way and S/L Butler the senior officer on duty. They made landfall over the Scheldt and reached the target to find hazy conditions and a little thin cloud at between 3,000 and 13,000 feet, despite which, they would be able to identify the buildings and huts in the light of illuminating flares. Three Oboe Mosquitos were on hand to deliver the initial marking, but inaccurately forecast winds caused the 83 Squadron heavy element to arrive late, by which time the main force crews had begun to orbit to await instructions. A communications problem prevented some crews from hearing the Master Bomber's broadcasts, but the aiming-point could be seen to be marked by red spotfires and green TIs. From the Master Bomber's perspective, the initial Oboe marker had been visible only to a few crews, and quickly burned out, and so he called for another Mosquito to drop a red spot fire onto the aiming-point. Before this was accomplished, however, the main force crews started to bomb and as smoke

began to obscure the ground, the Master Bomber, S/L Mitchell, quickly became uncomfortable about the close proximity of civilian residential property and called a halt to the bombing at 00.35, sending the rest of the force home, some of them after circling for more than twenty minutes. A few crews failed to hear the signal and continued to bomb, while a handful of others found last resort targets rather than jettison part or all of their hardware. Two 630 Squadron Lancasters failed to return, and news eventually came through that P/O Watt RNZAF and four of his crew had lost their lives when ME737 was shot down by a night-fighter to crash near Herenthout, some fifteen miles to the south-east of Antwerp delivering the flight engineer and bomb-aimer into captivity. The fate of P/O Jackson and his crew has never been determined, ND580 disappearing without trace, presumably in the sea.

On the 19th, following a week of minor operations, the station teleprinters worked overtime dispensing the details of operations that night against five marshalling yards, two coastal batteries and a radar station. 5 Group detailed 225 Lancasters for railway targets, 112 from 52 and 55 Bases for Amiens with eight Mosquitos, and 113 from 53 and 54 Bases for Tours accompanied by four Mosquitos. 630 Squadron loaded seventeen Lancasters with eleven 1,000 and four 500-pounders each and the one for the crew of W/C Deas with five 1,000-pounders and a selection of hooded flares, TIs and spotfires, before sending them on their way from East Kirkby between 23.06 and 23.32 with S/L Calvert the other senior pilot on duty. They set course for north-eastern France, where they found the target shrouded in a layer of eight to ten-tenths cloud at between 6,000 and 11,000 feet, through which the target was identified by red spotfires. However, when checked on H2S, they appeared to be up to five miles from the planned aiming-point and thirty-seven aircraft had carried out an attack before instructions came through by W/T at 01.24 to terminate proceedings and return home. The 630 Squadron element was in the third wave and returned most of its ordnance to the station store.

Meanwhile, at Tours, where a previous attack by 5 Group had targeted the railway installations on the outskirts of the town, this night's effort was directed at those in the central district between the rivers Loire to the north and La Cher to the south. The crews found largely clear skies over north-western France and visibility good enough through the four-tenths cloud to identify ground detail. The aiming-point was marked by red spotfires, and in view of the close proximity of civilian housing, the Master Bomber took great care and much time before issuing the order to bomb. This would extend the time on target, but fortunately, the Luftwaffe was absent, and the accuracy of the bombing was sufficient to cause massive damage to the target with only a little collateral damage and no losses.

For the first time in a year, Duisburg was posted as the target for a heavy raid on the 21st, for which a force of 510 Lancasters was drawn from 1, 3, 5 and 8 Groups, 5 Group responsible for 131 of them. They would be supported by twenty-two Mosquitos, and while this operation was in progress, seventy Lancasters from 5 Group and thirty-seven Halifaxes would undertake mining duties in the Nectarines and Rosemary gardens around the Frisians and off Heligoland, and in the Forget-me-not, Silverthorn and Quince gardens in the Kattegat and Kiel Bay regions of the Baltic. 630 Squadron briefed five crews for the main event and fourteen for mining, loading each of the Lancasters of the former with a cookie and ten deep SBCs of 4lb incendiaries and twelve standard SBCs of the 30lb denomination and the latter with five Mk VI mines to deliver to the Forget-me-not garden in Kiel harbour. The latter departed East Kirkby over an extended period between 21.47 and 23.27 with S/L Calvert the senior pilot on duty and according to the 57 squadron ORB, in the complete absence of information provided by 630 Squadron, some encountered night-fighters over Denmark and faced searchlights and flak as they began their timed runs to the release point. LL950 was shot down by a night-fighter somewhere over Jutland's western coastal region with no survivors from the crew of F/O Bailey, who, it will be recalled, had been dragged clear of the burning wreckage of their aircraft following the crash-landing at East Kirkby just one month earlier. The East Kirkby community also had to deal with the failure to return of a 57 Squadron crew.

The Ruhr-bound crews of P/Os Brown, Henriquez, Lindsay and Maxwell and F/O Smith took off between 22.49 and 23.27, the Maxwell crew ten minutes late, which would persuade them ultimately to abandon their sortie. At briefings, crews had been instructed to adhere to the plan for the outward route, which involved a few aircraft from 3 Group gaining height as they adopted a north-westerly course as far as Sleaford, so as not to cross into enemy radar cover earlier than necessary. The groups would rendezvous at 18,000 feet over the North Sea at 3° East to cross the enemy coast via the western Frisians at 20,000 feet and climb to 22,000 or 23,000 feet, before increasing speed for the run across the target. The spearhead of the bomber stream reached the western edge of the Ruhr to find it concealed beneath ten-tenths cloud with tops at between 11,000 and 20,000 feet, into which the red Wanganui markers with-yellow-stars fell almost before they could be seen. A number of crews commented on the data provided by the wind-finder system to be inaccurate, and this made it a challenge to establish positions. The main force crews used the explosion of cookies, the glow of fires and the evidence of intense flak as references and bombed from 15,000 to 22,000 feet either side of 01.30, before returning home with little useful information to report. The Lindsay and Henriquez crews attacked the primary target, the Brown crew an alternative, believed to be Cologne, while the mixed RCAF/RAF crew of F/O Smith RCAF failed to return, JB672 having fallen victim to a night-fighter over Holland and crashing without survivors near Kilder, between Arnhem and the German frontier. The loss of twenty-nine Lancasters was a reminder to the Command that the Ruhr remained a dangerous destination, although most of the missing aircraft had been brought down by night-fighters over Holland and Belgium and the North Sea on the way home. The leading night-fighter Ace, Martin Drewes of III./NJG1, alone accounted for at least three Lancasters. Returning crews were not enthusiastic about the outcome, and post-raid reconnaissance confirmed that a modest 350 buildings had been destroyed in the southern half of Duisburg and 665 others had been seriously damaged.

Just like its Ruhr neighbour, Duisburg, Dortmund was posted on the 22$^{nd}$ to host its first large-scale visit from the Command for a year and would face an all-Lancaster heavy force of 361 aircraft drawn from 1, 3, 6 and 8 Groups. While this operation was in progress, 220 Lancasters of 5 Group and five of the ABC variety from 101 Squadron were to target Braunschweig, which thus far had evaded severe damage at the hands of Bomber Command. 630 Squadron made ready sixteen Lancasters, loading each with a 2,000-pounder and a dozen 500lb J-Type cluster incendiaries before dispatching them from East Kirkby between 22.25 and 22.43 with W/C Deas the senior pilot on duty and S/L Butler navigating for F/L Hill. The bomber stream passed through the clearly-evident night-fighter activity from the Dutch coast all the way to the target, having to negotiate intense searchlight activity as they passed between Bremen and Osnabrück and patches of ten-tenths cloud over northern Germany. P/O Mallinson and crew were some distance into the outward flight when the rear turret became unserviceable and forced them to turn back. The forecast at briefings had suggested clear skies over Braunschweig but, in fact, the marker force encountered four to seven-tenths drifting cloud with tops at up to 7,000 feet, and although highly effective in the right weather conditions, the 5 Group low-level visual marking method could easily be rendered ineffective by cloud cover. The blind heavy marker aircraft dropped skymarkers by H2S, while the 627 Squadron Mosquito element went in at low level to release red spotfires. Some crews described "hopeless confusion" with flares and incendiaries spread over a distance, and many had to rely on their own H2S to establish their position. Some found a complete absence of marking and orbited for up to fifteen minutes until a few green TIs appeared and bombing took place on these or on incendiary fires from an average of 19,000 feet, in the case of the 630 Squadron contingent, between 01.16 and 01.43.

Considerable interference over R/T communications added to the problems, and although the Master Bomber could be heard in discussions with his Deputies, no instructions were received from him, and the attack lacked cohesion. Thirteen Lancasters failed to return, five of them having taken off from East Kirkby, and two of these, belonging to 630 Squadron, contained mixed-nationality crews. ND655 disappeared without trace with the crew of P/O Brown RAAF, and JB546 was shot down by a night-fighter to crash near Quakenbrück, some thirty-five miles from the Dutch frontier and 120 miles short of the target with fatal consequences for P/O Champness RAAF and three of his crew, while the three survivors were taken into captivity. Of the fourteen airmen in the two aircraft, eight were RAF, five RAAF and one RCAF. It was a bad night for 55 Base generally, which also registered the loss of three crews from 207 Squadron at Spilsby. At debriefing, crews reported heavy predicted flak bursting at 18,500 feet and intense searchlight activity co-operating with night-fighters, and a number of Lancasters were handed back to their ground crews with flak holes to patch. Post-raid reconnaissance confirmed that most of the bombing had fallen onto outlying communities, confirming in the minds of the residents that this was an intentional ploy by the RAF.

The main operation on the 24th involved 442 aircraft in an attack on two previously targeted marshalling yards at Aachen, Aachen-West and Rothe-Erde in the east. As the most westerly city in Germany, sitting on the frontiers of both Holland and Belgium, it was a major link in the railway network that would be a route for reinforcements to the Normandy battle front. Other operations on this night involved coastal batteries in the Pas-de-Calais and war-industry factories in Holland and Belgium, 5 Group detailing forty-four Lancasters, mostly from 55 Base, to attack the Ford and General Motors works in Antwerp, while fifty-nine from 53 and 54 Bases were assigned to the Philips electronics factory at Eindhoven in southern Holland. It was for the former that 630 Squadron made ready eleven of its own, loading each with eleven 1,000 and four 500-pounders, some with a long-delay fuse, before departing East Kirkby between 22.45 and 23.00 with F/Ls Hill and Rodgers the senior pilots on duty. They headed for the Norfolk coast, running into a bullseye (cross-country) exercise, and having to avoid weaving Lancasters and intense searchlight activity. Matters settled down as they crossed the North Sea towards the Scheldt Estuary, where they found slight ground haze but generally good visibility. The target was identified by illuminating flares, a yellow TI and red spotfires, and was bombed by the 630 Squadron crews from 6,000 to 8,000 feet between 00.40 and

00.52. On return, crews reported a good concentration of bomb bursts around the markers and were no doubt disappointed to discover later that the factory had escaped damage. Meanwhile, those bound for Eindhoven were more than an hour into the outward journey and some eight minutes from the target when the Master Bomber sent them home by W/T, presumably after a Met Flight Mosquito crew had found poor visibility in the target area. As a result, and because the long-delay fuses had been activated, hundreds of perfectly serviceable 1,000 pounders ended up on the seabed.

The night of the 27/28th was to be one of feverish activity, which would generate more than eleven hundred sorties, reflecting the close proximity of the invasion, now just ten days away. The largest operation would bring a return to the military camp at Bourg Leopold in Belgium, the previous attack on which, two weeks earlier, had been abandoned part-way through. There was also a repeat of the Aachen attack of the 24th, which had failed to destroy the Rothe-Erde marshalling yards at the eastern end of the city and needed further attention. 5 Group was not involved in either of the above, and instead prepared forces of one hundred Lancasters and four Mosquitos and seventy-eight Lancasters and five Mosquitos respectively to target marshalling yards and workshops at Nantes and the aerodrome at Rennes, situated some fifty miles apart in north-western France. The group would also support operations against coastal batteries, of which there were five on this night, including one at Saint-Valery-en-Caux, situated a dozen or so miles west of Dieppe, for which forty-seven Lancasters from 55 Base and three Mosquitos were detailed. 630 Squadron was responsible for fourteen of the Lancasters, which departed East Kirkby between 23.36 and 23.51 with W/C Deas the senior pilot on duty and each carrying eleven 1,000 pounders and four 500 pounders. All reached the target area to find clear skies and good visibility, and observed the initial flares to fall over the sea to the north-west of the town, the consequence of which was an instruction to orbit for up to twenty-five minutes until further flares and the red spotfires were released over the aiming-point. The Master Bomber called the main force in at 01.53 and bombing was carried out by the 630 Squadron crews between then and 02.04 from an average of 7,000 feet. The order to go home was issued at 02.09, by which time P/O Maxwell and crew had not been able to carry out an attack after bomb blasts obscured the spotfires. The consensus among returning crews was of an accurate attack.

On the 28th, 181 Lancasters and twenty Mosquitos were made ready to attack three coastal batteries overlooking the Normandy beaches, which, a week hence, would be the scene of Operation Overlord. The target for the 53 Base force was at Sainte-Martin-de-Varrevilles, situated close to what would be Utah Beach, the landing ground for the American 1st Division. On the 31st, 5 Group detailed eighty-two Lancasters and four Mosquitos to attack a railway junction at Saumur in the Loire Valley, and another sixty-eight Lancasters to deal with a coastal battery at Maisy, overlooking Omaha Beach. 55 Base Squadrons did not take part in these operations, but on the last occasion, sent four 57 Squadron Lancasters for mining duties in the Kraut garden in Lim Fjord, a narrow waterway in northern Jutland linking Ålborg with the coast at Hals.

During the course of the month the squadron took part in eleven operations and dispatched 148 sorties for the loss of six Lancasters and crews. The Hill crew was declared tour-expired and this meant that the long-serving S/L Butler would relinquish command of A Flight on his posting to pastures new in early June. His successor, the twenty-three-year-old F/L Arthur Foster DFC, arrived at the end of May and would be elevated to acting squadron leader rank accordingly. It is believed that he was posted in from a training unit having served previously with 61 Squadron, and sadly, his time at 630 Squadron would be brief.

# June 1944

June was to be a hectic month which would make great demands on the crews, beginning with the bombing of coastal batteries as the main priority during the first few days of the month leading up to D-Day. 5 Group opened its account on the 1st by returning to Saumur to attack a second railway junction, through which German forces could be transported to the invasion area. The day dawned cloudy and cold, and these conditions would persist throughout the first week, causing concern among the invasion planners. On 54 and 55 Base stations fifty-eight crews were briefed, sixteen of them from 630 Squadron, while out on the dispersals the armourers were filling each bomb bay with ten 1,000 and four 500 pounders. They departed East Kirkby between 21.58 and 22.21 with no senior pilots on duty and climbed out through a blanket of ten-tenths cloud, before setting course for the south coast and the Channel crossing. The cloud persisted until twenty miles from the target, when it dispersed completely to leave clear skies and good visibility under a three-quarter moon, which rendered the flare force almost superfluous. However, the first wave of the flare force was called in by the Master Bomber, W/C Jeudwine in a 54 Base Mosquito, and instructed to release from 15,000 feet at 01.08, and the first red spot fire from an Oboe Mosquito fell bang on the aiming-point two minutes later. The main force was called in at 01.15, but after five minutes smoke became a problem as it drifted across the area to obscure the spotfire that was still burning, and W/C Jeudwine issued a stand-by order at 01.20 while a green TI was dropped to maintain the aiming-point. Bombing resumed at 01.29 and apart from a few scattered sticks to the north, and on an island in the Loire to the south, the attack seemed to be accurate. Returning crews reported little opposition, fires in the yards and large explosions at 01.22 and 01.35, and the success of the raid was confirmed by photo-reconnaissance, which showed severe damage to the track.

Elements of 53, 54 and 55 Bases joined forces on the 3rd for an attack on a listening station at Ferme-d'Urville, situated on the Cherbourg peninsular to the west of the port, which had escaped damage when attacked by Halifaxes two nights earlier. 101 Lancasters were made ready, 57 Squadron representing East Kirkby in the absence of a 630 contribution, and on arriving in the target area the force was greeted by clear skies and good visibility apart from ground haze. The first of three Oboe Mosquitos dropped a red TI at 00.50, and this was followed by a second one seven minutes later, supplemented shortly afterwards by green TIs from the heavy marker aircraft. The main force bombs were delivered from 6,000 to 10,000 feet from around 01.00 and a large explosion was witnessed at 01.02. Returning crews reported a successful attack that had been focused in a five-hundred-yard radius of the aiming-point, and photographic reconnaissance confirmed that the listening station had ceased to exist.

Orders came through on the 4th to prepare for attacks that night on coastal batteries, three in the Pas-de-Calais to maintain the deception, and the one at Maisy, overlooking what would be the American landing grounds of Utah and Omaha beaches. 259 aircraft of 1, 4, 5, 6 and 8 Groups were made ready, the majority for the deception targets, while fifty-two of the Lancasters from 54 and 55 Bases were assigned to Maisy. 630 Squadron made ready seventeen Lancasters for these pre-dawn attacks, loading each with eighteen 500 pounders and dispatching them from East Kirkby between 01.20 and 01.37, again with no senior pilot on duty. They all reached the target area to encounter ten-tenths cloud with a base at around 4,000 feet, which necessitated the use of Oboe skymarkers, and many crews would complain later that they had been unable to pick up the instructions of the Master Bomber, W/C Grey of 207 Squadron, whose TR aerial, he would discover on landing, had been carried away. Positions were confirmed by Gee-fix, H2S and a faint red or green glow, and the bombing was carried out by the 630 Squadron crews from just above the cloud tops between 03.31 and 03.50, before they returned safely with nothing of value to offer at debriefing. It had been impossible to assess the outcome, and similarly cloudy conditions had thwarted two of the three attempts in the Pas-de-Calais, although the outcome there was of secondary importance to the deception aspect.

The night of the 5/6th was D-Day Eve, and, during its course, a record number of 1,211 sorties would be flown against coastal defences and in support and diversionary operations. 57 and 630 Squadrons each detailed sixteen crews, who attended the briefing at East Kirkby to hear no direct reference to the invasion, but unusually, strict instructions with regard to altitudes and there was a complete ban on dumping bombs into the Channel. They learned also that they would be among more than a thousand aircraft targeting ten heavy gun batteries along the Normandy coast, and that their specific objective was at La Pernelle, the most north-westerly, and although it was not disclosed to them, the closest to Utah Beach. The plan called for 52, 54 and 55 Bases to provide 122 Lancasters and four Mosquitos, among which would be a six-strong flare force provided by 83 Squadron led by W/C Northrop as Deputy Master Bomber to W/C Jeudwine. At the same time, 115 Lancasters and four Mosquitos from 53 and 54 Bases would be targeting a battery at Sainte-Pierre-du-Mont, which was the closest to Omaha Beach, and among the number were seventeen Lancasters of 97 Squadron to provide the illumination and marking. Each of the East Kirkby Lancasters received a bomb load of eleven 1,000 and four 500-pounders before the 630 Squadron contingent took off first between 01.12 and 01.31 with F/Ls Joblin and Rodgers the senior pilots on duty. They all arrived in the target area to find two layers of thin cloud at 7,000 and 10,000 feet, through which the Oboe markers went down at 03.32, to be followed by the first flares thirty seconds later. The low-level Mosquitos backed-up at 03.36, only for the first bombs to be dropped before W/C Jeudwine gave the order. He described the bombing as appalling and called for a halt at 03.45 to allow re-marking to take place, but the main force, as occasionally was the case, took no notice. Another red spot fire was delivered within thirty yards of the aiming point at 03.51, and the order was given to continue bombing at 03.57. Six minutes later, after additional cloud had rolled in, W/C Jeudwine called a halt to proceedings, but some elements of the main force again took no notice. Sgt Hayes and crew were unable to bomb after failing to spot the markers, but the others from the squadron joined in from 5,000 to 12,000 feet and on return would have little to report other than bomb bursts and a mushroom of black smoke.

Any homeward-bound crews looking down through the occasional gaps in the clouds in the early light of dawn were rewarded by the incredible sight of the greatest armada in history, ploughing its way sedately southwards towards the French coast. A total of five thousand tons of bombs was dropped during the night, and this was a new record. Only seven aircraft failed to return from these operations, three of them from Sainte-Pierre-du-Mont, two from 97 Squadron, including the one containing W/C "Jimmy" Carter and seven highly experienced others, all but one of whom held either a DFC or DFM.

Among the many deception and diversionary operations carried out during the night were the highly successful Operations Taxable and Glimmer, carried out respectively by 617 and 218 (Gold Coast) Squadrons employing "window" and precision formation flying to simulate fleets of ships heading for the Pas-de-Calais coast.

As the beachheads were established during the course of the 6th, preparations were put in hand to support the ground forces by attacking nine road and railway communications centres through which the enemy could bring reinforcements. 5 Group was assigned to two targets, at Argentan, located some thirty miles south-east of Caen, and a road bridge in Caen itself, for which forces of 112 Lancasters and six Mosquitos and 120 Lancasters and four Mosquitos respectively were assembled. 54 and 55 Bases were assigned to the latter, for which 630 Squadron loaded its thirteen participating Lancasters with eighteen 500-pounders, while the crews learned at briefing that 83 Squadron's S/L Mitchell was to act as Deputy Master Bomber to W/C James Tait. They departed East Kirkby between 00.18 and 00.45 with S/L Foster the senior pilot on duty for the first time, and all reached the target area to find ten-tenths cloud with a base at 5,000 feet. Whether or not that was responsible, W/C Tait did not see any Oboe markers and suspected that none had been delivered. However, the 83 Squadron illumination was good, and the low-level marking of the road bridge with red spotfires, backed up with green TIs was accomplished punctually and largely accurately, despite smoke drifting across from a fire to the north of the town. The bombing was carried out from below the cloud base at 3,000 to 5,000 feet, by the 630 Squadron crews between 02.38 and 02.55 in accordance with the Master Bomber's instructions, and bomb bursts were observed along with a large fire to port of the aiming-point. Six Lancasters failed to return, and among them was 630 Squadron's ND685, which crashed in the target area almost certainly the victim of light flak as a result of having to orbit while the markers were assessed and then having to make bombing runs just a few thousand feet over masses of enemy armour. P/O Wilson RAAF lost his life along with three others, while the flight engineer, navigator and bomb-aimer fell into enemy hands. Some returning crews reported light flak batteries on an airfield to the west, and others around Cherbourg, which came into play on the way home.

Four railway targets were earmarked for attention by a force of 337 aircraft on the 7th, while elements of 5 Group were being prepared to join forces with 1 and 8 Groups to attack a six-way road junction at Balleroy, situated fifteen miles west of Caen on the approach to the Foret-de-Cerisy, where it was believed the enemy was concealing a fuel dump and tank units. 630 Squadron put up thirteen of the thirty-eight Lancasters provided by 55 Base in an overall force of 112 Lancasters and ten Mosquitos, and they departed East Kirkby ahead of the 57 Squadron contingent between 23.00 and 23.26 with S/L Foster the senior pilot on duty and each crew sitting on eighteen 500-pounders. They arrived in the target area to encounter ten-

tenths cloud with a base at 8,000 to 10,000 feet with haze below, and while the initial Oboe markers appeared to be accurate and on time, others fell simultaneously some five miles to the south-south-west and attracted some bomb loads. The Master Bomber quickly gained control of the situation and redirected the focus upon the correct marker, which was pounded by concentrated bombing. The attack was carried out from 5,000 to 7,000 feet, by the 630 Squadron crews between 01.40 and 01.53, and a large explosion was observed at 01.44 among many smaller ones, each accompanied by a dense cloud of black smoke.

The 55 Base squadrons sat out 5 Group operations on the night of the 8/9th, which, in concert with the other groups, were devoted to the disruption of railway communications and involved a total of 483 aircraft assigned to five centres. 5 Group assembled a force of fifty-four Lancasters and four Mosquitos to attack railway installations at Pontabault, a town situated at the mouth of the Selune River in the Gulf of St Malo, south-west of the beachhead, and ninety-seven Lancasters and four Mosquitos to attend to a similar objective at Rennes in Brittany, thirty miles to the south-west. 617 Squadron would also operate on this night to employ the very first Barnes Wallis-designed 12,000lb Tallboy "earthquake" bombs against the railway tunnel at Saumur.

Enemy-occupied aerodromes in the battle area were to be the targets on the 9th for 401 aircraft from 1, 4, 6 and 8 Groups, while 5 Group concentrated on a railway junction at Etampes, south of Paris, for which 108 Lancasters and four Mosquitos were made ready. 630 Squadron loaded each of its seventeen Lancasters with eighteen 500-pounders, including two with long-delay fuses of twelve and thirty-six hours, before launching them from East Kirkby between 21.40 and 22.03 with F/Ls Joblin, Rodgers and Weller the senior pilots on duty. It is unclear at which point in the operation, whether outbound of homebound, that PB121 was attacked and set on fire by a night-fighter and crashed near Omerville to the west of Paris, killing F/Sgt Houghton AFM and five of his crew and delivering the bomb-aimer, the only commissioned member of the crew, as the sole survivor into enemy hands. Those reaching the target found eight to ten-tenths cloud with a base at 8,000 feet and patches of two to three-tenths lower down at 4,000 feet. The yellow TIs and red spotfires went down on time but the first spotfire fell some four hundred yards north-east of the aiming point at 23.59 and immediately attracted bombs. The Master Bomber called for crews to stand-by and stop bombing while the aiming point was re-marked with red spotfires backed up with green TIs, and bombing resumed at 00.13. Crews confirmed their positions by H2S and Gee-fix before bombing from 5,000 to 7,000 feet between 00.09 and 00.20, some after the Master Bomber had called a halt to proceedings at 00.17. Photo-reconnaissance confirmed that all tracks had been cut for a distance of four hundred yards to the north-east of the junction, but it revealed also that the town had sustained collateral damage, which caused more than 130 civilian fatalities. P/O Kerr and crew claimed the destruction of a Ju88, and P/O Lindsay and crew reported damaging another, in return for which six Lancasters failed to return.

The squadron was not involved in the 5 Group attack by 108 Lancasters on a railway junction at Orleans on the 10th, one of four similar targets for the night, and the group enjoyed the next night off altogether. The campaign against communications targets continued on the 12th at six locations, including Caen and Poitiers, for which 5 Group detailed forces of 109 Lancasters and four Mosquitos and 112 Lancasters and four Mosquitos respectively. 55 Base was assigned to the former, East Kirkby detailing thirty-three Lancasters, fifteen of them belonging to 630 Squadron, which each received a bomb load of thirteen 1,000-pounders, before taking to the air ahead of the 57 Squadron contingent between 23.34 and 23.54 with S/Ls Calvert and Foster the senior pilots on duty. They reached the target area to encounter six to ten-tenths cloud with tops at between 4,000 and 6,000 feet, which made it difficult to see the red spotfire and green TIs. Those arriving in the early stages of the attack bombed from above cloud from up to 10,000 feet, presumably on H2S, before the Master Bomber issued an order at 02.18 to cease bombing and orbit, while he assessed the situation. At 02.20 he ordered crews to bomb visually, which left them confused as to whether that meant coming beneath the cloud base to bomb TIs or the bridge itself or to wait for further illumination. In the event, there was insufficient time for all to break cloud and complete a run before the order to cease bombing was issued at around 02.30. Eight of the 630 Squadron crews were able to get their loads away from 5,000 or a little higher, but the others failed to beat the deadline, and brought most of their bombs home. The first bombing photos, taken at 02.29, confirmed the accuracy of the markers and that the bombing had fallen in the vicinity of the bridges and in the town immediately north of the river. Photo-reconnaissance revealed later that this had been the night's most scattered operation.

A new oil campaign began on this night, prosecuted by 286 Lancasters and seventeen Mosquitos of 1, 3 and 8 Groups, which had as their target the Gelsenkirchener Bergwerke A G refinery, a Bergius-process plant in the Horst district to the north-west of Gelsenkirchen city centre, known to the Germans as Gelsenberg A G and to Bomber Command as Nordstern. Such was the accuracy of the attack, which delivered fifteen hundred bombs on the site, that all production of vital aviation fuel was halted for a number of weeks at a cost to the Germans of a thousand tons per day.

It was at this time that W/C Guy Gibson VC arrived at East Kirkby with a specific brief to understudy the 55 Base operations officer. Following Operation Chastise, Gibson had been sent on a goodwill tour in the United States and found his career at a crossroads on his return. His mind was in turmoil and grappling with a number of important issues, including a possible political career as the Conservative parliamentary candidate for Macclesfield, an unfulfilled, long-term extra-marital romantic liaison, and a burning desire to return to operations before others grabbed the glory by being in at the end, while he languished in a non-operational backwater. Gibson hitched a ride with 57 Squadron flight commander S/L Drew "Duke" Wyness on an air-test and took the Lancaster's controls, and when visited by S/L "Mick" Martin, an original Dambuster, who was now flying a 515 Squadron Mosquito night-fighter with Bomber Command's 100 Group, the pair took a joyride and Gibson was much impressed by the "Wooden Wonder's" capabilities and became even more determined to fly operationally again.

The first daylight operations by Bomber Command since the departure of 2 Group a year earlier were conducted against Le Havre on the evening of the 14th. The port was home to E-Boats and other fast, light naval craft posing a threat to Allied shipping serving the beachhead. The two-phase operation took place under the umbrella of a massive fighter escort and was opened by a 617 Squadron attack on the concrete pens with Tallboys, closely followed by a predominately 1 Group force. 3 Group completed the assault at dusk, and few if any marine craft escaped the carnage unscathed.

Other operations on this night targeted railway installations at three locations in France, while elements of 4, 5 and 8 Groups were hastily assembled to attend to enemy troop and vehicle concentrations at Aunay-sur-Odon and Évrecy near Caen. 5 Group assembled a force of 214 Lancasters and five Mosquitos for the former, of which the sixteen representing 630 Squadron each received a bomb load of eleven 1,000 and four 500-pounders, before departing East Kirkby between 22.15 and 22.31 with no senior pilot on duty. The weather was generally clear with some low cloud, but this did not hamper the marking process, which proceeded punctually and accurately in accordance with the instructions of the Master Bomber, W/C Jeudwine. His Deputy, W/C "Joe" Northrop of 83 Squadron, carried out the first of his four passes across the aiming point to drop illuminating flares from 8,000 feet at 00.30, and the bombing began at 00.35, only to be halted after five minutes when the red spotfire disappeared from view, either having been obscured by smoke or simply blown out. W/C Northrop made a second run at 00.41 at 10,000 feet to deliver further flares and the target was re-marked at 00.43, allowing the bombing to resume at 00.53. W/C Northrop dropped green TIs from 11,000 feet at 00.54 and red TIs at 01.00 to complete his part in the process and the bombing continued from 6,000 to 10,000 feet until 01.06½, when the master Bomber called a halt. The evidence of fires and much smoke suggested a concentrated and highly effective attack, which proved to be an accurate assessment at no cost in aircraft and crews.

A force of 297 aircraft from 1, 4, 5, 6 and 8 Groups was assembled on the 15th to try to do to Boulogne what had been done to Le Havre twenty-four hours earlier. It was again left to 617 Squadron to represent 5 Group, and the operation was concluded with equal success, although the town itself suffered its worst experience of the war. While this was in progress, 5 Group dispatched 110 Lancasters and four Mosquitos to deal with a fuel dump at Châtellerault, situated between Tours and Poitiers in western France. Clear skies and good visibility greeted their arrival in the target area, and red spotfires and green TIs marked out the aiming-point for the attack from 7,000 to 10,000 feet either side of 01.00. Post-raid reconnaissance confirmed that eight out of thirty-five individual fuel storage sites within the target had been destroyed. Returning crews complained that the greatest danger to life and limb on French targets came from London flak and that fired by the Royal Navy.

55 Base squadrons had remained at home on this night, and on the 16th awaited orders for the coming night's activities. Just three days earlier, the first V-1 flying bombs had landed on London, and this prompted a second new campaign to open during the month, against the revolutionary weapon's launching and storage sites in the Pas-de-Calais region of north-eastern France. Four targets were earmarked for attention by 405 aircraft from all but 3 Group, 5 Group handed a storage site at Beauvoir, located some twenty miles inland from Berck-sur-Mer. Such sites were referred to in Bomber Command parlance as "constructional works", and many were, indeed, large concrete structures in various stages of completion, while others were small structures shaped like the letter J, known as "ski" sites, where flying bombs were stored before being launched from nearby ramps. 112 Lancasters were detailed, of which the nineteen representing 630 Squadron each received a load of eighteen 500

pounders, two with thirty-six-hour delay fuses, before departing East Kirkby between 22.30 and 23.01 with W/C Deas the senior pilot on duty. There was only one early return from the entire force, and all of the 630 Squadron participants reached the target area to find nine to ten-tenths cloud with tops at 6,000 to 8,000 feet. The Oboe markers went down on time, but few crews were able to see them through the cloud and resorted to bombing on the reflected glow. The bombing took place from 10,000 to 13,000 feet, by the 630 Squadron crews between 00.39 and 00.50, and was concluded by 01.00. P/O Lindsay and crew reported an unserviceable bomb sight, which prevented them from delivering an attack, and other crews could only report observing bomb bursts but no detail.

The oil campaign continued on this night in the hands of 1, 4, 6 and 8 Groups at the Ruhr-Chemie synthetic oil plant at Sterkrade-Holten, a district of Oberhausen in the Ruhr, but cloudy conditions caused the bombing to be scattered, and there was little impact on production. 5 Group's main force squadrons enjoyed a four-night break from operations thereafter, before embarking on their first involvement in the oil campaign, and during this period 617 Squadron went alone to attack "constructional works" at Watten and Wizernes with Tallboys in daylight on the 19th and 20th, but cloudy conditions affected accuracy at the former and caused the latter to be aborted.

5 Group had to wait until Mid-Summer's Night, the 21st, before becoming involved in the oil offensive, and was handed two targets to attack simultaneously. A force of 120 Lancasters and six Mosquitos was assembled from 52, 54 and 55 Bases to target the refinery at Wesseling, or to give it its full name, the Union Rheinische Braunkohlen-Kraftstoff Aktien Gesellschaft, situated on the East Bank of the Rhine south of Cologne, while a second force of 120 Lancasters and four Mosquitos drawn from the squadrons of 53 and 54 Bases was assigned to the Hydrierwerke-Scholven plant in the Buer district of Gelsenkirchen. Included in the numbers of both elements was a sprinkling of ABC Lancasters of 101 Squadron for RCM duties, and the latter force included a number of Oboe Mosquitos to carry out the initial marking. 630 Squadron made ready nineteen Lancasters for Wesseling, loading each with a cookie and sixteen 500-pounders, four of the latter with long-delay fuses, before sending them on their way from East Kirkby between 23.08 and 23.31 with S/L Foster the senior pilot on duty. What they could not know was that they were heading into the greatest disaster to afflict 5 Group thus far in the war, brought about by enemy night-fighters pouncing as soon as the enemy coast was crossed at the Scheldt Estuary. Many combats took place between there and the target, and those surviving the carnage and expecting to find the clear skies and conditions ideal for the 5 Group low-level marking method predicted at briefing, were greeted instead by ten-tenths low cloud at 3,000 feet and accurate predicted heavy flak. This meant, that low-level marking was not an option, and faced with this situation, the Master Bomber, W/C Tait, ordered a blind attack that forced the Lancaster crews to bomb on the red, green and later yellow TIs that were visible through the cloud and confirm their positions by H2S. The bombing was carried out from approximately 17,000 to 20,000 feet and apart from a large explosion at 01.45, there was little to indicate the conduct of the attack. After the war, a secret German report suggested a 40% loss of production at the site, but this was probably of very short duration as the limited number of casualties on the ground pointed to a scattered and largely ineffective raid.

Whatever success was gained came at the high cost of thirty-seven Lancasters, a massive 28%, and all but two of them belonged to 5 Group Squadrons, 44, 49, 57 and 619 Squadrons each losing six Lancasters, while 207 and 630 Squadrons each had five empty dispersals to contemplate in the cold light of dawn. There must have been a sense of disbelief at East Kirkby when eleven of its Lancasters containing seventy-seven crew members failed to return, and the shock was only tempered slightly with the news that one 630 Squadron crew had abandoned their Lancaster over Bedfordshire and all were safe. This was P/O "Blue" Rackley and crew, who, it will be recalled, had been forced to land on Corsica on return from Munich in April and their rear gunner had lost his life in the ensuing crash. Now, ME795 staggered across the Suffolk coast displaying a gaping hole in the forward fuselage, a shattered rear turret, a missing H2S cupola and severe damage to the tailplane control surfaces, all inflicted by a Ju88. When it became clear that a landing was out of the question, by which time they were in the vicinity of Henlow, Rackley ordered his crew to bale out and was last to leave the stricken Lancaster, which crashed at 03.38. According to Bill Chorley's Bomber Command Losses, the entire crew survived, but in his books, Silksheen and Bomber Squadrons at War, Geoff Copeman records that the rear gunner, Sgt Davies, who had been the sole survivor of P/O Murray's crew after the take-off crash for Stuttgart in February on their maiden sortie, failed to survive the descent. Apparently, his parachute had been rendered unusable, and he left the aircraft tied to the bomb-aimer only to be jolted free as the parachute jerked open and fell to his death. "Blue" Rackley, meanwhile, who seemed to attract drama, hit a moving train on landing, and was quite badly injured. Sometime later the news was received that 57 Squadron's ND471 had ditched off the Norfolk coast at 02.10 and the crew of P/O Nicklin RNZAF had been rescued later in the day by an ASR launch sent out from Yarmouth.

The missing 630 Squadron crews were those of S/L Foster DFC, P/O Hooper DFC, P/O Hart RCAF and P/O Smith, and there was not a single survivor from among the twenty-eight men involved. ND531 disappeared without trace with the crew of S/L Foster, which included another holder of the DFC, two of the DFM and one Mentioned in Dispatches (MiD), while ME843, ME782 and LM118 were all brought down by night-fighters and crashed respectively in the Dutch/German border region, two miles north-east of Turnhout in the Antwerp region of northern Belgium and two miles south of Boxtel, ten miles or so north-north-west of Eindhoven. The sad news was received from Fiskerton that W/C Malcolm Crocker, 630 Squadron's first commanding officer, had lost his life also while leading 49 Squadron from the front.

Meanwhile, the Scholven-Buer force arrived in the target area also expecting to find clear skies, instead of which they encountered ten-tenths cloud, which was the only flaw in the highly-effective 5 Group low-level marking method, which required the Mosquito element to go in beneath the cloud base and drop spotfires on the aiming point in the light of illuminating flares. However, when the cloud base was almost at ground level, nothing could be done and, on this occasion, the preliminary marking was carried out by Oboe Mosquitos, whose red spotfires were backed up by red and green TIs from the Lancaster marker element. The glow could be observed only dimly through the cloud and the attack was carried out on them, confirmed by Gee and H2S fixes. It was impossible to assess the outcome, and to compound any sense of disappointment, eight Lancasters from the group failed to return. A secret German report surfaced post-war for this operation also and suggested a 20% loss of production at the plant, but this was probably for a limited period only.

East Kirkby was allowed two free nights to lick its wounds, and none of its crews was consequently involved in operations on the 23rd, when more than four hundred aircraft of 3, 4, 6 and 8 Groups targeted four flying-bomb sites and 1 and 5 Groups were sent respectively against railway yards at Saintes and Limoges in western France. Ninety-seven Lancasters and four Mosquitos were detailed from 53 and 54 Base squadrons, and they found clear skies and good visibility, in which ground features like the river Vienne and the railway sidings stood out prominently. Red spotfires and green TIs marked out the aiming-point, which was bombed from 5,000 to 8,000 feet either side of 02.00 and several large explosions created clouds of smoke. 617 Squadron had attempted another Tallboy assault on the constructional works at Wizernes in daylight on the 22nd, but the attack had been abandoned in the face of ten-tenths low cloud. The squadron returned the bombs to store and brought them back to France on the 24th to score a number of direct hits.

Thirteen 630 Squadron crews were called to briefing on the 24th to learn of their part in a busy night of operations involving more than seven hundred aircraft targeting seven flying-bomb sites. Wesseling was still and open wound, but all trace of the missing had been removed and their billets repopulated with fresh faces, most of whom would ask the same question, "How long does it take to complete a tour and how many make it through?" In truth, crews joining Bomber Command at this stage of the war could finish within two months rather than the twelve to eighteen months it might have taken their predecessors. It is unlikely that any new faces attended briefing on this afternoon, when it was learned that "the targets for tonight" were at Pommeréval and Prouville, situated respectively some fifteen miles south-east of Dieppe, and east of Abbeville, for each of which 103 Lancasters and four Mosquitos were made ready. The 630 Squadron element took off for the former between 22.21 and 22.37 with F/Ls Hawker, Joblin, O'Dwyer and Rodgers the senior pilots on duty and eighteen 500-pounders in each bomb bay, two with a six-hour delay fuse. All reached the target area, where the weather conditions were favourable, and W/C Tait was again on hand in the role of Master Bomber to watch the Oboe marker going down on time at 23.50 and assess that it was five hundred yards south of the aiming point. He directed the flare force to illuminate another Oboe marker that was much closer, and then sent in the low-level Mosquitos to mark the aiming point with red spotfires. This delayed the opening of the attack by two minutes, before the main force Lancasters delivered concentrated bombing from 6,000 to 9,000 feet, those from 630 squadron between 00.02½ and 00.17, and all of the bomb bursts were observed to be within a few hundred yards of the aiming point.

More than seven hundred aircraft were detailed for operations against six flying-bomb sites on the 27th, while two railway yards occupied the attention of other elements. There were two targets for 5 Group, a flying-bomb site at what the 5 Group ORB identified as Marquise/Mimoyecques, situated some five miles inland from Cap Gris-Nez, and railway yards at Vitry-le-Francois south-east of Reims. Mimoyecques is actually five miles north-east of Marquise and the 57 Squadron ORB identified the former rather than Marquise as the target for thirteen of its Lancasters in a force of eighty-six provided by 52 and 55 Bases.

Mimoyecques had been targeted earlier in the day by 4 Group Halifaxes with Path Finder support and would continue to attract attention over the ensuing days.

Originally planned as one of two V-3 super-gun sites, each containing twenty-five barrels angled at 50 degrees and aimed at London, test failures and delays meant that a single three-barrel shaft stretching a hundred metres into the limestone hill, five miles from the coast and 103 miles from its target, was all that existed at the time. Each fifteen-metre-long smooth-bore barrel, which was designed on the multiple-charge principle to progressively boost the acceleration of the one-ton projectile as it travelled towards the muzzle, was to be capable of pounding London at the rate of hundreds per day without let-up. It was protected by a concrete slab thirty metres wide and five-and-a-half metres thick, which was correctly believed by the designers to be impregnable to conventional bombs. The 630 Squadron element of fourteen Lancasters departed East Kirkby between 22.58 and 23.11 with the same four flight lieutenant pilots as for the previous operation leading the way and eleven 1,000 and four 500-pounders in each bomb bay. They completed the outward flight within seventy-five minutes under clear skies and in good visibility and the attack began at 00.48½ with punctual and accurate marking with red TIs, onto which the East Kirkby crews delivered their payloads until the Master Bomber called a halt at 01.01. It was clear that the bombing had been concentrated on the markers, but it was impossible to assess if any damage had occurred.

While this operation was in progress, the second 5 Group force of 103 Lancasters and four Mosquitos from 53 and 54 Bases carried out an attack on the railway yards at Vitry-le-Francois. They were greeted by varying amounts of cloud reported at between zero and seven-tenths at around 7,000 feet, but the visibility was good, and the aiming-point was clearly marked by red spot fires and green TIs. Bombing took place from 4,500 to 8,000 feet between 01.44 and 01.54, at which point the Master Bomber called a halt and ordered crews with bombs still aboard to take them home. 50 Squadron's commanding officer, W/C Frogley, was critical of the decision to abandon the attack, suggesting that, if the first spotfire had not been accurate, the bombing should never even have started. In fact, it had been smoke obscuring the aiming-point that prompted the Master Bomber to send the final wave home with their bombs.

During the course of the month the squadron undertook eleven operations and dispatched 174 sorties for the loss of six Lancasters, five crews and a single airman.

# July 1944

Sadly, July would bring further traumas for 5 Group, the first occurring early on, while the disaster of Wesseling remained an open wound. The month began as June had ended, with flying-bomb sites providing employment for over three hundred aircraft on both the 1st and 2nd. It was the 4th before the "Independent Air Force" was invited to re-enter the fray, when it was called upon to attack a V-Weapon storage site in caves at St-Leu-d'Esserent, some thirty miles north of Paris. The caves had originally been used for growing mushrooms, and they were protected by some twenty-five feet of clay and soft limestone, to say nothing of the anti-aircraft defences brought in by the Germans. The operation involved not only seventeen Lancasters, a Mustang and a Mosquito from 617 Squadron, but also 211 other Lancasters and eleven Mosquitos from the group, with three ABC Lancasters to provide RCM cover and three Path Finder Oboe Mosquitos to carry out the marking of an initial reference-point. There were actually two aiming-points, the road and railway communications to the area dump for the main force, and the supply site, a tunnel complex at Creil, a settlement located three miles north-east of St-Leu, for 617 Squadron.

55 Base supported the operation with fifty-two Lancasters, thirty-seven made ready at East Kirkby, where the twenty representing 630 Squadron each received a bomb load of eleven 1,000 and four 500-pounders before taking off between 22.59 and 23.31 with S/L Calvert the senior pilot on duty. A number of crews from other squadrons responded to what appeared to be a "Return to base" signal, which was almost certainly a spoof message sent by the Luftwaffe in a tactic employed successfully in the past by the RAF. The others pressed on to reach the target area under largely clear skies and in good visibility, which would prove to be of equal benefit to the night-fighters making contact with the bomber stream during the outward flight and maintaining a presence also over the target and on the way home. There were no searchlights, but the expected volume of flak was thrown up at the main force element as it ran across the aiming-point to deliver the high-explosive payload from an average of 16,000 feet onto red and green TIs between 01.33 and 01.45. Thirteen Lancasters failed to return, three of them on their way back to East Kirkby, and among them was 630 Squadron's ME867, which was racing for the French coast near Dieppe and was just thirty miles short when intercepted and shot down by a night-fighter to crash at around 02.00 at Lannoy-Cuillere with no survivors from the crew of P/O Taft. Post-raid reconnaissance revealed that a large area of subsidence had blocked the side entrance to the caves and that the road and railway links had been cut over a distance of four hundred yards.

While the above operation was in progress a force of 280 Lancasters from 1, 6 and 8 Groups attacked marshalling yards at Orleans and Villeneuve-St-George. Among eleven Lancasters missing from the latter was one belonging to 35 (Madras Presidency) Squadron containing the crew of S/L Alec Cranswick DSO DFC, one of the brightest stars in Bomber Command, who lost his life on what was his official 106th sortie but is believed to have undertaken others not recorded in his logbook.

On the 6th, more than five hundred aircraft were engaged on operations against V-Weapons targets, and 617 Squadron was assigned to the V-3 super-gun site at Mimoyecques. Direct hits were scored with the 12,000lb Tallboy earthquake bomb, which was designed to penetrate deep into the ground and destroy concrete structures by the effect of shock waves. An unexpected bonus of the weapon was its ability to drill though many feet of reinforced concrete and detonate inside a building, which would prove to be useful against U-Boot bunkers. A provisional reconnaissance revealed four deep craters in the immediate target area, one causing a large corner of the concrete slab to collapse. The extent of the damage underground would not be apparent to the planners at Bomber Command, but the shafts and tunnels had been rendered unusable and would remain so and many workers underground were buried as the constructional works collapsed around them. Although W/C Cheshire did not know it, this was to be his final operation, not only with 617 Squadron, but also of the war in Europe. His one hundred-operation career would see him awarded a Victoria Cross, and his successor as commanding officer of 617 Squadron would need to be someone of immense stature, which was found in the person of the previously-mentioned W/C James "Willie" Tait.

The authorities were not convinced that the site at St-Leu-d'Esserent had received terminal damage and scheduled another attack on it for the late evening of the 7th. By the time it was launched, more than 450 aircraft from 1, 4, 6 and 8 Groups had carried out the first major operation in support of the Canadian 1st and British 2nd Armies trying to break out of Caen. The target had been changed from German-fortified villages to an area of open ground north of Caen, where almost 2,300 tons of bombs were dropped somewhat ineffectively, and, ultimately, the decision to shift the point of aim proved to be counter-productive by causing damage to the northern suburbs of the city rather than to German forces.

5 Group detailed 208 Lancasters and fifteen Mosquitos for the second assault on St-Leu, the 630 Squadron element of seventeen departing East Kirkby in the wake of the 57 Squadron contingent between 22.28 and 22.46 with W/C Deas the senior pilot on duty. They arrived in the target area to find medium-level cloud, which prevented the moonlight from providing illumination, although, below the cloud level the visibility was good. The Master Bomber was W/C Ed Porter DFC, who had recently relinquished command of 9 Squadron to join the 5 Group Master Bomber fraternity at Coningsby, and he oversaw the delivery of the Oboe yellow TI at 01.06, which was followed by the first stick of flares four minutes later. The first red spotfire went down at 01.08, a hundred yards south of the aiming-point, but in line with the direction of the bombing run and backing-up by red and green TIs continued until 01.13. The marking was assessed as sufficiently accurate to call in the main force crews at 01.15, and those from 630 Squadron dropped their loads of eleven 1,000 and four 500 pounders each from an average of 13,000 feet between 01.15 and 01.25, the time at which the Deputy Master Bomber, 83 Squadron's S/L Eggins, assumed control and sent the force home after the Master Bomber's VHF was found to be indistinct.

Twenty-nine Lancasters and two Mosquitos failed to return after night-fighters got amongst them, and this represented 14% of the force, 55 Base suffering another bad with 207 Squadron hardest-hit, losing five Lancasters. There was a sombre dawn for the East Kirkby community, which would have to come to terms with four empty dispersal pans, three belonging to 57 Squadron Lancasters and one that should have been occupied by 630 Squadron's commanding officer, W/C Deas DSO DFC & Bar. NE688 was a few minutes into the return flight when shot down to crash near Villers-en-Arthies, roughly midway between Paris and Rouen, and only the wireless operator survived to fall into enemy hands. W/C Deas had been on his sixty-ninth sortie and was a most popular and efficient commanding officer, whose loss was a major blow to the squadron and would be keenly felt by all at East Kirkby. Photo-reconnaissance revealed that both ends of the tunnel complex had collapsed, as had a section in the middle, and the approach road and rail links had been heavily cratered and blocked.

There was no immediate opportunity for the afflicted squadrons, particularly 106 of 54 Base and 207, which had lost five crews each, to "get back on the horse", and there must have been a great air of sadness while the populations of RAF Metheringham and Spilsby each came to terms with the loss of thirty-five familiar faces in one night. A special congratulatory message arrived on the participating stations from A-O-C, AVM Sir Ralph Cochrane, who considered it the finest effort by the group to successfully press home the attack in the face of the fiercest opposition.

On the 10th, 5 Group detailed six Lancasters from East Kirkby, three from each squadron, to conduct a mining operation in the Kattegat region of the Baltic. We are not informed as to which of the Silverthorn gardens the crews of P/O Henriquez and F/Os Brittain and Hayes had been assigned as they took off between 22.17 and 22.31 with instructions to abandon their sorties in the event of a lack of cloud cover. The Henriquez crew turned back, probably when over northern Jutland, leaving the others to fulfil their brief to plant their vegetables from high level by H2S, with eight-tenths cloud below them at 4,000 feet.

W/C Leslie Milne Blome-Jones arrived at East Kirkby on the 12th to succeed W/C Deas as 630 Squadron's commanding officer. A "Man of Kent" born on the Island of Sheppy in January 1912, he had a glittering and varied operational career behind him and a reputation as a no-nonsense outspoken officer with a predilection for leading from the front. He had joined the RAF in 1936, and in 1940 was a member of 103 Squadron flying Fairey Battles with the Advanced Air Striking Force (AASF) during the ill-fated battle for France. The AASF was decimated during one particular week in May 1940 and struggled to maintain a presence for a few further weeks before its withdrawal to England in mid-June. It was shortly before the withdrawal that Blome-Jones flew four sorties and undertook one more in a Battle in July before attending a Wellington conversion course, during which he carried out three further sorties. In May 1941, after completing nineteen Wellington sorties with 103 Squadron, he was screened and became an instructor, remaining away from the operational scene until December 1942, when he joined 21 Squadron in 2 Group, with which he flew five daylight operations in a Lockheed Ventura. This was a development of the Lockheed Hudson, the performance of which was not up to the tasks asked of it, and it soon developed a reputation as a "flying coffin". In early 1944 he undertook a Lancaster conversion course and spent a number of weeks gaining experience with 61 Squadron before joining 207 Squadron as a flight commander in April. His first operation with 207 Squadron was the highly contentious and ultimately successful if expensive attack on the Panzer training camp at Mailly-le-Camp on the 3rd of May, and by the time of his arrival at East Kirkby, he had eleven Lancaster operations under his belt.

Operations were posted and then cancelled on each of the four days after St-Leu until the 12th, when eleven 630 Squadron crews joined an equal number from 57 Squadron for a briefing to learn the details for that night's operation against railway installations at Culmont-Chalindrey in the Grand Est region of eastern France. Two aiming-points were planned, at the western and eastern ends, for which a force of 157 Lancasters and four Mosquitos was made ready, and crews were informed that another operation by elements of 1 Group would be taking place further south on a railway junction at Revigny, and that this, hopefully, might dilute the night-fighter response. The East Kirkby Lancasters each received a bomb load of eight 1,000 and four 500-pounders, those representing 630 Squadron departing East Kirkby between 21.42 and 21.53 with S/L Millichap the senior pilot on duty and undertaking his first sortie since his posting to the squadron in June. They flew south for the Channel crossing, and on arrival at the French coast a few enemy night-fighters made their presence felt, one, a Ju88, shot down by a 57 Squadron Lancaster. Eight-tenths low cloud prevailed until shortly before the target area was reached, from which point the conditions improved to provide clear skies, and, promisingly, no sign of defensive activity from the ground. The controller at the eastern aiming-point experienced VHF communications problems, which delayed that part of the attack, and eventually, the entire force was directed to the western aiming-point. A pause in the bombing from 01.52 allowed the aiming-point to be re-marked, after which bombing continued from 5,000 to 8,000 feet until around 02.16. Explosions were observed, followed by fires that remained visible for fifty miles into the return flight, but the high proportion of delayed action fuses in use prevented an immediate assessment of results, and it would be left to post-raid reconnaissance ultimately to confirm an effective operation. Conditions over Lincolnshire had deteriorated and Lancasters landed wherever they could and would straggle back to base on the following day. Cloud had interfered with the 1 Group operation at Revigny and only half of the force had bombed by the time the Master Bomber called a halt, a disappointment compounded by the loss for little gain of ten Lancasters.

A new policy was introduced on the 14th that raised most pilot officers to flying officer rank, which meant that an NCO, on receiving a commission, would progress directly to that rank, bypassing pilot officer. This certainly applied in 5 Group, but to what extent it was universal in Bomber Command is uncertain. Nine crews from each squadron were informed at the East Kirkby briefing that day that their target was to be the huge marshalling yards at Villeneuve-St-Georges situated on the southern rim of Paris for which their Lancasters each received a bomb load of eighteen 500-pounders, two with a 72-hour delay fuse. They would be part of a force of 111 Lancasters, six Mosquitos and an American twin-engine P38 Lightning, the last-mentioned containing the Master Bomber, W/C Jeudwine. The 630 Squadron crews took off between 21.56 and 22.03 with W/C Blome-Jones the senior pilot on duty for the first time and all reached the target area to find a large amount of cloud with a base at 5,000 feet, but clear conditions below. W/C Jeudwine was having compass trouble, and would arrive on target twelve minutes late, so contacted his Deputy, 83 Squadron's W/C Joe Northrop, to take matters in hand. Joe could clearly see the target and judged the Oboe marker to be within fifty yards of the planned aiming-point, but drifting smoke from early bombing obscured the ground and he called for a pause at 01.38. The 5 Group marker force lobbed the TIs within the confines of the yards, and the bombing resumed at 01.45, proceeding smoothly thereafter and precisely according to plan. Bombing took place on red and green TIs from 6,000 to 9,000 feet between 01.36 and 02.00 and most of the hardware hit the yards, while a proportion also fell outside to the east. Meanwhile, 1 Group had returned to Revigny, but had been thwarted by ground haze, which forced the Master Bomber to abandon the attack before any bombing could take place. Seven Lancasters were lost for no gain, and it would fall to 5 Group to finish the job a few nights hence at great expense.

Flying-bomb sites and railways dominated the target list on the 15th, and 5 Group was handed a railway junction at Nevers, a city on the northern bank of the Loire in central France. 630 and 57 Squadrons each contributed eight Lancasters to the force of 104, with four Mosquitos to carry out the low-level marking, and they were loaded with nine 1,000 and four 500-pounders, before the 630 Squadron element departed East Kirkby between 21.53 and 22.00 with F/Ls Hawker, O'Dwyer and Rodgers the senior pilots on duty. They bypassed the Channel Islands on their way to the Brittany coast and reached the target after an outward flight of more than three-and-a-half hours to be greeted by clear skies and a little haze. The first two red spotfires proved to be inaccurate and had to be cancelled with Yellow TIs, but not before they had attracted a number of bomb loads, possibly as a result of contradictory instructions from the Master Bomber at 01.58 and 01.59. However, once corrected, the red spotfires and green TIs attracted the main force bomb loads, those from the East Kirkby participants from around 5,000 feet between 01.59 and 02.18. A very large explosion occurred at 02.09, which might have been from an ammunition train or dump, but the use of largely delayed-action ordnance prevented an immediate assessment of results. Photographic reconnaissance later in the day revealed that the site had been all but obliterated, and there was much damage to rolling stock.

Seventeen crews from each of the East Kirkby squadrons attended briefing at midnight on the 17/18th to learn of their part in a tactical support operation to be carried out at dawn by a force of 942 aircraft, of which 201 of the Lancasters were to be provided by 5 Group. It was the start of the ground forces' Operation Goodwood, which, General Montgomery intended, would be a decisive breakout into wider France as a prelude to the march towards the German frontier. The aiming-points were five enemy-held villages to the east of Caen, Colombelles, Mondeville, Sannerville, Cagny and Manneville, all of which stood in the path of the advancing British 2nd Army. The 630 Squadron element took off between 03.27 and 04.06 with W/C Blome-Jones and S/L Millichap the senior pilots on duty and each crew sitting on eleven 1,000 and four 500-pounders, and all reached the target area to find their aiming-point, the Mondeville steel works, already marked by red and yellow TIs, but about to be swallowed up and obscured by drifting smoke. The target, which the Germans had converted into a strongly defended fortress, was actually situated south of the River L'Orne in an industrial suburb of the city itself, to the east of the marshalling yards. The 630 Squadron crews delivered their payloads from 6,000 to 10,000 feet between 05.44 and 06.13 in accordance with instructions from the Master Bomber, and as far as could be determined, they fell accurately onto the markers. The RAF dropped five thousand tons of bombs to good effect onto the two German divisions in just half an hour, and the Americans followed up with a further two thousand tons.

Crews returning from the above operation took to their beds after breakfast to get as much sleep as possible, before many were called into action again that night. Following two failed attempts by 1 Group to cut the railway junction at Revigny in France's Marne region at a cost of seventeen Lancasters, the job was handed to 5 Group, which assembled a force of 109 Lancasters, four Mosquitos and a P38 Lightning containing the Master Bomber, W/C Jeudwine. It was to be a busy night of operations, which included another railway target at Aulnoye and a flying bomb site at Acquet for 3 and 4 Groups respectively, and oil targets at Wesseling and Scholven-Buer for 1, 6 and 8 Groups, in addition to which, support and diversionary activities brought the total of sorties for the night to 972. Ten crews from each of the East Kirkby squadrons attended briefing at teatime to learn of their part in what promised to be an unspectacular and routine operation, seven of those from 630 Squadron about to undertake their second sortie of the day. F/L Joblin was the senior pilot on duty and, indeed, the first of the entire force to take off, at 22.36, to be followed by the rest of the squadron over the ensuing fourteen minutes. It would be a further hour until the Mosquitos of 627 Squadron departed Woodhall Spa and later still before the P38 took off. Eleven 1,000 and four 500-pounders swung from their fixings in each Lancaster bomb bay as the force passed east of London to cross the south coast near Hastings and the head of the Revigny-bound force reached French airspace near Dieppe at 00.40. This was just a few minutes before the 4 Group Halifaxes departed it on their way home, and ahead lay another hour's flight to the target. The 3 Group raid at Aulnoye was concluded about twenty minutes later, and once these aircraft had cleared the enemy coast, 5 Group would be on its own over a very hostile land, with the enemy night-fighter controller on top of the developing situation. The Revigny force then passed through an intense searchlight belt some twenty miles inland, before PB244 was attacked by an unidentified enemy night-fighter at 01.10, which F/O Kemp's rear gunner sent crashing to the ground, only to have to fend off another inconclusive encounter immediately afterwards.

The bomber stream continued to be harried all the way into eastern France by night-fighters, which had been fed into the stream shortly after it entered enemy airspace, and it was at this stage of the outward flight that matters began to go awry. In just forty-five minutes, sixteen Lancasters fell victim to night-fighters and one to flak, and among them was 630 Squadron's PB236, which crashed at 01.21 at Neuvy, some ten miles west-north-west of Sezanne on the western edge of the Marne region, with fatal consequences for the crew of P/O Sargent. Those arriving at the target found clear skies but haze obscuring ground detail, a problem which would have been solved had the first wave of flares, delivered at about 01.30, not fallen too far to the east. More flares were ordered, and the bombing was put back by five minutes, while Wanganui markers were dropped by Mosquito, and the situation was assessed. F/O Maxwell RAAF and crew responded to the Master Bomber's instructions to delay their attack, and while orbiting to port ME796 was attacked by a night-fighter and set on fire, whereupon the wireless operator and gunners were ordered to bale out and once on the ground were spirited away by the local Resistance. Despite also having time to save themselves, F/O Maxwell and the other three occupants remained on board as the aircraft lost height, apparently because Maxwell was trying to find open ground for a crash-landing to avoid possible civilian casualties in the nearby villages. The bombs had actually been jettisoned from low level, while held in searchlight beams and no sooner had the bombs gone, than a flak shell took off a wing and the Lancaster crashed at 01.30 between two villages and burned, killing all four occupants.

At 01.34 three aircraft were seen falling in quick succession with smoke coming from their engines and exploding on impact, clearly with their bombs still on board. One of these was 630 Squadron's LM537, which was the flak victim, and F/O Dennett RAAF and his crew all lost their lives. The whole attack seemed chaotic, and the use of many delayed-action bombs meant that it was difficult to see what was happening on the ground as the East Kirkby crews crossed the target at 7,000 to 10,000 feet between 01.43 and 01.57 and bombed on a red spotfire in accordance with the instructions of the Master Bomber. Heading homeward just to the south of the rural Champagne region, LM117 was brought down by flak at 02.06, but not before F/O Brittain RAAF and his crew had taken to their parachutes. Sadly, the wireless operator had been wounded and would succumb shortly afterwards, while the pilot, bomb-aimer and mid-upper gunner retained their freedom, leaving three others to fall into enemy hands. Photo-reconnaissance revealed that the operation had been successful in cutting the railway link to the battle front, but had cost twenty-four Lancasters, almost 22% of those dispatched. *(For a full and highly detailed account of the three Revigny raids, read the amazing book, Massacre over the Marne, by Oliver Clutton-Brock.)*

Long before the residents of East Kirkby had any inkling of what was befalling the four 630 Squadron crews, and one from 57 Squadron, another drama was unfolding over Scotland. Having taken off for a navigation exercise a few minutes before the operating crews got away, 630 Squadron's ME729 began to experience engine problems, and was abandoned near Ayr at 00.59 by the pilot, F/O Sparkes. Whether the other three occupants also abandoned the aircraft is uncertain, but unlikely, as none survived. It would be some time before news of the fate of the 630 and 57 Squadrons crews filtered through to East Kirkby, and all they knew for certain, was that five of their aircraft were missing, each with seven men on board. In fact, thirteen crew members had survived, and a goodly number of them would manage to evade the enemy net.

5 Group crews stood-by on the 19th for a possible daylight operation, and it was evening before orders came through to prepare for an attack on a flying-bomb storage site at Thiverny, situated just to the north of St-Leu-d'Esserent and separated from the recently attacked site at Creil by the river Oise. A force of 103 Lancasters and two Mosquitos was detailed, nine of the former provided by 630 Squadron, which departed East Kirkby between 19.20 and 19.27 with S/L Millichap the senior pilot on duty, S/L Miller navigating in the crew of F/Sgt Bowers and ten 1,000 and four 500-pounders in each bomb bay. The attack was to take place in daylight under the protection of a Spitfire escort, which was picked up at the south coast and all from the squadron reached the target in fine weather conditions, but with ground haze creating challenging conditions in which to identify the aiming-point. Late preliminary marking by the Path Finder element and communications problems between the Master Bomber, S/L Charles Owen, and his Deputy added to the frustrations and led to most crews having to bomb visually in the face of moderate to intense heavy flak bursting as high as 18,000 feet. The 630 Squadron crews were over the target between 21.30 and 21.39 at altitudes ranging from 13,000 to 18,000 feet, and although few enemy fighters were sighted, F/Sgt Bowers and crew in PB244 N-Nan claimed the destruction of one, the type of which was unidentified. In his excellent biography of Gibson, Richard Morris suggests that he had wangled himself into the pilot's seat of this aircraft, and according to Gibson's logbook, returned with an aiming point photograph, but no corroboration is provided in the ORB. While it is believed that Gibson's account is true, it is also a fact that his logbook is an unreliable source of information. Reconnaissance revealed some loose bombing, but sufficient aiming-point photographs were brought back to suggest that the railway tracks to the storage caves had been cut, while the caves themselves were undamaged.

On a busy night of operations on the 20th, when three of the four campaigns were to be prosecuted, oil at Bottrop and Homberg in the Ruhr and V-Weapons sites at Ardouval and Wizernes, elements of 1, 5 and 8 Groups were detailed to attack railway yards and a triangular junction at Courtrai (Kortrijk) in Belgium. 630 Squadron contributed eleven Lancasters to the 5 Group force of 190 Lancasters and five Mosquitos, and they departed East Kirkby between 23.01 and 23.12 with F/Ls Hawker and O'Dwyer the senior pilots on duty and eleven 1,000 and four 500-pounders in each bomb bay. They all reached the target area to find it free of cloud, if slightly obscured by ground haze, but the Oboe marking was well-placed in the marshalling yards and backed up by green TIs, onto which the squadron contingent delivered its payloads from 10,000 to 14,000 feet between 00.56 and 01.03. They returned home safely to report a large, orange explosion at 00.57 and a successful outcome, which was confirmed by post-raid reconnaissance revealing both aiming-points to have been obliterated, while locomotive and repair shops had been partially destroyed along with a large amount of rolling stock. The success was achieved for the loss of nine Lancasters, most of them belonging to 1 Group.

Following two nights at home for 5 Group and a two-month break from city-busting, Harris sanctioned a major raid on the naval and shipbuilding port of Kiel, home to the Deutsche Werke, Germania Werft and Howaldtswerke shipyards, all producers of U-Boots. A force of 629 aircraft was assembled on the 23rd, of which ninety-nine of the Lancasters were provided by 5 Group, six of them contributed by 630 Squadron, while three others were to join three from 57 Squadron to sneak in under cover of the main event to mine the waters of the Forget-me-not garden in Kiel Harbour. The 630 Squadron ORB is utterly confused and lists six crews, five of them twice, all recorded as part of the bombing brigade, while there is no mention at all of the gardeners, which appear to have departed East Kirkby first to be followed into the air by the bombers between 22.46 and 22.58 with F/Ls Jobling and O'Dwyer the senior pilots on duty and unusually for an urban target, each crew sitting on a bomb load of eleven 1,000 and four 500 pounders. They headed for the rendezvous point, where they formed up behind an elaborate "Mandrel" jamming screen laid on by 100 Group, before setting course for Denmark's western coast. *(In November 1943, 100 Group had been formed to take over the Radio Countermeasures (RCM) role, which had been the preserve of 101 Squadron since its introduction a number of months earlier. 101 Squadron, however, would remain in 1 Group and continue to provide RCM for the remainder of the war.)*

According to Bill Chorley's Bomber Command Losses, F/O Hayes and crew took off in PB211 at 22.44 bound for the Forget-me-not garden but ditched some thirty-six miles off Cromer and only the navigator and rear gunner managed to survive in the water for seven hours, before being picked up by the coastal minesweeper, HMS Coursor. Meanwhile, the head of the bomber stream arrived unexpectedly and with complete surprise in Kiel airspace, its presence rendering the enemy night-fighter controller confused and unable to bring his resources to bear. Kiel was covered by a nine to ten-tenths veil of thin cloud with tops at 4,000 feet, and a skymarking plan was put into action, which enabled the main force crews to bomb on the glow, first of the flares, and then of fires. The 630 Squadron crews are assumed to have bombed from 14,000 to 20,000 feet between 01.27 and 01.32, aiming at the glow of red and green Wanganui markers as they disappeared into cloud. Flak was mostly in barrage form and exploding at 15,000 to 22,000 feet, without being overly troublesome. It was not possible to determine the outcome of the raid, but the glow of fires remained visible for a hundred miles into the return journey, which suggested that it had been effective. This was confirmed by local reports, which conceded that this had been the town's most destructive raid of the war and had inflicted heavy damage on the port and shipyards and cut off water supplies for three days and gas for three weeks. Many delayed-action bombs had been dropped, and these continued to cause problems for some time. While the above was in progress, the two remaining and unidentified 630 Squadron gardeners fulfilled their briefs by planting six vegetables each into the allotted locations by H2S.

5 Group divided its forces on the 24th to enable it to support the first of a three-raid series in five nights on the city of Stuttgart, and an oil refinery and fuel dump at Donges. Situated on

the northern bank of the Loire to the east of St-Nazaire, the latter target had been attacked successfully by elements of 6 and 8 Groups on the previous night, but clearly required further attention. 5 Group detailed ninety-nine Lancasters for southern Germany in an overall force of 614, while 104 Lancasters and four Mosquitos were made ready for western France, with five 8 Group Mosquitos in attendance. 630 Squadron would support both operations with eight Lancasters for Stuttgart, each loaded with a 2,000-pounder and a dozen 500lb J-Type cluster bombs, and seven for Donges carrying eleven 1,000 and four 500-pounders, and the former departed East Kirkby first between 21.31 and 21.54 with S/L Millichap the senior pilot on duty. They were followed into the air between 22.00 and 22.32 by the second element led by F/Ls Hawker, Joblin, O'Dwyer and Rodgers. Bound for Stuttgart, F/O Bolton became unwell, and he and his crew were back on the ground after three hours and forty minutes, leaving the others to continue on across France, where at around 01.30, PA992 crashed near Tramont-Emy, some eighty miles west of the German frontier at Strasbourg. It was a mixed USAAF/RAF/RCAF crew captained by Flight Officer Adams USAAF, and he was one of five survivors and four evaders, while both gunners lost their lives. Those reaching the target were greeted by nine to ten-tenths cloud with tops at 4,000 to 7,000 feet, which required the employment of Wanganui flares to mark the aiming-point. The bombing was carried out on the red glow on the cloud base from 18,000 to 22,000 feet from around 01.50 in accordance with the instructions of the Master Bomber, and crews set course for home fairly satisfied with the outcome, although it was impossible to make an accurate assessment. At debriefings across the Command, crews reported a glow of fires covering an area of perhaps five square miles, which remained visible for eighty miles into the return journey. No local report came out of Stuttgart for this night, but it had been a successful and destructive raid, although gained at a cost of seventeen Lancasters and four Halifaxes.

Meanwhile, 290 miles to the west of Stuttgart, clear skies and good visibility greeted the 5 Group crews, who were able to pick out ground detail in the light of the illuminator flares. Bombing by the 630 Squadron element took place on concentrated red and green TIs from 8,000 to 11,000 feet between 01.43 and 01.51 in accordance with the Master Bomber's instructions, and the glow of fires through thick smoke, along with a large explosion at 01.49, indicated a successful outcome. Post-raid photo-reconnaissance confirmed the success of the operation, revealing the site to have been devastated at a cost of three Lancasters.

5 Group split its forces again on the 25th to support the second of the raids on Stuttgart with eighty-three Lancasters from 52, 54 and 55 Bases and a daylight attack on an aerodrome and signals depot at Saint-Cyr involving ninety-four Lancasters and six Mosquitos from 53 and 54 Bases. *(There are at least four locations called Saint-Cyr, and it is believed that the one targeted on this night was in the Ile-de-France to the west of Paris.)* 630 Squadron briefed twelve crews for the former operation, while loading its Lancasters with a 2,000 pounder and a dozen 500lb J-Type cluster bombs each and they departed East Kirkby between 21.20 and 21.46 with S/L Calvert the senior pilot on duty. They rendezvoused with the rest of the 550-strong force as they made their way via Reading to the south coast and crossed the Channel to make landfall on the French coast and adopt a route similar to that employed twenty-four hours earlier. The crews of F/L O'Dwyer and F/O Fenning returned early because of mechanical defects, the former from a position deep inside enemy territory but before the bomber stream entered Germany near Strasbourg, accompanied by layers of cloud, which

over the target was at five to ten-tenths with tops in places as high as 20,000 feet. There was haze below the cloud level to create further challenges for the marker force, and the red and green TIs appeared to the main force crews to be somewhat scattered. The 630 Squadron crews bombed from around 17,000 to 21,000 feet between 01.53 and 02.20, and the glow from the resulting fires remained visible for a hundred miles into the return flight. Despite the evidence, there appeared to be little optimism at debriefings, and no report came out of Stuttgart to provide a clue to the outcome. In fact, this was probably the most destructive of the three raids in this current series, but it would be only after the third one that cumulative reports came out of the city to confirm much destruction and heavy casualties.

The hectic round of operations continued for 5 Group on the 26th with preparations for an attack on two aiming-points in the marshalling yards at Givors, situated on the western bank of the River Rhône in south-eastern France. 178 Lancasters and nine Mosquitos were made ready, eight of the former by 630 Squadron, which departed East Kirkby between 21.05 and 21.17 with W/C Blome-Jones and S/L Millichap the senior pilots on duty, seven 1,000 and four 500-pounders in each bomb bay, one with a thirty-six-hour delay fuse, and a round-trip of eleven hundred miles ahead of them. Bad weather had been anticipated, but the conditions during the outward leg over France were even worse than forecast, with icing and electrical storms contributing to the early return of fourteen aircraft. The East Kirkby contingents were not affected by the conditions and completed the almost five-hour outward flight to the target to be greeted by a continuation of the severe weather in the form of rain, thunderstorms and lightning. The cloud was down to around 7,000 feet with poor visibility below, and the flare force Lancasters made a number of runs across the target, orbiting in between awaiting instructions. There were occasional glimpses of the ground, but the Master Bomber was experiencing great difficulty in getting Mosquito TIs onto the two aiming points. Eventually, one of the Deputies managed to put a green TI onto the southern aiming-point, and the main force crews began to bomb at around 02.00, those from 630 Squadron crews carrying out their attacks from 4,700 to 7,500 feet between 02.07 and 02.29, using the light from flares and aiming at green TIs, all in accordance with instructions. ND527 was heading home towards the Clermont-Ferrand region when crashing at Saint-Ignat at 02.45 with no survivors from the mixed RCAF/RAF crew of F/O Wilson RCAF. Little useful information could be offered to the intelligence section at debriefings, but post-raid reconnaissance revealed that the tracks to the north of the junction were closed, and the locomotive depot in the yards had been damaged.

The night of the 28/29th would prove to be busy, eventful and expensive as the Command prepared for major operations against Stuttgart and Hamburg and a number of smaller undertakings involving a total of 1,126 aircraft. The final raid of the series on Stuttgart was to be an all-Lancaster affair of 494 aircraft drawn from 1, 3, 5 and 8 Groups, while 307 Lancasters and Halifaxes of 1, 6 and 8 Groups carried out the annual last-week-of-July attack on Hamburg, a year and a day after the devastating firestorm of Operation Gomorrah. 5 Group put up 176 Lancasters, eleven of them made ready by 630 Squadron, each of which received a bomb load of a 2,000-pounder and a dozen 500lb J-Type cluster bombs. They departed East Kirkby in the wake of the 57 Squadron element between 21.51 and 22.00 with S/L Calvert the senior pilot on duty and were not represented among the five 5 Group early returns. The bomber stream flew across France in bright moonlight above the cloud layer and exposed themselves to the night-fighter hordes that had infiltrated the bomber stream as it closed on the target. It was the Luftwaffe's Nachtjagd that would gain the upper hand on this night and claimed two 57 Squadron Lancasters at around 00.30 and 01.20. Those arriving in the target area found a layer of up to ten-tenths thin cloud over the city, with tops in places at around 10,000 feet, which prompted the Path Finders initially to employ skymarker flares (Wanganui), and then later, green TIs, at which the 630 Squadron crews aimed their bombs from around 16,000 to 18,000 feet either side of 02.00. ND797 was homebound with the long-serving crew of F/L Joblin DFC RNZAF on board, when it was brought down by a night-fighter to crash at around 02.30 between Magstadt and Sindelfingen, some ten miles west-south-west of Stuttgart, and although three crew members are reported to have jumped, only the bomb-aimer survived to fall into enemy hands. Thirty-nine Lancasters failed to return, fourteen of them from 5 Group, and night-fighters also caught the Hamburg force on its way home, and an additional twenty-two aircraft were shot down, bringing the night's casualty figure to sixty-one aircraft. Although it was difficult to make an accurate assessment of this night's attack on Stuttgart, the series had severely damaged the city, leaving its central districts devastated, with most of its public and cultural buildings in ruins, while 1,171 of its inhabitants had lost their lives.

Twelve 630 Squadron crews were briefed and put on stand-by at East Kirkby late on the 29th in anticipation of an early-morning tactical support operation in the Villers Bocage-Caumont region of the Normandy battle area south-west of Caen. Thirteen 57 Squadron crews also attended the briefing, while over at Spilsby fifteen 207 Squadron crews were informed of their part in the proceedings. They were to be part of an overall force of 692 aircraft to carry out attacks on six enemy positions facing predominantly American forces, 57 and 207 Squadrons at Cahagnes and 630 Squadron some six miles away to the south-east at Aunay-sur-Odon, on the other side of a major road junction. The 630 Squadron element departed East Kirkby between 05.31 and 05.50 with S/L Calvert the senior pilot on duty and twenty 500-pounders in each bomb bay and approached the target over ten-tenths cloud with tops at 5,000 feet and a base at 3,500 feet with haze below. They were just five minutes from the start of the bombing run when the Master Bomber sent them home with their loads intact at 07.58 and only two of the six targets were actually attacked.

5 Group prepared for two daylight operations on the 31st, one of them an evening attack on a flying bomb storage tunnel at Rilly-la-Montagne, some five miles south of Reims, for which a force of ninety-seven Lancasters and three Mosquitos was assembled. This included sixteen Lancasters of 617 Squadron, led by its recently appointed successor to Cheshire, W/C Tait, and three Lancasters each representing 630 and 57 Squadrons. A second operation was to be directed at locomotive facilities and marshalling yards at Joigny-la-Roche, situated north of Auxerre and some ninety miles south-east of Paris, and would involve 127 Lancasters and four Mosquitos of 1 and 5 Groups including nine and seven of the former provided respectively by 630 and 57 Squadrons. The two 630 Squadron elements departed East Kirkby together between 17.20 and 17.37 with S/L Millichap the senior pilot on duty and ten 1,000 and four 500-pounders in each bomb bay and made their way south to rendezvous with the rest of the two forces and pick up the fighter escort. 83 Squadron formed into two vics, one at 15,000 feet and the other at 18,000 feet, to lead the Rilly force to the target, where the weather conditions were sufficiently clear to enable a visual identification of the aiming point. The

1,000 and 500-pounders went down from around 17,000 feet at 20.20, and once the tallboys detonated, dust and smoke made it difficult to assess the outcome.

Meanwhile, the Joigny-la-Roche force had arrived in the target area to find no more than three-tenths cloud with tops at 7,000 feet, and good enough visibility also to enable a visual identification of the aiming-point. The marking was concentrated, as was the bombing onto the red TIs, and the 630 Squadron crews delivered their payloads from 12,000 to 14,000 feet almost as one shortly before 20.30. 57 Squadron's ND954 was unable to maintain formation on the way home and crashed at 21.45 near Caen, killing F/L Spencer and four of his crew and delivering the two survivors into enemy hands. This was a particularly sad loss involving a crew on their thirty-first sortie and was the only failure to return from what post-raid reconnaissance confirmed as a successful operation.

This was the final operation of one of the busiest months of the war to date, during which the squadron took part in nineteen operations that generated 191 sorties and cost twelve Lancasters, eleven crews and three individual airmen. As daylight operations were becoming more frequent, squadrons began to apply identity markings to their aircraft, and in the case of 630 and 57 Squadrons, this was achieved by painting the outer fin surfaces red.

## August 1944

August would bring an end to the flying bomb offensive, and also see a return to major night operations against industrial Germany. Flying bomb sites were to dominate the first half of the month and would be targeted in daylight on each of the first six days beginning with the commitment of 777 aircraft to operations against numerous flying bomb-related sites on the afternoon of the 1st, although there were serious doubts about the weather conditions, which were poor over England. 5 Group's targets were at La Breteque, situated in Normandy, some ten miles east-south-east of Rouen, Mont Candon, a mile or two south-west of Dieppe, and Siracourt, located some thirty miles east of the coastal town of Berck-sur-Mer. Forces of fifty-three Lancasters, fifty-nine Lancasters and a Lightning and Mosquito and sixty-seven Lancasters and four Mosquitos respectively were made ready, the first mentioned supported by 630 Squadron with four Lancasters, each of which received a bomb load of eight 1,000- and four 500-pounders. The crews of F/Os Fenning, Kemp, McNeil and Mitchell departed East Kirkby in that order between 16.27 and 16.35 and joined forces with the others as they made their way towards the south. The formation was led by a vic of Lancasters from 83 Squadron, which included the Deputy Master Bomber, F/L Meggeson, a former member of 57 Squadron. Conditions became clear over the Channel, but the cloud built again to nine-tenths stratocumulus with tops at 4,000 feet over the target, and F/L Meggeson took the decision upon himself to abandon the operation. At almost the same time, 18.33, he received a confirmatory call by VHF from the Master Bomber, by which time one crew had spotted the target through a gap and had taken the opportunity to bomb it. It was a similar story at the other 5 Group targets, and those assigned to other groups, and in total only seventy-nine aircraft bombed. Crews were eager to operate against the enemy and were scathing in their condemnation if the meteorological people got the weather wrong and wasted the efforts of all of those involved in launching a raid. Sadly, weather forecasting in the 1940s was an art, not the science it is today.

On the following afternoon, 394 aircraft were assigned to three supply sites and one launching site, 5 Group contributing 194 Lancasters, two Mosquitos and the P38 Lightning to those at Bois-de-Cassan and Trossy-St-Maximin. A dozen Lancasters were made ready by 630 Squadron to participate in the attack at the Trossy-St-Maximin storage facility, situated north of Paris and uncomfortably close to St-Leu d'Esserent. They were part of a heavy force of ninety-four Lancasters and two Mosquitos and took off between 14.26 and 14.39 with F/L Hawker the senior pilot on duty, and a bomb load beneath the feet of each crew of nine 1,000 and four 500-pounders, some of the latter with a delay fuse of up to thirty-six hours. There were complaints that the formation leaders flew too fast, and there were comments also about excessive weaving, but all from East Kirkby reached the target to find three to seven-tenths patchy cloud. The Oboe proximity markers went down on time, and were backed up with TIs, and once the bombing started, the defences opened up with accurate flak that caused damage to twenty-seven aircraft. Despite that, most of the formation passed over the aiming-point and plastered it from 15,000 to 18,000 feet between 17.01 and 17.05. Post-raid reconnaissance revealed many new craters, a large rectangular building stripped of its roof and sides, and the southern end of two road-over-rail bridges demolished.

Despite the effectiveness of the operation, the same site was included among targets for more than eleven hundred aircraft on the following day, the reason given to the 1 and 5 Group crews at briefing to justify that was the importance of the site to the Third Reich, which demanded that no building be left intact, and one or two may have escaped damage during the previous day's attack. 187 Lancasters, one Mosquito and the P38 Lightning were made ready as 5 Group's contribution to the operation, the ten 630 Squadron participants departing East Kirkby between 11.41 and 11.50 with S/L Millichap the senior pilot on duty and eleven 1,000 and four 500-pounders in each bomb bay. They were to attack about fifteen minutes after 1 Group, and as they approached the target smoke could be seen rising to 8,000 feet, and this combined with a fierce flak defence to present the crews with challenging conditions. They bombed from around 16,000 to 17,000 feet between 14.31 and 14.33 by visual reference, having been prevented by the smoke from picking up the markers, but the attack was not as concentrated as on the previous day and much of the bombing fell short. Many aircraft returned to their respective stations bearing flak damage, and at some debriefings complaints were aired that there had been too much chat on VHF between the Master Bomber and his Deputy. Photo-reconnaissance was unable to confirm that the site had been obliterated, and it would need to be attacked again on the following day, a job that would be handed to 6 Group.

W/C Gibson's brief spell at East Kirkby ended with his posting as a senior air staff officer (SASO) to the 54 Base main station at Coningsby on the 4th, where he would put to use the experience gained while understudying the 55 Base operations officer. His time at East Kirkby, however, had reinvigorated his desire to return to operations and that became his sole focus and led him to his untimely death. The 5th dawned bright and clear and brilliant sunshine glinted off the Perspex of twelve 630 Squadron Lancasters as they took off from East Kirkby in the wake of the 57 Squadron element between 10.52 and 10.59, bound once more for the familiar airspace over St-Leu-d'Esserent. They were part of a 5 Group force of 189 Lancasters and one Mosquito, which in turn represented about 25% of the effort by 4, 5, 6 and 8 Groups against two flying-bomb sites, the other in the Forét-de-Nieppe, close to the

Belgian frontier. S/L Millichap was the senior pilot on duty as they climbed out over the station, each carrying eleven 1,000 and four 500-pounders, and lost the services of F/O Lennon and crew to engine trouble. The lead formation remained well to starboard of track for most of the outward flight, and only adjusted its course when some thirty seconds from the target, which created difficulties for those following and attempting to set up their bombing run. It was, at least, an almost intact force that homed in on the target to find it partly protected by up to six-tenths patchy cloud with tops at about 12,000 feet. This prevented the Master Bomber from picking up the aiming-point until thirty seconds from it, and smoke added to the challenges, hiding the yellow TIs from the view of the main force bomb-aimers, and most picked up the aiming point by means of ground features. The East Kirkby crews ran through a spirited flak defence and bombed from 16,100 to 17,500 feet between 13.32 and 13.35, before returning home to report what they assessed as a somewhat chaotic and scattered attack. Others thought it to have been reasonably concentrated and PRU photos seemed to confirm that view with images of fresh damage and heavily cratered approaches.

Six 630 Squadron crews were in their Lancasters before 09.00 on the 6th to carry out the checks before departing for a flying-bomb launching site at Bois-de-Cassan in the L'Isle-Adam, a few miles to the south-west of St-Leu-d'Esserent. They were part of a 5 Group force of ninety-nine Lancasters and the P38 Lightning and departed East Kirkby in the wake of the seven-strong 57 Squadron element between 09.29 and 09.34 with each captained by a pilot of flying officer rank. They joined up with the rest of the formation as they made their way south, the heavy element led by 83 Squadron's G/C Laurence Deane with F/L Drinkell acting as his deputy, but Deane began to experience problems with his navigation homing equipment as he crossed the English coast outbound and decided to hand over to Drinkall. When about forty miles inland of the French coast, a large cumulus cloud extended up to 30,000 feet to bar the way, and F/L Drinkall communicated his intention to take the force below it, descending to 16,000 feet. G/C Deane warned him not to go below 15,000 feet, and advised him not to enter the cloud, but to circumnavigate it to starboard. However, they were immediately enveloped in cloud, and G/C Deane did his best to hang on to F/L Drinkall's tail as he continued to descend, and the two eventually became separated. Emerging on the other side of the cloud, Deane saw a large formation in the distance and followed it, but the passage through the cloud had caused the formation to become widely scattered and it could not be reformed. Thirty-eight aircraft bombed after picking up the aiming point visually, those from East Kirkby from 12,500 to 17,000 feet between 12.14 and 12.21, but fifty-eight others did not, and all had to contend with a fierce flak and fighter defence. Three Lancasters failed to return, and among them was that of F/L Drinkall and crew, who all lost their lives. Photo-reconnaissance revealed some fresh damage to the eastern side of the target, but two large buildings on the main roadway immediately south of the aiming point remained intact, and further operations would be required.

Other than night flying tests (NFTs), there was little activity during the day on the 7th, the first time during the month that no daylight operations had been mounted. It was from teatime onwards that the feverish activity began to prepare 1,019 aircraft for attacks on five enemy positions facing Allied ground forces in the Normandy battle area. The aiming-point for 179 Lancasters and one Mosquito from 5 Group was the fortified village of Secqueville, situated some fifteen miles east of Le Havre. Fourteen 630 Squadron Lancasters each received a bomb load of eleven 1,000 and four 500-pounders before departing East Kirkby ahead of the 57 Squadron element between 21.04 and 21.17 with F/L O'Dwyer the senior pilot on duty and joined up with the others as they travelled south. The target could be seen by the approaching bombers to be under clear skies, although haze shrouded ground detail to an extent, and star shells were fired from the ground to illuminate the aiming-point. This enabled the Path Finder aircraft to drop red TIs onto it for the main force crews to aim at, and the first phase of bombing was concentrated and lasted fifteen minutes. By the time that the 630 Squadron crews began their bombing runs, however, smoke had obscured the markers, persuading the Master Bomber to call a halt to proceedings at 23.25 and send everyone home. LM262 failed to arrive back at East Kirkby having crashed on the Normandy coast near St-Valery-en-Caux, and F/Sgt Patterson RNZAF, a native of Fiji, perished with three members of his crew, while the flight engineer and navigator fell into enemy hands and the wireless operator evaded a similar fate.

A rare day off for 5 Group crews on the 8th led to another for them on the 9th until late afternoon, when briefings took place for that night's operation against an oil storage dump in the Forét-de-Châtellerault, situated south of Tours in western France. It was to be predominantly a 5 Group show involving 171 Lancasters and fourteen Mosquitos, but with five 101 Squadron Lancasters to provide RCM cover. 630 Squadron loaded fifteen Lancasters with ten 1,000 and four 500-pounders each, before dispatching them from East Kirkby between 20.27 and 20.53 with F/L Hawker the senior pilot on duty. The force arrived in the target area to find no cloud, but the presence of considerable ground haze created poor visibility for the marker crews attempting to identify the two aiming-points. The flares dropped by the first two waves of the marker force were scattered, and this prompted the Mosquito marker leader to drop a Wanganui flare as a guide to the third flare-force crews. This meant that some crews had to orbit for up to twenty minutes before the Master Bomber was satisfied that the green TIs were in the right spot and called in the main force, upon which they produced accurate bombing, resulting in three large explosions and volumes of black smoke, which, within five minutes, completely obscured the aiming-point. A pause in the bombing was called, before it recommenced, until the lack of a verifiable marker compelled the Master Bomber to call a halt. All but one of the 630 Squadron crews carried out an attack from around 4,800 to 8,000 feet between 00.02 and 00.27, while one was thwarted by the smoke obscuring the TIs.

The Gironde Estuary, situated on France's south-western Biscay coast, narrows as it leads inland towards the south-east, before dividing to become the Garonne River to the west and the Dordogne to the east. Its banks and islands were home to a number of important oil production and storage sites at Pauillac, Blaye, Bec-d'Ambe and Bassens, and the region was a frequent destination for gardening activities. Bordeaux was a vitally important port to the enemy as a gateway to the Atlantic for its U-Boots and was heavily defended along the entire length of the waterway. Orders were received on 54 and 55 Base stations at teatime on the 10th to prepare sixty-two Lancasters and five Mosquitos to bomb oil storage facilities at the Bassens site, located on the eastern bank of the Garonne to the north-east of the city. 630 and 57 Squadrons made ready five Lancasters each, loading them with 11,000lbs of bombs in the form of five armour-piercing 2,000 pounders and a single 1,000 pounder and dispatched them from East Kirkby between 18.38 and 18.49 with S/L Millichap at the head of the 630

Squadron quintet. They headed towards the Dorset coast, joining up on the way with the other elements, which included nine Lancasters from 83 Squadron to act as the flare and marker force. The flight out was in daylight, which enabled the Deputy Master Bomber to recognise that the formation had become somewhat disorganized with about twenty main force aircraft ahead of the flare force, and the remainder behind it to starboard, but catching up and veering further and further to starboard, until they were some ten to twenty miles off track. Fortunately, the situation rectified itself, and the force arrived in the target area to find clear skies with a little ground haze. As they ran in on the aiming-point, a limited amount of heavy flak began to burst at 16,000 to 18,000 feet, while the considerable light flak fell short, and neither proved to be troublesome. Within thirty seconds of the flares illuminating the ground, the TIs were burning close to the aiming-point, and the East Kirkby crews bombed from 16,000 to 19,000 between 22.32 and 22.45. As they turned for the long flight home, they were confident of a successful attack after observing black smoke rising, but in the absence of multiple explosions it was difficult to accurately assess the outcome.

On the 11th, while 617 Squadron took care of the U-Boot pens at La Pallice, thirty-nine other Lancasters and two Mosquitos from 5 Group ventured a further one hundred miles further south to attack a similar target at Bordeaux under the protection of six Serrate-equipped Mosquitos of 100 Group, which had been escorting Bordeaux-bound Bomber Command forces since the 4th. *(Serrate was a radar device that homed in on Luftwaffe night-fighter radar to turn the hunters into the hunted and it was highly successful, creating among Luftwaffe night-fighter crews "Moskito Panik".)* 630 and 57 Squadrons each made ready five Lancasters, loading them as for the previous operation, and sent them on their way from East Kirkby between 11.59 and 12.10 with no senior 630 Squadron pilot on duty. They reached the target to be greeted by excellent conditions, which enabled the entire dock complex and the aiming point to be identified from a distance. Up to a dozen flak guns targeted the force as it ran in and six Lancasters sustained minor damage but held their course to deliver the contents of their bomb bays accurately across the pens. No enemy fighters were encountered, and Spitfires were on hand off the Brest peninsula to escort the bombers the rest of the way home. At debriefings crews reported a lack of smoke or other evidence of damage to the pens, and, in truth, the concrete roofs were impervious to conventional bombs and vulnerable only to the "earthquake" weapons employed by 617 Squadron.

For the evening operation, 5 Group was switched to communications targets at Givors, located about twenty miles to the south of Lyon in south-east-central France, where the town's marshalling yards to the north and a railway junction to the south were the aiming points for a force of 175 Lancasters and ten Mosquitos. The 55 Base squadrons were assigned to the former, for which 630 Squadron loaded each of its ten Lancasters with seven 1,000 and four 500-pounders, one of the latter with a seventy-two-hour delay fuse. They departed East Kirkby between 20.22 and 20.30 with F/L Rodgers the senior pilot on duty, accompanied as second pilot by the recently arrive F/O Monk. The fact that a pilot called F/O Nunns had also recently arrived on posting gave rise to a degree of mirth. They arrived in the target area to find clear skies and a little haze, favourable conditions which the seemingly usual organised chaos of contradictory or confusing instruction via VHF and W/T threatened to waste, in spite of which the 5 Group ORB would describe the W/T control as excellent and the VHF R/T as good. The initial marking was accurate, but the backing up erratic, which delayed permission to bomb until 01.12, by which time some crews had been forced to orbit three times while the Master Bomber and his Deputy discussed the accuracy of the markers. At 01.14½ the Master Bomber ordered the bombing of a concentration of red TIs, which most crews were unable to see, but they did spot a rough crescent of isolated reds across the yards which the East Kirkby crews bombed from 6,150 to 8,800 feet between 01.07 and 01.23 after confirming their positions by Gee and H2S. Despite the wrinkles, both aiming-points were eventually well-illuminated and marked, and the bombing was concentrated in the correct place. They all returned to home airspace critical of some aspects of the raid, but confident that it had been concluded successfully. Photo-reconnaissance revealed heavy damage to both aiming-points, with the ground badly-cratered and many tracks severed, and the middle span of the railway bridge over the river Rhône had received a direct hit.

The main operation on the 12$^{th}$ was an experiment to gauge the ability of main force crews to locate and attack an urban target on the strength of their own H2S equipment in the absence of a Path Finder element. This resulted from the huge volume of operations generated by the four concurrent campaigns, each of which called upon the finite resources of 8 Group, compelling it, in the short term at least, to spread itself more and more thinly. The conclusion of the flying-bomb campaign at the end of the month, together with the end of tactical support for the ground forces, would remove the pressure, and the planned independence of 3 Group through the G-H bombing system from the autumn would solve the problem altogether. In the meantime, however, no one knew what demands might be made of the Command, and it would be useful to see what main force crews could do when left to their own devices. The target was to be Braunschweig, for which a force of 379 aircraft was assembled, seventy-two of the Lancasters provided by 5 Group. 630 Squadron loaded each of its eight Lancasters with a 2,000-pounder and twelve 500lb J-Type cluster bombs and launched them from East Kirkby in the wake of the 57 Squadron element between 21.29 and 21.35 with F/L Rodgers the senior pilot on duty.

It was a night of heavy Bomber Command activity at numerous locations involving more than eleven hundred sorties, 297 of which were participating in a second large operation over Germany directed at the Opel tank factory at Rüsselsheim, some two hundred miles to the south-west of Braunschweig, but as events would prove, this did not weaken the enemy night-fighter defences, and powerful elements of the Nachtjagd were waiting for the Braunschweig force as it crossed the German coast at around 18,000 feet. Night-fighter flares were in evidence from then until the coast was crossed again on the way home, and it became an expensive night for the Command as a whole. The Braunschweig force made its way eastwards under clear skies, before encountering nine to ten-tenths thin cloud in the target area with tops at 7,000 feet. This was not a problem, as the whole purpose of the operation was to locate and bomb the target blind. The 55 Base crews bombed from around 18,500 to 22,800 feet in a ten-minute slot shortly after midnight and observed the glow of fires beneath the cloud, and some of the bombing did, indeed, hit Braunschweig, but there was no concentration, and many outlying towns also reported bombs falling. Twenty-seven aircraft failed to return from this operation, an unhealthy 7%, and this was in addition to a further twenty from the disappointing tilt at the Opel factory, which would require further attention.

While the above was in progress, a "rush job" called upon the services of 144 crews to attack German troop concentrations, which were attempting to escape the Allied net through a road junction north of Falaise and make it back into Germany. 5 Group supported the attack with twenty-five Lancasters, three of them representing 630 Squadron, which departed East Kirkby along with five from 57 Squadron between 00.12 and 00.32, bearing aloft the crews of W/C Blome-Jones, S/L Millichap and F/O Archer and bomb loads of eleven 1,000 and four 500-pounders. They found a blanket of ten-tenths stratus cloud over the target with tops at 2,000 feet, through which the green TIs were clearly visible and bombed from 5,800 to 8,000 feet between 02.18 and 02.23. Post-raid reconnaissance confirmed that the area around the junction was heavily cratered and the roads leading from it mostly blocked.

The main activity during the afternoon of the 14th was an operation in support of Canadian divisions in the Falaise area, which involved 805 aircraft targeting seven enemy troop positions. 5 Group took part, by sending sixty-one Lancasters to Quesnay Wood, which was concealing a concentration of German tanks. The eight 630 Squadron Lancasters each received a bomb load of eleven 1,000 and four 500-pounders before departing East Kirkby in the wake of the 57 Squadron element between 12.20 and 12.25 with no senior pilot on duty but a Monk and Nunns on the order of battle. They all arrived in the target area, where the Master Bomber issued clear instructions to bomb on the yellow TIs, which, because of rising smoke, were not always visible. Those unable to see the TIs bombed the upwind edge of the smoke, the East Kirkby crews from around 6,000 to 8,700 feet shortly after 14.20. Master Bombers were on hand to control the bombing at each of the other aiming-points because of the close proximity of the opposing armies, but despite the most stringent efforts to avoid friendly fire incidents, some bombs did fall into a quarry occupied by Canadian troops, killing thirteen men. injuring fifty-three others and destroying a large number of vehicles.

5 Group had actually begun the day with an attack by elements of 617 and 9 Squadrons on the derelict French cruiser Gueydon at berth at Brest, which, it was believed, the enemy might sink strategically along with other ships in the harbour to render it unusable if liberated. In the evening, 128 Lancasters and two Mosquitos were made ready to send back to Brest for another go at the Gueydon, a tanker and a hulk, and among those taking part were four 630 Squadron crews and eight from 57 Squadron. The crews of W/C Blome-Jones, F/Os Bolton and Docherty and F/Sgt Herbert departed East Kirkby between 17.30 and 17.45 and arrived over the port to find clear skies and excellent visibility, but also a fierce flak defence, which would cause a number of aircraft to return bearing the scars of battle. The 55 Base squadrons bombed from 16,000 to 18,500 feet between 20.23 and 20.33, and a number of direct hits were observed on both vessels, with smoke issuing out of the tanker. Photo-reconnaissance revealed that the tanker had settled on the bottom, and the cruiser had suffered a similar fate with its decks awash.

In preparation for his new night offensive against Germany, Harris called for operations against enemy night-fighter airfields in Holland and Belgium, in response to which, a list of eight such targets was prepared for attention. Those at Eindhoven, Soesterberg, Volkel, Melsbroek, St-Trond, Tirlemont-Gossancourt and Le Culot were to be targeted in daylight during the course of the morning and early afternoon of the 15th, and Venlo that night, involving, in all, 1004 aircraft. 5 Group was handed Deelen in central Holland and Gilze-Rijen in the south and prepared forces of ninety-four Lancasters and five Mosquitos for the former and 103 Lancasters, four Mosquitos and the P38 Lightning for the latter. The P38 must have been the two-seat variant as it allegedly contained S/L Ciano, who was nicknamed "Count" in reference to his famous namesake, the Italian Foreign Minister, and W/C Guy Gibson, the latter still working his way back onto operations. 52 and 55 Bases was assigned to Deelen, and 630 Squadron loaded its eleven participating Lancasters with the usual eleven 1,000 and four 500-pounders, before launching them from East Kirkby in the wake of the 57 Squadron element between 10.03 and 10.10 with F/L Rodgers the senior pilot on duty. They found the target under clear skies in excellent visibility and were able to identify the aiming point visually as they ran in through the accurate fire from up to twenty flak guns. The bombing took place on yellow TIs from 16,000 to 18,000 feet between 12.08 and 12.11½, in accordance with instructions from the Master Bomber, and many detonations were observed on the aerodrome, post-raid reconnaissance confirming 230 craters on the runways and damage to hangars and other buildings.

The new offensive began with simultaneous attacks on Stettin and Kiel on the night of the 16/17th, 5 Group contributing 145 aircraft to the overall all-Lancaster force of 461 assigned to the former. At East Kirkby, fourteen 630 Squadron Lancasters each received a bomb load of a 2,000-pounder and twelve 500lb J-Type cluster bombs, before taking off between 20.56 and 21.21 with W/C Blome-Jones the senior pilot on duty. Taking to the air at the same time were nine from 57 Squadron bound for the main event and six others as part of a thirty-strong 5 Group force sneaking in under cover of it to mine the waters of the Young Geranium garden, which is believed to be in the Stettiner Haff, a body of water linking Stettin with the Baltic at Swinemünde some thirty miles to the north. It took some three-and-a-half hours for the bombing brigade to reach Stettin, where they were greeted by up to nine-tenths high cloud with a base at 18,000 to 20,000 feet and sufficient breaks to register clear visibility below. Concentrated red and green TIs could be seen marking out the aiming-point, and the 55 Base crews bombed these from 17,200 to 21,000 feet between 01.03 and 01.22 and reported fires taking hold. Not all returning crews were confident about the outcome, some suggesting that concentrations of red and green TIs had fallen wide of the aiming point to the north and west and caused the bombing to be scattered. In fact, it had been a highly successful operation, which destroyed fifteen hundred houses, numerous industrial premises and sank five ships in the harbour, while seriously damaging eight more. A modest five Lancasters were lost, among them LL972 from 630 Squadron, which crashed in the target area, killing F/L Henriquez, a native of Jamaica, and the other seven men on board.

Five 630 Squadron crews were called to briefing early on the 18th to be told of that morning's operation against two flying-bomb dumps in the Forét-de-L'Isle Adam, north of Paris for which a force of 158 Lancasters, six Mosquitos and the P38 Lightning was assembled. 83 Squadron would take the lead and provide the back-up marking on the heels of the low-level Mosquitos at the two aiming points in the east and west. They departed East Kirkby between 12.04 and 12.10 with F/L Rodgers the senior pilot on duty and each Lancaster carrying eleven 1,000 and four 500 pounders, all with a half-hour delay fuse. They headed south in squadron formation to rendezvous with the rest of the force and pick up the fighter escort, and when over the mid-point of the Channel at 13.15, sixty or seventy USAAF Liberators passed across the bows of the gaggle heading east a thousand feet higher, persuading the lead Lancaster to change course. This may have been what prompted comments by some crews on return, that not all had observed station keeping as set out at briefing, and that would result in aircraft bombing out of the planned sequence and on wrong headings. On arrival in the target area, they encountered five to seven-tenths cloud with tops at around 8,000 feet, which hampered identification of both aiming-points, and instructions were issued to not bomb unless a clear view of the target had been established. Some were able to pick out the aiming-points assisted by smoke markers, and four of the 630 Squadron crews bombed from around 10,000 feet either side of 14.10, observing a number of bursts, while those unable to pick up the aiming-point jettisoned part of their load and brought the rest home. Whether or not F/O Kemp RCAF and his predominantly RCAF crew carried out an attack is uncertain as PB244 failed to return. News was received eventually to confirm that Kemp and three others were on their way home after evading capture, leaving one man in enemy hands and two dead. Photos snapped from main force aircraft suggested that the attack had overshot to the north, and this was confirmed from images taken by the Photographic Reconnaissance Unit (PRU).

Later in the afternoon, among a handful of small-scale operations, 5 Group sent a force of twenty-six Lancasters to attack the oil storage depot at Bassens near Bordeaux, 630 Squadron loading nine Lancasters with six SAP American 1,900-pounders and launching them from East Kirkby between 15.38 and 16.08 with S/L Millichap the senior pilot on duty. Time-on-Target was 20,00, and as the Lancasters approached they were able to identify the town and docks through the slight haze and pick out the aiming point. Bomb bursts were observed but not on the oil facility, and while smoke was seen rising it was not indicative of emanating from an oil fire. LM262 was hit by flak during the run-up, but P/O Bolton continued on to deliver the bombs and was observed to head off in a north-easterly direction shedding height and pieces of Lancaster. Six members of the crew are known to have baled out before the Lancaster broke up and crashed at St-Crepin, some fifteen miles east of Rochefort, and P/O Bolton and four others were able to evade capture. The body of the Canadian navigator was found near the village of Muron with his parachute undeployed, and the bomb-aimer had probably been mortally wounded by the flak.

A spell of wet, cloudy and sometimes windy weather set in for the ensuing week, and although crews were alerted daily for operations, little came of it apart from a small mining operation by seven aircraft in the Cinnamon garden off the port of La Pallice during the evening of the 20th. A popular member of the East Kirkby community, 57 Squadron's S/L Drew "Duke" Wyness, was posted to 617 Squadron on the 25th to assume the role of flight commander, and some six weeks hence, he and his crew would become victims of a war crime, when murdered in cold blood on the orders of a local civilian Nazi official after ditching in the River Rhine.

When major operations resumed that night, more than nine hundred aircraft were assembled to take part in three major operations, against Rüsselsheim and nearby Darmstadt in southern Germany and Brest, while a further four hundred aircraft would be engaged in a variety of smaller endeavours. The largest operation would be the all-Lancaster affair involving 461 aircraft from 1, 3, 6 and 8 Groups in a return to the Opel tank works, while 334 others attended to eight coastal batteries around Brest. 5 Group was assigned to Darmstadt, a university city and centre of scientific research and development, and one of a few almost virgin targets considered to be worthy of attention. A force of 191 Lancasters and six Mosquitos included fifteen of the former made ready by 630 Squadron, which departed East

Kirkby between 20.40 and 20.55 with F/Ls Long, Mallinson, O'Dwyer and Rodgers the senior pilots on duty and a cookie and ten No 14 cluster bombs in each bomb bay. There were no early returns, but the Master Bomber was forced to turn back, leaving his two 83 Squadron Deputies, F/L Meggeson DFC and S/L Williams DFC to step into the breach. The target area was free of cloud and some ground haze was present, but this would have been a minor inconvenience had VHF communication not proved to be weak and if the flares dropped by five aircraft of the illuminator force at 01.05 had not fallen too far to the west. The Deputy Master Bombers experienced difficulty in passing on instructions, and when the low-level Mosquitos reported at 01.07 that they were unable to locate the aiming point, H-hour was pushed back to 01.22, although bombing actually began at 01.19. Soon afterwards, someone left their VHF on transmit, creating a noise that drowned out all voice communications, at the same time that W/T became jammed by the Germans. One of the Deputies was heard indistinctly instructing the crews to "bomb on the box" (H2S), and then he and the other Deputy were shot down. The main force crews did their best to comply, among them those from East Kirkby, who were over the target at 6,000 to 10,000 feet between 01.12 and 01.49 and described a widely scattered attack. This was the consensus at debriefings, and many crews admitted to seeking out alternative targets in the face of sparse marking, most choosing to join in the raid on Rüsselsheim just fifteen miles to the north-west and close to the route home.

It was daylight as the 630 Squadron crews crawled into their beds on the 26th, and many of them would find themselves back on the order of battle that night for a very long-range operation. Later, all ground personnel were informed that they were to be posted out of 57 and 630 Squadrons to become part of 55 Base HQ, a move that alleviated administrative pressures but outraged those involved, who felt that their identity as part of the squadron family was being torn from them.

The German port of Königsberg, now Kaliningrad in Lithuania, is located on the eastern side of the Bay of Danzig and was being used by the enemy to supply its eastern front. It lay some 860 miles in a straight line from the bomber stations surrounding Lincoln, which increased to a round trip of 1,900 miles when routing across Denmark was taken into account. This made it the most distant location ever targeted by Bomber Command and was exceeded only by SOE flights to Poland. Such a distance required sacrificing bombs for fuel, and it was a reduced load of a single 2,000 pounder and twelve 500lb J-Type cluster bombs that was loaded into each of 630 Squadron's fourteen Lancasters, while the petrol bowsers at East Kirkby were in constant demand during the afternoon to supply the needs of twenty-nine Lancasters. They were part of an overall force of 174 Lancasters but would not be heading for Jutland's western coast alone, as a second force consisting of 372 aircraft from 1, 3 and 8 Groups would be adopting a similar route on their way to Kiel. Having been briefed for Königsberg twice before without going, there was some doubt among the crews as to whether or not this one would go ahead. Confirmation came when the first 630 Squadron Lancaster began to roll at East Kirkby at 19.53 to be followed by the others over the ensuing thirteen minutes with F/Ls Long, Mallinson, O'Dwyer and Rodgers the senior pilots on duty. Accompanying the force to the target area would be ten Lancasters carrying mines for delivery into the sea-lanes in the Tangerine garden off Pillau at the entrance to the estuary serving Königsberg. Ahead of them lay a ten to eleven-hour marathon, which all but one of the 630 Squadron crews would complete.

When they arrived in the target area almost five hours later, after flying through electrical storms and icing conditions over Denmark, the skies were clear and the visibility good, and they were greeted by around a hundred searchlights and an intense flak defence. The flare force went in at 14,000 to 15,000 feet between 01.05 and 01.12, to be followed minutes later by the heavy markers at a lower level. The TIs fell in two concentrations, 350 yards to the north-west of the aiming point and 1,200 yards to the north-east, prompting the Master Bomber to add his own between the two and call for his to be backed up. Unfortunately, the backing up focused on the north-eastern TIs and these attracted the main weight of bombs. The East Kirkby crews bombed on red TIs from around 10,000 feet between 01.10 and 01.30 and, on return, were fairly enthusiastic about the outcome, reporting punctual marking, concentrated bombing and fires that could be seen, according to some, from 250 miles into the return journey. Photo-reconnaissance revealed that the main weight of the attack had, indeed, fallen into the town's north-eastern districts, where fire had ripped through many building blocks at a cost of just four Lancasters, two of them from East Kirkby. 630 Squadron's ME650 crashed at Skarrild in central Jutland, whether out or inbound is unknown, and there were no survivors from the crew of F/O Bowers, which contained two members of the RCAF and one of the RAAF. After an analysis had been carried out it was decided that the job was not yet done, and a second operation would have to be mounted.

The final operations in the long-running flying-bomb campaign were conducted by small Oboe-led forces against twelve sites on the 28th, and Allied ground forces took control of the Pas-de-Calais a few days later.

Having established that a decisive blow had not been delivered on Königsberg, a return was posted on the 29th, and twelve 630 Squadron crews called to briefing at 17.30 to learn that they were to be part of a 5 Group force of 189 Lancasters. They departed East Kirkby in the wake of the thirteen-strong 57 Squadron element between 20.08 and 20.21 with S/L Eyre, the new B Flight commander, the senior pilot on duty for the first time, and because of the extreme range, each Lancaster loaded with a 2,000-pounder and thirteen No 14 cluster bombs. In fact, the entire force again carried between them only 480 tons of bombs to deliver onto the four aiming-points. Sneaking in under cover of the main event, ten Lancasters were to deliver four mines each into the Tangerine garden on the approaches to Pillau, and the four representing 630 Squadron took off among the bombing element with F/L Long the senior pilot on duty. The bomber stream made its way across the North Sea and Denmark and reached the target to encounter eight to ten-tenths cloud with a base at around 10,000 feet, the Master Bomber, W/C Woodroffe, one of 5 Group's most experienced raid controllers, deciding at that point on a visual attack and instructed the first flare force wave to drop below the cloud, a move that kept the spearhead of the main force circling for twenty minutes before the marking began. The later arrivals could see the markers going down as they approached to carry out what was a complex plan of attack, that proceeded with the first flares falling at around 01.05 and continuing at regular intervals thereafter. At 01.24, the third flare force wave was instructed to illuminate the red spot fire, and a minute later an instruction was given to overshoot by four hundred yards to the east of the aiming-point. At 01.26 a marker aircraft was told to run over the red marker and overshoot by three hundred yards, while, at 01.27, another was ordered to overshoot by six hundred yards east of the aiming-point, before the visual backers-up were sent to track over the reds and greens and overshoot by three hundred yards. The flare force was invited to go home at 01.30, and at 01.34 the visual marker crews were instructed first to back up the greens by six hundred yards on a westerly heading, and two minutes later, the concentrations of reds and greens. The East Kirkby crews identified the target by the red and green TIs and searchlight concentrations and confirmed their positions by H2S before bombing from 9,000 to 16,000 feet between 01.23 and 01.56.

The Master Bomber called a halt to bombing at 01.52 and sent the force home, at which time some main force crews still had their bombs on board, having circled for up to thirty minutes, often coned and constantly under a flak barrage. Understandably, they and others in the same situation became increasingly agitated at the controller's refusal to let them bomb until further backing up had taken place. Enemy night-fighters were much in evidence over the target and would play their part in bringing down fifteen Lancasters. Meanwhile, the gardeners had fulfilled their briefs and returned safely from uneventful sorties, in the case of F/Sgt Flood and crew after fifteen minutes short of twelve hours aloft. At debriefings across 5 Group stations, scathing comments about the performance of W/C Woodroffe were rife, and his stubbornness was blamed for the high casualty rate of 7.9%. They maintained that the backers-up had confirmed the marking to be accurate, despite which, he kept some crews orbiting for up to forty minutes. ND982 was absent from its dispersal pan, and no trace of the Lancaster and the crew of F/O Twidle RNZAF would ever surface. Post-raid reconnaissance confirmed that the operation had been an outstanding success, which destroyed over 40% of the town's residential and 20% of its industrial buildings.

The flying-bomb campaign may now have ended, but a new one against V-2 rocket storage and launching sites began on the 31st with raids on nine suspected locations in northern France. 5 Group sent three forces of forty-nine, forty-six and fifty-two Lancasters with two Mosquitos each to target sites respectively at Auchy-les-Hesdin, Rollancourt and Bergueneuse, all situated some twenty miles inland from the coast at Berck-sur-Mer. Elements of 55 Base were assigned to the last-mentioned, for which 630 Squadron made ready eight Lancasters and dispatched them from East Kirkby between 16.00 and 16.11 with F/L Long the senior pilot on duty and bomb loads of eleven 1,000 and four 500-pounders. All reached the target area to find five-tenths cloud with a base at 6,000 feet and tops as high as 18,000 feet, out of which issued occasional heavy rain showers. The Master Bomber ordered the force to orbit until the cloud had drifted clear, and once Mosquitos had dropped smoke markers, he descended to beneath the cloud to establish their accuracy. Satisfied, he called in the main force crews, and those from East Kirkby bombed visually from 5,000 to 14,000 feet between 18.06 and 18.36. The operations appeared to be successful, and this concluded a month of feverish and record activity for most heavy squadrons, during which 630 Squadron had taken part in twenty-three operations and dispatched 203 sorties for the loss of six Lancasters and their crews, although a number of evaders were on their way home.

*Top left: Crew and ground crew of Lancaster JB288*

*Top right: F/Sgt Arthur McGill KIA*
*Above left: Sgt William France (Big Bill) KIA*
*Middle: Sgt William Pearson (Little Bill) PoW*
*Right: F/Sgt Ernest Farnell KIA*
*Left: Sgt G E Watts (PoW)*

*Lancaster LE-U*

*F/O J W Hoare and crew including Sgt T G Bowie (FE)*

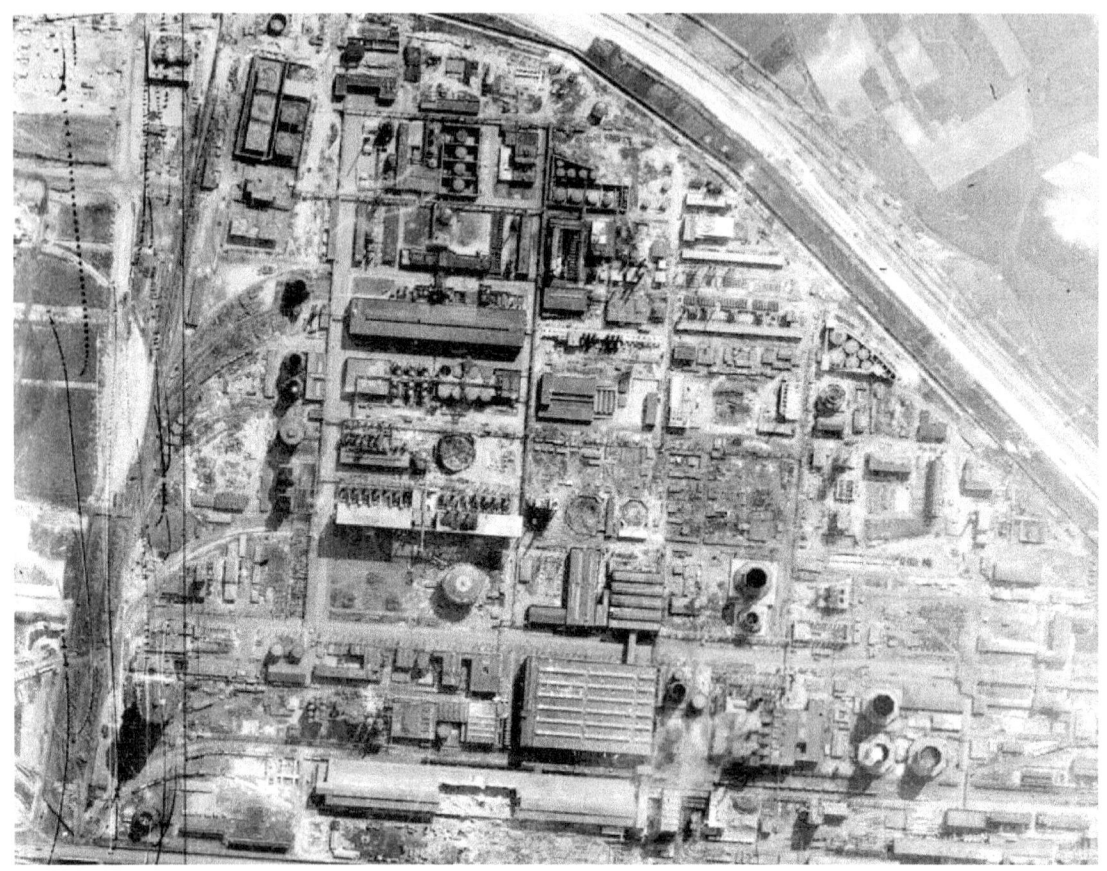
*Damage to the synthetic oil plant of Ruhrchemie AG at Sterkrade-Holten, Germany*

*The German light cruiser Köln underway during the later 1930s.*

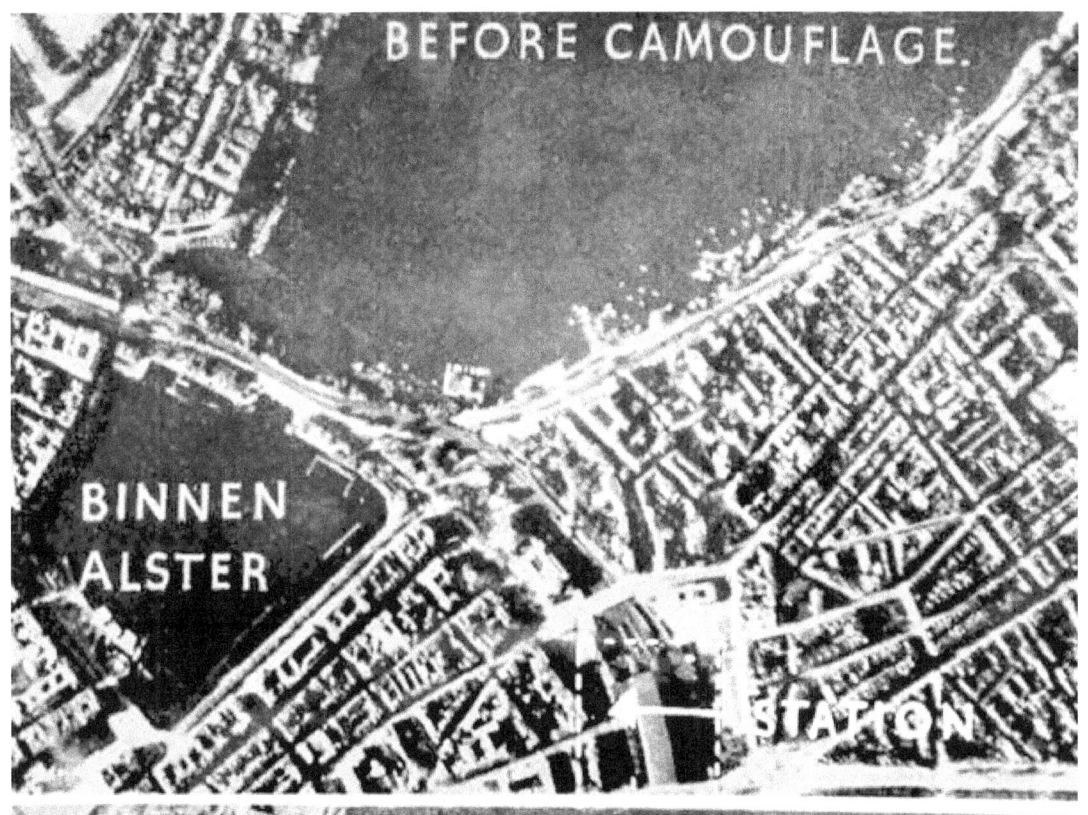

*The Defence of Hamburg*
*Initial decoy methods in and around Hamburg included the disguising of the distinctive lakes in the centre of the city. The intention was that bombers using the Binnenalster as an aiming point would drop their bombs harmlessly into the watery decoy. (Photo by kind permission of Malcom Brooke Military Histories)*

*'A' Flight, 19th April 1944*

QUADRON
AIR FORCE

*630 Squadron Lancaster LE-W*
*L-R: Sgt Joe Cook (RG), F/O Ron Norgrove (BA), Sgt S (Jock) Cruikshank (W.Op), Sgt S C H 'Tich' Priest (MUG), F/O A MacLean (Pilot), Sgt J H Mitchell (FE), Sgt G M Sanders (Nav). Below: Same crew smartened up!*

*Sgt George Dove. KIA 29th January 1944.*   *Sgt Ronald Quinn KIA 12th September 1944.*

*F/O Joseph Feldman RCAF*   *F/Sgt Denis Muddiman*
*Both killed on 12th May 1944 in Lancaster ND580 during a Bourg-Leopold operation. The aircraft was lost without trace, and all are commemorated on the Runnymede Memorial to the Missing.*

*Three Groundcrew with Joe Baldwin (W.Op) and Ted Watson (FE)*
*Left: Ted Watson*

*Sgt Ted Watson (FE), F/O Len Knowles (BA), Sgt Jim Keneally (RG), Sgt Jock Gillespie (MUG), F/O Jerry Monk (Pilot), Sgt Bill Whenray (Nav)*

*Sgt C R Batcup (FE), W/O Steve Nunns (Pilot), Sgt Geoffrey Dent (BA), F/Sgt Frank Baker (Nav), Phillip Carroll (W.Op),Sgt Keith Nelson (MUG), Sgt Jim Elliott (RG). Below: Same crew with groundcrew.*

*F/Sgt Harold Charles Leeton Mackintosh piloting a Wellington Aircraft. These images were taken from the bomb aimer's position. From Australia, Harold enlisted on 20$^{th}$ July 1941 and after training in Australia he was attached to 630 Squadron RAF. He was lost over Plittersdorf whilst on operations over Germany on 21/22$^{nd}$ February 1944.*

*F/Sgt Harold Mackintosh RAAF*

*Sgt James Keneally. Rear gunner in various crews including that of F/Sgt Monk.*

*Boys and Girls of 630 Squadron*

*Bomb Aimers probably 630 Squadron*

*Sgt E C 'Bill' Burnand (W.Op)*

*F/O J C Clingin (Pilot), Sgt K Brookes (FE), Sgt Harry Price (Nav), F/L G Arkieson (BA), Sgt Ken Farthing (W.Op), Sgt D Twomey (MUG), Sgt R Louden (RG)*

*Above: The Clingin crew and (left) their Lancaster PA266*

*Dinghy Drill in Sleaford Pool*

*The Clingin crew with Lancaster PA266*

*Lancaster LM258 LE-F The Spirit of Canada 1944*

*The Orchiston Crew*
F/O Jack Gill (BA), P/O Kenneth Orchiston (Pilot), Sgt Winston Clough (FE), F/Sgt Peter Dutchak (MUG), F/Sgt Derek Pearse (Nav), Sgt Jack Palmer (W.Op), Sgt Alexander Kiltie (RG). Location and identity of Stirling are unknown.

*P/O Sassoon Crew*
Back L-R: F/O John Hopwood (KIA), F/Sgt Ivor Lynn, (PoW), P/O Richard Sassoon (KIA). Front: F/Sgt Murray Munro (KIA), F/O Patrick Fleming (PoW). F/Sgt William Jenkins (KIA). Sgt S C Walton (FE) not shown but was also killed. Took off in Lancaster RF122 to bomb Wahren railway yards but were shot down over Leipzig.

*630 Squadron, unknown date at East Kirkby*

*630 Squadron 1944*

*The Gewerkschaft-Rheinpreussen Synthetic Oil (Fischer Tropsch) Plant at Homberg, before attacks by RAF Bomber Command*

*BBC war correspondent Richard North interviews the crew of Avro Lancaster "S for Sugar" of 630 Squadron RAF on their return to East Kirkby, Lincolnshire, after bombing the marshalling yards at Juvisy-sur-Orge, France.*

*F/Sgt Gordon Burness DFM who had previously served with 44 Squadron*

*F/O Douglas Twidle (Pilot)*
*KIA 30$^{th}$ August 1944.*

*F/Sgt John Turnbull.*
*KIA 2$^{nd}$ January 1944.*

*S/L Roy Calvert and Crew*
*Back L- R: F/O Allan Connor DFM RAAF (W.Op), S/L Roy Calvert DFC\* RNZAF (Pilot), W/O G 'Crooky' Cruickshank DFC (MUG), F/O M 'Beau' Beaudoin RCAF (Nav). Kneeling: P/O Bill Mooney DFC (FE), F/Sgt D 'Tich' Freeman RAAF (RG), Not in photo Sgt Bob Hogg (BA).*

*F/O John Langlands (PoW)*

*F/Sgt Alan Drake KIA 31$^{st}$ March 1944 in F/O Langlands crew.*

**Now Presumed Dead**

**SGT. H. M. COFFEY**

Sgt. Air Gunner Harry M. (Bud) Coffey, only son of Mr. and Mrs. Harry M. Coffey, 285 Charlotte Street, previously reported missing after air operations, is announced as believed killed.

The official notice received by his parents reads as follows: "Regret to advise International Red Cross quoting German information states your son, Sgt. Harry M. Coffey lost his life, March 31, but does not give additional particulars. Pending further confirmation your son is to be considered missing, believed killed."

*Sgt Harry Coffey KIA 31$^{st}$ March 1944 in F/O Langland's crew. Their Lancaster ME664 was attacked at 20,000 feet by a night-fighter and being out of control came down near Ruhla central Germany.*

*P/O Don Cheney RCAF
Survived ten sorties to Berlin before a posting to 617 Squadron.*

| FILE No. | AIRCRAFT TYPE | RAF NUMBER | SQUADRON | RAF STATION |
|---|---|---|---|---|
| 47 | LANCASTER | ND530 | 630 | E. KIRKBY |

Form 2871/A — RESTRICTED — OFFICIAL USE ONLY

# LOSS RECORD FORM

| DATE | TAKE OFF TIME | TARGET/MISSION | FATE |
|---|---|---|---|
| 15.03.44 | 19.12 | STUTTGART | Shot down over Soissons, France |

Barnes L A
P/O, RAF
Pilot

**EVADED**
REMARKS

Walker K A
Sgt, RAF
F/Eng

**EVADED**
REMARKS

Geisler M
F/O, RAF
Navigator

**P.O.W**
REMARKS

Gregg M E
Sgt, RAF
Bomb Aimer

**P.O.W**
REMARKS

Plowman G E
Sgt, RAF
W/Op

**P.O.W**
REMARKS

Overholt J H
Sgt, RCAF (20)
Air Gunner

**KIA**
REMARKS
St-Gilles Churchyard

Fox T A
Sgt, RAF
Air Gunner

**KIA**
REMARKS
Vevey (St Martin's) Cemetery

REMARKS

*Loss record for P/O Len Barnes' Crew*

*Sgt Eric Arthur Snell*

*A very wintry East Kirkby*

*Flight engineer Sgt George Mather (right inboard side of the wing) clearing snow from the wing of Lancaster LE-Z before a raid in January 1945.*

*Gutted and bomb-blasted buildings and installation of the synthetic oil plant of Braunkohle Benzin A. G. at Bohlen, Germany.*

*F/Sgt William Gorton (FE)*

*F/Sgt Joseph Jones (W.Op)*
*Lost without trace 1st January 1945.*

*F/O George E Billing was the pilot of Lancaster PD317 on the 7th January 1945. The aircraft took off from East Kirkby at 1645 but the port inner engine failed soon after take off. The bombs were jettisoned and the crew returned to base but on landing at 1759, the Lancaster bounced and the pilot opened the throttles in an attempt to go round again. However, the port wing dropped and the Lancaster cartwheeled across the airfield. F/O Billings was injured resulting in the amputation of his arm. The navigator F/Sgt A hobson and mid upper gunner Sgt D A Holloway were killed in the crash. The rest of the crew recovered from their injuries.*

*F/O George Billing*

*Back: Sgt Gordon Rabbetts, Sgt Vincent Southworth, Sgt John Sills. Front: Sgt Ronald Smith, F/O Bernard Hall, F/O Victor Meade. On 17th May 1945 Lancaster RF124 took off on a training flight when the aircraft was seen to dive out of the cloud inverted after flying erratically and crushed at Wednesfield near Wolverhampton where it exploded and burnt out. All seven members of the crew died in the crash. The cause of the accident could not be determined but it was considered possible that an engine fire could have occurred in the air leading to loss of control.*

*Ruins of Ludwigshafen Oppau IG Farben BASF Chemiewerk 1945*

*Sgt George Boden KIA 1st January 1945.*

*F/Sgt D Dawson*

*Memorial to 630 and 57 Squadrons, East Kirkby
(Gary Radford)*

# September 1944

The destructive power of the Command was now almost beyond belief with each of its heavy bomber groups capable of laying waste to a German town and city at one go, and from this point until the end of the war, this would be demonstrated in awesome and horrific fashion. Much of the Command's effort during the new month would be directed towards the liberation of the three French ports remaining in enemy hands, Le Havre, Boulogne and Calais, but in the meantime, operations began for 5 Group with an attack on shipping at Brest on the 2nd, for which sixty-seven Lancasters were detailed from 55 Base. Eleven 630 Squadron Lancasters received a bomb load of eleven 1,000 and four 500-pounders before departing East Kirkby between 11.07 and 11.25 with F/L O'Dwyer the senior pilot on duty and flew immediately into cloud as they headed south. A 57 Squadron Lancaster was observed to emerge from the cloud base in a steep dive and crash near the village of Crick, some five miles south-east of Rugby, at 11.45 with a full bomb load on board. The others flew through thunderstorms on the way out, and on arrival in the target area, were greeted initially with a layer of five to seven-tenths cumulus cloud between 2,000 and 9,000 feet affording a range of visibilities between good and poor. However, as the cloud appeared to be drifting away, they were ordered to orbit until the aiming-point could be identified visually, after which the bombing was carried out unopposed from 10,800 to 12,700 feet between 14.33 and 15.22 and was observed to straddle the quays, although some of it hit the town also. Post-raid reconnaissance revealed damage to a number of the vessels at berth and in the dry dock.

Preparations were put in hand on the following morning to launch attacks on six Luftwaffe-occupied aerodromes in southern Holland, for which forces totalling 675 aircraft were assembled, 5 Group detailing 103 Lancasters and two Mosquitos from 55 and 54 Bases for its target at Deelen, located thirty miles to the east of Utrecht in central Holland. The 630 Squadron ORB incorrectly identifies the target as the town of Deelen in Germany, which lies some seventy miles south of the Dutch Deelen on the south-western fringe of the Ruhr. The seventeen 630 Squadron Lancasters were loaded with the usual eleven 1,000 and four 500-pounders each before departing East Kirkby between 15.11 and 15.31 with S/L Eyre the senior pilot on duty. They encountered cloud on the way out that created challenging conditions for formation-keeping and the lead formation appeared to adopt a course to the north of the briefed track. At the target they found varying amounts of cloud cover up to nine-tenths with tops at 7,000 feet and were ordered to orbit to await gaps to appear through which to identify the aiming-point visually, and even then, some had to make a second run to gain a clear sight. The East Kirkby crews bombed from 13,700 to 16,500 feet between 17.31 and 17.42, and despite a spirited flak defence from the airfield, there were no losses and returning crews were relatively confident that they had fulfilled their brief. It would be the 6th before photo-reconnaissance provided a partial cover of the target area and revealed at least sixty craters around runway intersections and taxiways.

Most of 5 Group remained at home over the ensuing five days, while enemy strong-points in and around Le Havre received daylight visitations from other elements of the Command on the 5th, 6th, 8th and 9th. These operations took place during a spell of unhelpful weather conditions, and the attacks on the 8th and 9th were not fully pressed home. Mönchengladbach was posted as the target for 113 Lancasters and fourteen Mosquitos of 5 Group on the 9th, for which briefings took place at 01.30. The sixteen 630 Squadron crews learned that they were to attack the centre of this town located on the western fringe of the Ruhr, which, with the "Bridge too far" Operation Market Garden looming, was expected soon to be within striking distance of the advancing Allied forces. They would have to wait until the early hours of the 10th before departing East Kirkby between 02.35 and 03.15 with F/L Long the senior pilot on duty, and there would be no early returns as they made their way via Ostend to the target. They found clear skies and good visibility as they followed on the heels of the flare forces, which had started a little early at 05.05 and continued until 05.14, at which point Master Bomber, W/C Charles Owen, sent them home and called in the main force to attack. The East Kirkby crews identified the aiming-point by means of red TIs and bombed from 16,000 to 18,000 feet between 05.17 and 05.30, observing large explosions at 05.21 and 05.23 and the glow of fires from the Dutch coast up to eighty miles away. There were no losses, and photo-reconnaissance confirmed the claims of the crews, that they had participated in a highly successful raid, which had left the town centre in ruins.

A further attack on German positions around Le Havre was carried out on the 10th and involved almost a thousand aircraft, 5 Group supporting the effort with 108 Lancasters and two Mosquitos from 53 and 54 Bases. They were greeted at the French coast by clear skies and just a little ground haze, which enabled the crews to identify the target visually and release their bombs onto red TIs from around 10,000 to 13,000 feet roughly between 17.15 and 17.30 and observe the area become enveloped in smoke.

The 11th brought the final attacks on the environs of the port, and involved 218 aircraft drawn from 4, 5, 6 and 8 Groups, 5 Group contributing ninety-three Lancasters from 53, 54 and 55 bases, fifteen of them representing 630 Squadron. They departed East Kirkby in the wake of the 57 Squadron element between 05.38 and 05.51 with S/L Millichap the senior pilot on duty and arrived in the target area under clear skies with slight haze to locate their aiming points to the north and south of the outer defences just after dawn. Each aiming point had been given the name of a car manufacturer, and the one assigned to East Kirkby was Cadillac 1, where the attack was due to begin at 07.30. However, there were no markers on the northern aiming-point, and nothing was heard from the Master Bomber, which left the crews to their own devices. The East Kirkby crews bombed visually from 10,000 to 13,000 feet from 07.30 until the first red and green TIs were seen to go down at 07.43, and aimed at these, thereafter, until turning for home at 07.50. Photo-reconnaissance confirmed accurate and concentrated bombing, and within hours of this operation the German garrison surrendered to British forces.

Twelve of the 630 Squadron crews who had participated in the morning operation found themselves back in the briefing room later, along with five others, to learn of their part in 5 Group's return to Darmstadt, which had escaped serious damage at its hands during the final week of August. A force of 221 Lancasters and fourteen Mosquitos was assembled and those at East Kirkby each received a bomb load of a cookie and fourteen 500lb cluster incendiaries, before taking off ahead of the 57 Squadron element between 20.38 and 20.52 with W/C Blome-Jones the senior pilot on duty. The force arrived in the skies over southern Germany to find them clear of cloud, and despite some ground haze, the visibility was good as the flare force went in at 17,000 feet at 23.52, homing in on a green Mosquito-laid TI. The Master bomber seemed satisfied with the illumination and required no further flares, leaving the backers-up to drop their TIs over the ensuing four minutes before sending them home at 23.59. The main force followed up with extreme accuracy and concentration, those from East Kirkby bombing on red and green TIs from 12,000 to 13,800 feet between 23.50 and 00.09. The city centre became engulfed in flames, which spread outwards to consume large parts of the built-up area, and the glow, according to some, could be seen from the French coast, 250 miles away. The conditions had been ideal for the 5 Group marking method, and photo-reconnaissance confirmed the main weight of the attack to have fallen in the centre and surrounding districts to the south and east. Unknown to the crews as they headed homewards, the attack resulted in a genuine firestorm, in which more than twelve thousand people died and a further seventy thousand, 60% of a total population of 120,000, were made homeless. It was an horrific and devastating blow, which would be repeated at small to medium sized towns across Germany with increasing frequency as worthwhile urban targets became harder to find. The operation cost 5 Group twelve Lancasters, and among them was 630 Squadron's PD283, which crashed at 00.15 at Schmidthachenbach, midway between the target and the Luxembourg border and there were no survivors from the crew of F/O Faulkner. This would prove to be the squadron's last operational loss for ten weeks, the longest loss-free period during its wartime career.

Orders were received on 5 Group stations on the 12th to prepare for a return to southern Germany that night, this time to target the city of Stuttgart, home to major contributors to Germany's motor, electronics, chemicals and aircraft industries. Twelve 630 Squadron crews attended the briefing at East Kirkby and learned that they were to be part of a force of 195 Lancasters and fourteen Mosquitos, which would be accompanied by nine ABC Lancasters from 1 Group's 101 Squadron, while a simultaneous operation by 378 Lancasters and nine Mosquitos of 1, 3 and 8 Groups would take place at Frankfurt, a hundred miles to the north. The East Kirkby Lancasters each received a bomb load of a cookie and fourteen 500lb incendiary cluster bombs before the 630 Squadron element took off between 18.50 and 19.15 with F/L Mallinson the senior pilot on duty. They mostly enjoyed an uneventful flight across France to enter Germany near Strasbourg and find Stuttgart to be under clear skies with moderate visibility and ground haze, and, therefore, ideal conditions for the low-level marker Mosquitos. The marking and backing up were very accurate, and the main force bombing concentrated upon the city centre, with a slight tendency to creep back towards the north-eastern district of Bad Canstatt and beyond into Feuerbach. The East Kirkby crews bombed on red TIs, many witnessing a huge explosion at 23.25, which lasted for about five seconds and reported the glow from the fires to be visible for a hundred miles into the return flight. At debriefing, one 57 Squadron crew claimed to have heard a suspicious voice issuing peculiar instructions while using the main force call sign but not that of the Master Bomber. A PRU aircraft photographed the city on the following morning and found the entire centre to be obscured by the smoke from numerous and widespread fires. Only four Lancasters were missing from this operation, and East Kirkby welcomed all of its crews home. Local sources in Stuttgart described the central districts as "erased", and it seems that a firestorm had erupted in northern and west-central districts, wiping them from the map. Almost twelve hundred people lost their lives, the highest death toll ever in this much-bombed city.

Other than the first of three attacks on the battleship Tirpitz by 617 and 9 Squadrons on the 15th, 5 Group undertook no further operations until the morning of the 17th, and this meant that it was not involved in the previous night's operations in support of the ill-fated Operation Market Garden, Montgomery's plan to seize the Rhine bridges in Holland in an attempt to foreshorten the crossing into Germany for the final push to victory. A force of 762 aircraft was assembled to attack troop positions at seven locations around the port of Boulogne, an assault which would be staggered over a four-hour period and benefit from a 5 Group effort of 195 Lancasters and four Mosquitos. At East Kirkby the seventeen Lancasters representing each squadron received bomb loads of a dozen 1,000 and four 500-pounders before the 630 Squadron contingent took off between 06.44 and 06.55 with F/Ls Mallinson and O'Dwyer the senior pilots on duty. The 55 Base squadrons were in the first wave of aircraft to attack one of two aiming-points assigned to 5 Group, and they found clear skies and good visibility along with red TIs at which to aim their payloads. One 630 Squadron crew, identified in the ORB as flying in LE-G, suffered a hang-up at bomb release, but the others bombed successfully from around 7,000 feet shortly after 08.30. The second 5 Group element went in an hour later to contribute to the three thousand tons of bombs that were dropped, paving the way for Allied ground forces to move in shortly afterwards to accept the surrender of the German garrison. This left only Calais of the major French ports still under enemy occupation.

5 Group stations received orders on the 18th to prepare for an operation that night against the port of Bremerhaven, located on the eastern bank at the mouth of the river Weser, some thirty miles north of Bremen. It was to be a classic 5 Group-style attack, employing the low-level visual marking method and involved 206 Lancasters and seven Mosquitos. At East Kirkby, 630 Squadron loaded its sixteen Lancasters with either an all-4lb incendiary load or a 2,000-pounder and twelve 500lb J-Type cluster bombs, before sending them on their way between 18.26 and 18.47 with S/L Millichap the senior pilot on duty. F/O Atkinson and crew were attacked by a Ju88 when some twelve miles short of the target and jettisoned the contents of the bomb bay during successful evasive action. The others arrived in the target area to find favourable weather conditions and good visibility and ran in on the aiming-point at medium level, releasing their loads in accordance with the Master Bomber's instructions onto red TIs from around 21.00 onwards. A number of huge explosions were witnessed at 21.02 and 21.07, and as they headed out of the target area, crews could see many large fires spreading throughout the built-up area, the glow from which remained visible for at least 150 miles. Post-raid reconnaissance revealed that this first major attack on the port, carried out by what, at the time, could be considered to be a modest force, had devasted the built-up areas north and south of the harbour entrance, wiping out installations and warehousing, and only the most northerly and southerly suburbs had escaped complete destruction. Local reports produced a figure of 2,670 buildings reduced to rubble and thirty-thousand people bombed out of their homes, all at the modest cost to 5 Group of a single Lancaster and a Mosquito. Sadly, the Lancaster was from East Kirkby and belonged to 57 Squadron, and only the bomb-aimer escaped with his life to spend the final seven months of the war as a guest of the Reich.

Seventeen crews from each squadron assembled for briefing at East Kirkby on the 19th and learned that they were to be part of a predominantly 5 Group attack on the twin towns of Mönchengladbach and Rheydt, which represented a shallow penetration into Germany, just ten minutes from the Dutch border, and therefore, a short round trip of four-and-a-half to five hours followed by a night in bed. A force of 217 Lancasters and ten Mosquitos would be accompanied by ten ABC Lancasters from 101 Squadron, and flying in one of the Mosquitos as Master Bomber was W/C Guy Gibson VC, DSO, DFC, who, as previously mentioned, had been agitating to get back into the war before it was over and didn't want his service to end in a backwater, while others gained the glory by being in at the death. Gibson was a warrior, and the war had brought out of him qualities, which, in peacetime, may have lain dormant. War had also given him a direction, and he revelled in the company of fellow operational types, particularly those of the officer class. Having been torn away from the operational scene following the success of the Dams operation, his direction had gone, and he had become listless, frustrated and discontented. His time in the operational wilderness had not, however, deprived him of his arrogance and self-belief, and when the opportunity to fly as Master Bomber on the coming raid presented itself, he grabbed it. He was driven the three miles from Coningsby to Woodhall Spa to collect his 627 Squadron Mosquito, which, for whatever reason, he rejected, and swapped with F/L Mallender, causing a degree of resentment. Gibson had already set the tone for the evening by rejecting the advice of W/C Charles Owen, who had been Master Bomber at this target ten nights earlier and had advised him to leave the target by a south-westerly route, and cross north-eastern France to the coast, and also to observe orders to remain above 10,000 feet. Gibson insisted that he would fly home via a direct route across Holland at low level and would not be dissuaded. He took off ahead of the 627 Squadron element at 19.51, to meet up with the main force element over the target, where two aiming-points were to be marked.

The 630 Squadron participants took off between 18.44 and 19.13 with S/L Eyre the senior pilot on duty and each Lancaster carrying a 2,000 pounder and twelve 500lb J-Type cluster bombs, most of which would reach the target. F/O Monk and crew returned early for an undisclosed reason, leaving the others to press on, some to report icing clouds at around 9,000 feet as they made their way to the target over Belgium, choosing to keep below the cloud base, before climbing fast to 15,000 feet as the cloud dispersed. The marking was complex, with a green marker to be dropped on a factory in a western district of Mönchengladbach, and a yellow marker on railway yards in the north, while a red marker was to be placed on railway yards in Rheydt, two miles to the south. It would have been a demanding plan even for an experienced Master Bomber, which Gibson was not, but even so, his instructions were heard clearly and all seemed to be going to plan, with accurate and punctual marking for the green and yellow forces, but late, though accurate marking for the red force, and some of the red force crews were diverted to the green aiming-point. The 55 Base squadrons were among those assigned to the green force, and identified it by flares and TIs, before bombing from around 10,000 to 11,500 feet shortly before 22.00. They observed the target to be well ablaze with the glow visible for at least a hundred miles into the return flight, and post-raid reconnaissance confirmed a highly destructive attack on both towns for the loss of four Lancasters and a Mosquito. Gibson had returned low over Holland, just as he said he would, and had crashed on the outskirts of Steenbergen in south-western Holland, with fatal consequences for him, and Coningsby's recently appointed station navigation officer, S/L James Warwick, whom Gibson had pressganged into accompanying him. The likelihood is, that Gibson's lack of familiarity with the Mosquito led to the failure to locate the fuel transfer cocks, and the engines simply became starved of fuel at too low an altitude carry out a forced landing.

It was now time for attention to be turned upon Calais as the final port still under enemy occupation, but only one 5 Group Lancaster was involved in the first round of attacks on enemy positions on the 20th, after which, the group remained inactive until the 23rd. Orders came through on that morning to prepare 136 Lancasters and five Mosquitos for an attack that night on the aqueduct section of the Dortmund-Ems Canal south of Ladbergen, a target associated with the group since 1940. It was also the scene of a disaster in September 1943 for 617 Squadron, which would be on scene also on this night to open the attack with Tallboys, to which the raised banks containing the waterway were particularly vulnerable. Germany's canal system was a vital component in the transport network and facilitated the import of raw materials and the export of finished goods to support the war effort. Its wide thoroughfares allowed the passage of large barges, and as the slack in Germany's war production was taken up during 1944, traffic was being pushed through at increasing levels. While this operation was in progress, a second 5 Group force of 108 Lancasters, four Mosquitos and the P38 Lightning would hit the Handorf night-fighter airfield some ten miles to the south to prevent it from interfering. The main operation on this night, however, would be conducted by 549 aircraft from 1, 3, 4 and 8 Groups seventy miles to the south-west at Neuss, situated across the Rhine opposite Düsseldorf, and this, hopefully, might help to split the enemy defences.

630 Squadron prepared twenty-one Lancasters for Handorf, loading each with a dozen 1,000 and four 500-pounders before sending them on their way from East Kirkby between 18.33 and 19.09 with S/Ls Eyre and Millichap the senior pilots on duty. They all reached the target area to encounter a layer of ten-tenths cloud between 8,000 and 9,500 feet, but with good visibility beneath, but the Master Bomber found himself unable to direct the attack and experienced great difficulty in communicating that to his Deputy because of intense interference on VHF. Identification and marking of the aiming-point proved to be problematic despite the flare force illuminating a wide area, and only two green TIs and several isolated yellows could be seen by a few crews. There would be complaints later that there was no control, and some crews orbited and remained in the target area for up to thirty-five minutes before bombing either on green TIs at Handorf or on yellows at the alternative target of Münster. It is difficult to identify which aiming-points were attacked by the East Kirkby crews, and an analysis revealed that only twenty-two crews in total bombed Handorf. An assessment of the results was out of the question, but post-raid reconnaissance revealed no new damage at a cost of a single 55 Base Lancaster belonging to 207 Squadron at Spilsby. Among eighty-nine Lancaster attacking the canal were some from 617 Squadron, returning with Tallboys as the main element of this night's assault, a year after its disastrous experience at the same target. The Ladbergen section consisted of two parallel branches, which carried the waterway over the River Glane and above the level of the surrounding countryside, making it particularly vulnerable to shockwave bombs. Tallboys were probably responsible for breaches in both branches, which left a six-mile stretch of the canal drained and unnavigable. The support operation at Hansdorf was inconclusive and did not prevent the loss of fourteen Lancasters from the Dortmund-Ems Canal contingent.

The second of the series of raids on enemy positions around Calais was mounted by 188 aircraft on the 24th, for which 5 Group detailed thirty Lancasters from the 53 Base stations of Skellingthorpe and Waddington. They climbed away into the most adverse weather conditions with a cloud base at 200 feet and as they approached the French coast, many crews picked up a series of signals between 18.20 and 18.26 telling them to "cease bombing". 126 others continued on to find the target concealed beneath ten-tenths cloud with a base hovering at around 2,000 to 2,500 feet and carried out their bombing runs at that height to deliver 1,000 and 500-pounders onto red TIs. It was a similar story on the following day, when only a third of more than eight hundred aircraft were able to deliver their bombs, before the Master Bomber called a halt to proceedings in the face of low cloud. The campaign continued on the 26th, with two separate raids against seven enemy positions around Cap Gris Nez and nearer Calais involving more than seven hundred aircraft. This time the conditions were favourable, and bombing was observed to be concentrated around the aiming points.

On the afternoon of the 26th, twenty 630 Squadron crews and nineteen from 57 Squadron attended briefing and learned that the night's operation was to be against Karlsruhe in southern Germany, for which 216 Lancasters of 5 Group were made ready, along with eleven Mosquitos and ten ABC Lancasters from 101 Squadron to provide RCM cover. It was to be a two-phase attack with a two-hour gap between and the 53 and 55 Base elements assigned to the second phase. This meant a late take-off for the two squadrons, between 00.20 and 00.55, with S/L Millichap the senior pilot on duty for 630 Squadron and all but one of its Lancasters loaded with 2,700 x 4lb incendiaries, while the crew of F/O Nunns was sitting on a cookie and eight 1,000-pounders. F/O Davies and crew turned back within the first hour with an unserviceable mid-upper turret, and they were followed home a little later by F/O Herbert and crew, whose electrical system and W/T had failed. The others flew out over France with ten-tenths cloud beneath them, which persisted all the way to the target, but thinned to a narrow band with the base estimated to be at between 6,000 and 7,000 feet. The plan was to bomb through the cloud on H2S, guided by Wanganui flares, and some approaching crews observed a red TI cascade above the cloud at 03.54. The East Kirkby crews focused on the glow of red and green TIs and bombed them from around 12,000 feet, the 630 Squadron element between 04.00 and 04.11 in accordance with the instructions of the Master Bomber. All returned safely to East Kirkby to report what appeared to be a city in flames and the glow of fires visible for up to 150 miles into the return journey. There were no plottable bombing photos, but reconnaissance confirmed that the attack had been spread throughout the city and had left a large part of it devastated.

As the crews returned to their stations after 07.00, elements of 1, 3, 4 and 8 Groups were preparing to leave theirs for a further attack on the Calais area. On arrival, the Master Bomber ordered the 340-strong force to come below the cloud base to bomb visually, and another successful operation ensued. At the same time 350 aircraft of 6 and 8 Groups were divided between oil plants at Bottrop and Sterkrade in the Ruhr, where complete cloud cover hampered target identification and bombing was carried out on skymarkers based on H2S-fixes.

Later that day, nineteen 630 Squadron crews attended briefing for an operation that night against Kaiserslautern, an historic city on the edge of the Palatinate Forest, some thirty miles west of Mannheim. It would be the first major attack of the war on this location, for which a force of 217 Lancasters, including ten of the ABC variety from 101 Squadron and ten Path Finder Mosquitos, was made ready. Nine of the 630 Squadron Lancasters were loaded with a

2,000 pounder and a dozen 500lb J-Type cluster bombs each for use against railway workshops, while the remainder carried all-incendiary loads consisting of 2,700 x 4lbs to drop on the city. They departed East Kirkby between 21.55 and 22.14 with F/L O'Dwyer the senior pilot on duty and climbed into clear skies, which gave way to a build-up of cloud over the Channel. They crossed the French coast in the Dunkerque region, at which point the cloud increased to ten-tenths and persisted to near the target with a base at a lowly 2,800 feet. F/O Nunns and crew had reached the St-Quentin area in PD253 when the port-outer engine burst into flames, persuading Nunns to turn for home and order the crew to bale out, while he remained at the controls and headed home, dumping the bomb load into the North Sea on the way. The others continued on to find the target partially covered by a thin layer of five to eight-tenths cloud with tops at 3,000 feet, with a further layer at 6,000 to 7,000 feet, through which the punctually delivered and accurately placed red and green TIs were visible. A green TI in the centre of the town became the objective for the main force crews in accordance with the Master Bomber's instructions at 00.58, while red spotfires pointed the way to the railway workshops. The bombing took place from 3,500 to 5,500 feet between 01.00 and 01.15 and was observed to be concentrated. Two yellow explosions were seen at 01.02, and fires were beginning to take hold as the force retreated towards the west. Reconnaissance revealed massive damage within the city, caused by more than nine hundred tons of bombs, and an estimated 36% of the built-up area was reduced to ruins. By the end of the day, F/O Nunns and crew had been reunited at East Kirkby.

The final raids on German positions around Calais were carried out by 490 aircraft of 1, 3, 6 and 8 Groups on the 28th, and the garrison surrendered to Canadian forces shortly thereafter. On the 29th, five Lancasters from each squadron had six mines winched into their bomb bays for delivery to the Rosemary garden in the Heligoland Bight and departed East Kirkby either side of 19.00. The details of the 630 Squadron crews are missing from the ORB, and we know only that all returned safely after planting their vegetables in the briefed locations. 55 Base numbers were boosted when 619 Squadron moved into Strubby on the 28th, and 44 (Rhodesia) Squadron joined 207 Squadron at Spilsby on the 30th.

During the course of the month the squadron participated in thirteen operations and dispatched 203 sorties for the loss of a single Lancaster and crew.

## October 1944

Now released from the bulk of its obligations to SHAEF, Bomber Command could return with a will to industrial Germany, and from this point until the end of hostilities, it would suffer an unprecedented assault by a force at peak strength. There was nothing to occupy 5 Group for the first two days of the new month, until contributing 128 Lancasters to an operation that was part of a campaign against the island of Walcheren in the Scheldt estuary, where heavy gun emplacements were barring the approaches to the much-needed port of Antwerp some forty miles upstream. Attempts to bomb these positions in September had proved unsuccessful, and it was decided to flood the land, both to inundate the batteries, and to render the terrain difficult to defend when the ground forces moved in. A force of 252 Lancasters was drawn from 1, 5 and 8 Groups and made ready on the 3rd to attack the seawalls at Westkapelle, the most westerly point of the island. 5 Group would occupy four of eight waves of thirty aircraft each, with Tallboy carrying 617 Squadron Lancasters standing off to be deployed only if absolutely necessary. A breach was opened by the fifth wave, which was extended to more than a hundred yards by those following behind, and the flood waters had reached the town by the time that the last Lancasters turned for home.

55 Base had not been invited to take part in the above and had to wait until 5 Group's first major outing of the month before being called into action for a daylight attack on the port of Wilhelmshaven on the 5th. The Kriegsmarinewerft shipyards had produced some of Germany's most famous warships, including the Deutschland Class "pocket battleships" Admiral Scheer and Admiral Graf Spee in 1934 and 1936 respectively, the heavy cruiser, Scharnhorst, in 1939 and the Bismarck Class Tirpitz battleship in 1941, along with twenty-seven Type VII U-Boots between 1941 and 1944. Once a frequent target for Bomber Command, it had been left to the American 8th Air Force for twenty months by the time that a force of 227 Lancasters, one Mosquito and the P38 Lightning was assembled in its honour. The East Kirkby Squadrons contributed forty-one Lancasters between them, twenty-one belonging to 630 Squadron, which took off between 07.40 and 07.58 with S/L Eyre the senior pilot on duty and ten 1,000 and four 500lb J-Type cluster bombs in each bomb bay. A new tactic had been briefed for this operation to present a broad front at the target rather than a spearhead, and in order to facilitate the forming-up process, the Master Bomber led the force around the northern side of Heligoland, before heading for Jade Bay on Germany's north-western coast. As forecast, they found the target concealed beneath a layer of ten-tenths cloud at between 3,000 and 5,000 feet with good visibility above and individual crews fixed their positions on H2S or by observing others. The tactic proved to be unworkable as the Master Bomber struggled to control such a large force attacking on a broad front and many aircraft were pushed wide and off course. He instructed crews to bomb on instrument at the primary target or seek out any suitable built-up area as an alternative, and two 630 Squadron crews chose the latter option and bombed at Sengwarden to the north-west of the town and Jever to the west. No results were observed, and there was no possibility of making an assessment, but the impression of a scattered attack was confirmed later when reconnaissance photos were studied.

That night, a heavy force of 530 Lancasters from 1, 3 and 8 Groups raided the city of Saarbrücken for the first time in numbers for two years, and almost six thousand houses were destroyed for the loss of just three Lancasters. This high return-low loss outcome would be repeated throughout the month and on to the end of the war, with only isolated occasions on which the defences gained the upper hand.

A second Ruhr campaign opened at Dortmund, for which a 3, 6 and 8 Group force of 523 aircraft was made ready on the 6th, while 5 Group had its own target to prepare for and detailed 237 Lancasters and seven Mosquitos for what would prove to be the thirty-second and final raid of the war on the city of Bremen. 630 Squadron loaded sixteen of its eighteen Lancasters with twenty deep SBCs containing a total of three thousand 4lb incendiaries and two with a cookie and nine 1,000-pounders and dispatched them from East Kirkby between 17.34 and 17.56 with S/L Eyre the senior pilot on duty. Taking off among them also were three additional Lancasters bearing the crews of F/L Gordon and F/Os Davies and Herbert, who, in company with two from 57 Squadron, were to sneak in under cover of the main event to deliver mines to the Young Yams garden in the river Weser. Having climbed out and set course, they left the cloud behind and headed into crystal clear skies with a three-quarter moon, which would provide ideal conditions for the 5 Group low-level marking method and hand the hapless city on a plate to the bombers. The attacks were carried out by the East Kirkby crews on red and green TIs from around 17,000 feet either side of 20.30 in the face of many searchlights and the usual intense and accurate flak response. They left behind them a city in flames, the glow from which remained visible on the horizon for a hundred miles and more. The gardeners, meanwhile, planted six vegetables each in the allotted location and returned safely with the others to report an effective night's work. The success of the operation was confirmed by post-raid reconnaissance and local reports, which described a huge area of fire and catalogued the destruction of more than 4,800 houses and apartment blocks, and severe damage to war industry factories, all achieved at the modest cost of five Lancasters.

Earlier in the day it had been announced that the number of sorties to complete a tour had been reduced from thirty-five to thirty-three, and this had been an unexpected bonus to some crews, who could spend the evening celebrating in the mess rather than exposing themselves to risk over Germany. However, this was not the final word on the length of a tour, which continued to demonstrate the characteristics of elastic.

53 Base's strength increased on the 7th with the reformation at Bardney of 227 Squadron from A Flight of 9 Squadron and B Flight of 619 Squadron. While this process was taking place, forces of 351 and 340 aircraft were being assembled by 3, 4 and 8 Groups and 1, 3 and 8 Groups respectively to attack the German frontier towns of Cleves (Kleve) and Emmerich following the failure of Operation Market Garden. Situated five miles apart and separated by the Rhine, both would suffer massive damage, while 5 Group returned to Walcheren with 121 Lancasters and three Mosquitos to target the seawalls near Flushing. 630 Squadron loaded sixteen of its Lancaster with fourteen 1,000-pounders each, all with a one-hour delay fuse, and dispatched them from East Kirkby between 11.43 and 12.06 with S/L Eyre the senior pilot on duty. All reached the target area to identify the two aiming-points visually and by red TIs, which had been accurately placed in the centre of the dyke on the seaward side, in spite of which the early bombing was observed to fall short. A new wind was broadcast to the main force, and this seemed to rectify the situation, enabling crews to deliver their payloads from around 6,000 to 8,500 feet from 14.00 onto the TIs. The deployment of delay fuses did not prevent some bombs from detonating on impact and the dyke was already beginning to crumble as the force turned for home.

617 Squadron had also been in action on this day to attack the heavily defended Kembs barrage, a dam-like structure across the Rhine deep in southern Germany at the point where the frontiers of Germany, France and Switzerland meet. The former 57 Squadron flight commander, S/L Drew "Duke" Wyness, was part of the low-level force briefed to deliver their Tallboys from around 600 feet in broad daylight and were one of two to be brought down. Wyness ditched in the Rhine and three of the crew reached the French bank, never to be seen again, while Wyness and three others were captured and murdered. Wyness and his crew would be fondly remembered by the East Kirkby community and their loss keenly felt.

Focus remained on the Scheldt defences, and the gun battery at Fort Frederik Hendrik near Breskens on the East Scheldt was targeted by elements of 1 and 8 Groups on the 11th, while 115 Lancasters from 5 Group were assigned to others near Flushing on the North Bank of the West Scheldt. At the same time sixty-one Lancasters and two Mosquitos from 5 Group were to attempt to breach the seawalls at Veere, situated on the eastern side of Walcheren opposite Westkapelle. 55 Base was to be involved at Flushing and Veere, 630 Squadron assigning nine Lancasters to Flushing docks and five to Veere and loading each with either fourteen 1,000-pounders or twelve 1,000 and four 500-pounders. They departed East Kirkby between 13.00 and 13.17 with S/L Eyre the senior pilot on duty, and on arrival in the target area encountered varying amounts of well-broken cloud between two and seven-tenths with tops at 4,000 to 5,000 feet. The 630 Squadron ORB is typically short on detail but based on the scant information provided by the 57 Squadron record, we can assume that the attacks on Flushing were carried out from 4,200 to 7,600 feet between 14.47 and 14.54 and at Veere from 4,000 to 7,500 feet between 14.41 and 15.01. Two 630 Squadron crews believed that they heard the codeword, "Bluebeard", the signal to cease bombing, and withheld their loads accordingly, but it became clear at debriefing that no such signal had been sent by the Master Bomber. Post-raid reconnaissance revealed several breaks in the dyke at Veere, the largest of two hundred yards, and an area of flooding of 800 x 250 yards but no new damage to the gun positions.

On the 14th, W/C Blome-Jones concluded his tour as commanding officer, ultimately to be awarded the DFC, the citation reading: "Wing Commander Blome-Jones has successfully completed his second tour of operations. As squadron commander, he has always elected to fly on the most dangerous and difficult missions. When on a sortie to Bourg-Leopold in Belgium, he was unable to locate the target. Despite fighter opposition and very bad weather, he circled the area until the target was located. His skill and determination as a pilot and captain, and his cool handling of his aircraft in the face of opposition have earned for him the absolute confidence of his crew. In the face of heavy anti-aircraft fire, he has bombed warships in Brest harbour and circled over Givors for thirty-two minutes in bad weather in order to identify and eventually attack it. His skill, courage and devotion to duty are worthy of the highest praise."

The new commanding officer was W/C John Grindon, and he would see the squadron through to the end of the bombing war. Grindon was a native of Newquay in Cornwall, where he was born in 1917, just a few weeks before his father was killed at Ypres. He was educated at Dulwich College and the RAF's University of the Air at Cranwell, and after passing out in 1937 joined 98 Squadron, before moving on to 150 Squadron in 1939. Equipped with the Fairey Battle, 150 Squadron became part of the Advanced Air Striking Force, which moved to France on the day before the declaration of war. Grindon was absent from the squadron on a navigation course during May 1940, when 150 Squadron and the others equipped with Battles suffered massive casualties during the German advance across the Low Countries and France and were effectively knocked out of the war. He spent the next four years as an instructor in Canada and as a staff officer at Bomber Command, before re-entering the operational scene as a flight commander with 106 Squadron at Metheringham in July 1944. He completed sixteen sorties with 106 Squadron, beginning at Kiel on the night of the 23/24th of July, and ending at Bremen on the 6/7th of October.

The 14th was the day on which were fired the opening salvoes of Operation Hurricane, a terrifying demonstration to the enemy of the overwhelming superiority of the Allied air forces ranged against it. Bomber Command ordered a maximum effort from all but 5 Group to attack Duisburg, for which 1,013 Lancasters, Halifaxes and Mosquitos answered the call. The American 8th Air Force would also be in business on this day, targeting the Cologne area further south with 1,250 bombers escorted by 749 fighters. The RAF force took off at first light, picked up its own fighter escort, and delivered 4,500 tons of high-explosives and incendiaries into Duisburg shortly after breakfast time, causing unimaginable destruction. That night, similar numbers returned to press home the point about superiority, bringing the total weight of bombs over the two raids to 9,000 tons from 2,018 sorties in fewer than twenty-four hours. The only involvement by 5 Group were single sorties by a Lancaster and a Mosquito to conduct a photo-reconnaissance of the operation.

However, 5 Group took advantage of the evening activity over the Ruhr to return to Braunschweig, the scene of quite a number of unsatisfactory previous attempts to land a really telling blow. A force of 232 Lancasters and eight Mosquitos was made ready, of which twenty of the former were provided by 630 Squadron and each loaded with a 2,000-pounder and sixteen No 14 cluster bombs, before departing East Kirkby between 22.25 and 23.15 with S/L Eyre the senior pilot on duty. They flew out over the Lincolnshire coast and made landfall on the Den Helder peninsula, before traversing 250 miles of Holland and Germany to arrive in the target area under conditions ideal for the low-level marking by Mosquitos. Approaching the target at 18,000 feet from the south-west over Salzgitter and Hallendorf, the homes respectively of the massive Reichswerke Hermann Göring steelworks and oil plant, crews had to run the gauntlet of searchlight cones and heavy flak for the three minutes it took to pass through. They were greeted by clear skies and good visibility on the other side, which facilitated accurate marking with red and green TIs by the heavy brigade, and although the early stages of bombing tended to undershoot, the Master Bomber quickly brought it back on track, calling for crews to overshoot by up to nineteen seconds. The 630 Squadron contingent passed over the aiming-point at around 17,000 to 19,500 feet between 02.30 and 02.40 and delivered their loads accurately to contribute to a highly effective raid.

The return flight was conducted by the entire force at 3,500 feet to fox the night-fighter controller and was covered by cloud, but passing to the south of the Ruhr, the effects of the attack on Duisburg were clearly visible over to starboard. At debriefing, there were complaints that main force crews had jettisoned incendiaries all the way back as far as the Rhine, and thereby illuminated the track for any stalking night-fighters. In the event, only a single Lancaster failed to return from what was, indeed, confirmed to be an outstanding result, which had wiped out the entire centre of this historic city, and visited damage upon almost every other district. *(Author's note. I have a very good friend, who was born on D-Day in the village of Geitelde, about four miles south-west of Braunschweig, and one of many small communities on the outskirts of the town. Years after the war, he learned from the locals, that they believed Bomber Command had intentionally bombed the surrounding villages, to force the populations into the city before the "big" raid took place with them in it. In view of the four previous attacks, which had fallen predominately outside of the town, it is easy to see how this belief occurred).*

On the night of the 15/16th, the 630 Squadron crews of F/Ls Archer and Gordon departed East Kirkby at 18.40 and 18.53 respectively bound for one of the Silverthorn gardens in the Kattegat region of the Baltic. They were part of the support and diversionary effort for the last heavy raid of the war on Wilhelmshaven, which was being conducted by five hundred aircraft from all but 5 Group. On arrival in the target area, they encountered seven-tenths cloud in layers up to 14,000 feet, which combined with the failure of their H2S, prevented them from establishing their positions, and it is believed that they brought their six Mk IV mines each back to base. Local sources in Wilhelmshaven reported severe damage in commercial and residential districts but relatively few casualties.

Stubborn resistance by the occupiers on Walcheren demanded further operations against the seawalls at Westkapelle, for which a 5 Group force of forty-seven Lancasters and three Mosquitos was made ready on the 17th. Five of the eleven Lancasters at East Kirkby belonged to 630 Squadron, and each had fourteen delayed-action 1,000 pounders winched into their bomb bays, before taking off between 12.42 and 13.08 with F/L Lewis the senior pilot on duty. They arrived at the target to find favourable conditions and bombed on red TIs from 5,000 to 5,250 feet between 14.00 and 14.16, observing most loads to fall between the TIs and the existing breach. Each returned home safely with an aiming-point photo, while a reconnaissance aircraft remained over the target from 14.55 to 15.10 to record the delayed-action bomb blasts. Disappointingly, the photos would reveal no extension to the breach in the dyke.

There were no operations for the heavy squadrons that night, but night flying training went on as usual, and this was to inflict upon 630 Squadron its first fatalities since Darmstadt five weeks earlier. NF961 came down in north Yorkshire to crash at 02.35 near Osmotherley on the western side of the Cleveland Hills, possibly as the result of icing, and there were no survivors among the crew of F/O Brammer.

An operation of significance on the morning of the 18th represented a major step forward in Bomber Command's evolution and brought with it for 3 Group the same level of independence enjoyed by 5 Group. The G-H bombing system had been under development for around two years and mirrored to an extent the American method of releasing bombs on observing the leader's fall away. While the American system was exclusively for daylight operations, the RAF system was equally effective at night and in 3 Group hands would prove to be particularly effective against precision targets like oil refineries and railways. As one of a few relatively intact German cities, Bonn, situated some twenty miles to the south-east of Cologne, was selected as the target for the first massed live trial on the assumption that fresh damage would be easily identified to assess the performance of G-H. The operation was not entirely successful, but time and practice would iron out the wrinkles.

Following a night off, forty-one crews were called to the East Kirkby briefing room on the 19th to learn the details of that night's operation against Nuremberg, which was to be a 5 Group affair involving a new record of 263 Lancasters and seven Mosquitos, while 560 aircraft from the other groups plied their trade at Stuttgart, some ninety miles to the south-west in two phases four-and-a-half hours apart. The twenty-strong 630 Squadron element took off between 17.18 and 17.38 with F/Ls Archer, Gordon and Lewis the senior pilots on duty and a 2,000-pounder and twelve 500lb J-Type cluster bombs in each bomb bay. There were no early returns among the East Kirkby contingent and the outward flight across France was uneventful, allowing a largely intact bomber stream to arrive in the target area to encounter a wedge of eight to ten-tenths cloud at between 3,000 and 10,000 feet, with poor visibility below. The marker force laid down flares and backed them up with others along with red and green TIs, which were observed to be somewhat scattered, and bombing had to take place on their glow seen through the cloud. The 630 Squadron crews carried out their attacks from 15,500 to 19,000 feet either side of 21.00 in accordance with the Master Bomber's instructions, which included a call to overshoot by two hundred yards after the early bombing was seen to fall short. At debriefings, the presence of jet-propelled fighters was mentioned, and one 630 Squadron crew positively identified a Me262. The impression given by the glow of fires was of an effective attack, but returning crews were uncertain as to the outcome and post-raid reconnaissance revealed the bombing to have fallen not on the intended city centre aiming-point, but predominantly into the more industrial southern districts, where almost four hundred houses were destroyed along with forty-one industrial buildings.

It was back to Walcheren on the 23rd for 112 Lancasters of 5 Group, including a contribution from the 55 Base squadrons of six Lancasters each to target the coastal battery at Flushing. At East Kirkby the bomb bays of the 630 and 57 aircraft were filled with fourteen 1,000 pounders before they took off between 15.11 and 15.19 with no senior pilots on duty. They were greeted at the target by eight to ten-tenths cloud with a base at between 3,000 and 5,000 feet, and poor visibility below caused by haze and rain. The force was led in on what appeared to be a decent approach but was ordered to "orbit port" as the lead crews experienced great difficulty in identifying their respective aiming-points. A second run was no more revealing, even for those crews who ventured down as low as 2,000 feet, and twenty would still have their bombs on board when ordered to go home. The East Kirkby crews were among eighty-eight to deliver their bombs, in their case from 3,800 to 4,800 feet between 16.24 and 17.25, and post-raid reconnaissance revealed evidence of seventy bomb bursts, including four near-misses, and the destruction of a number of buildings on the site.

That evening, a new record force of 1,055 aircraft was sent against Essen as part of the Hurricane "message", and in view of the destruction already inflicted upon the city, and the likelihood that there was little left to burn, 90% of the 4,538 tons of bombs were of the high explosive rather than incendiary variety. Six hundred buildings were destroyed, while a further eight hundred sustained serious damage, and the city's status as a major centre of war production was effectively ended. This number was achieved without 5 Group, which took the night off and committed only twenty-five Lancasters to gardening duties in northern waters on the following night. The 630 Squadron crews of F/Ls Archer and O'Dwyer and F/O Miller and Lt Adams of the USAAF departed East Kirkby between 17.25 and 17.40 bound for the Kattegat region of the Baltic with no reference to a specific location. However, the 57 Squadron element taking off at the same time was bound for the Kraut garden, located in the Lim Fjord that runs between Ålborg and Hals in northern Jutland, and we can reasonably assume that this was the destination also for the 630 Squadron quartet. They reached the target area to find ten-tenths very low cloud with tops at between 2,000 and 6,000 feet and established their positions by H2S-fix, before delivering their six mines each into the briefed locations and returning safely from uneventful sorties. Essen was pounded again by more than seven hundred aircraft in daylight on the 25th and suffered the destruction of a further eleven hundred buildings, before Operation Hurricane moved on to Cologne on the 28th, when a force of seven hundred aircraft destroyed more than 2,200 apartment blocks in districts north-east and south-west of the city centre, and much damage was inflicted upon power, railway and dockland installations.

5 Group occupied the 28th with the preparation of a force of 237 Lancasters and seven Mosquitos for an operation that night against the U-Boot pens at Bergen in Norway. 630 Squadron loaded its nineteen Lancasters with eleven 1,000-pounders each and dispatched them from East Kirkby ahead of the 57 Squadron element between 22.15 and 22.35 with W/C Grindon leading the squadron into battle for the first time. They reached the target area after a three-and-a-half-hour outward flight, having battled their way through electrical storms, and having been told to expect clear conditions. Some doubts had been expressed about the forecast, however, and these were confirmed when the force was met by eight to ten-tenths cloud at between 4,000 and 8,000 feet and in places as high as 14,000 feet, which obscured the aiming-point. This would not have been a problem over Germany, but the risk to Norwegian civilians was uppermost in the mind of the Master Bomber as he pondered his options before calling for the main force crews to descend. Even then, most were unable to pick out any markers, and the situation was exacerbated by intermittent VHF reception, which persuaded 83 Squadron's F/L Cornish to fly up and down the coast acting as a communications link between the Master Bomber and the main force. The flare force contingent did what it could from between 12,500 and 15,000 feet, and some main force supporters flew as low as 4,500 feet without being able to identify the target. Forty-seven aircraft bombed, including one from 630 Squadron and two from 57 Squadron aiming at red TIs from around 6,000, while the others orbited up to four times until the Master Bomber called a halt and sent them home at 02.10. Conditions in the 55 Base region were unsuitable for receiving returning aircraft and most landed at stations in Yorkshire.

The final operations against Walcheren were undertaken by 5 Group on the 30th, when two forces of fifty-one Lancasters and four Mosquitos each were sent against coastal batteries at Westkapelle and Flushing. 630 Squadron contributed a dozen Lancasters to the Westkapelle attack, and they departed East Kirkby between 10.17 and 10.42 with S/L Millichap the senior pilot on duty and fourteen 1,000-pounders with a one-hour delay fuse in each bomb bay. They ran into four to seven-tenths cloud at 6,000 feet over the target, despite which, visibility was good, and the aiming-point was identified visually and marked by red TIs. Some of these became buried in the dunes and were partially concealed, leading to a little overshooting, but the East Kirkby crews were able to deliver their payloads accurately from 3,000 to 4,000 feet between 12.09 and 12.28. That evening, nine hundred aircraft returned to Cologne to deliver four thousand tons of predominantly high-explosive bombs, and almost five hundred from 1, 3, 4 and 8 Groups went back again twenty-four hours later to complete the destruction of the Rhineland capital city. Ground forces began their assault on Walcheren on the 31st, and a week of heavy fighting preceded the island's capture. Even then, the clearing of mines from the approaches to Antwerp kept the port out of commission for a further three weeks.

During the course of the month the squadron took part in thirteen operations and dispatched 158 sorties for the loss of a single Lancaster and crew while training.

# November 1944

The new month began for 5 Group with a daylight operation on the afternoon of the 1st, against a synthetic oil plant referred to by the raid planners simply as Homberg, a name with an evil reputation among 3 Group squadrons, which had suffered heavy casualties in repeated attacks on the plant during the summer. The Gewerkschaft Rheinpreussen A G production site lay in the Meerbeck district of the town of Moers, which is situated a mile-and-a-half to the west of Homberg on the West Bank of the Rhine opposite Duisburg. Its reputation probably meant less to the likes of 5 Group squadrons, whose hearts were more likely to be set racing by the mention of the Wesseling refinery south of Cologne. 630 Squadron briefed nineteen crews as part of an overall 5 Group force of 226 Lancasters and two Mosquitos, which were to be joined by fourteen 8 Group Mosquitos to provide the Oboe marking. Before the crews made their way to their aircraft, they received the good news that the number of sorties for a tour had been reduced again to thirty, which would be a cause for celebration among the select few who had already reached that milestone.

The 630 Squadron element departed East Kirkby between 13.26 and 13.54 with W/C Grindon the senior pilot on duty and eleven 1,000 and four 500-pounders in each bomb bay. They all reached the target area to find it completely obscured by cloud with tops at between 6,000 and 9,000 feet, and the lead section of the bomber stream arrived either before the Wanganui flares went down or were on top of them before they became evident. Faced with an intense and accurate flak response coming up at them through the cloud, some crews apparently simply turned for home. The marking was confused by bad timing and the release point flares were well-scattered over a circle with a ten-mile radius, prompting a backer-up from 83 Squadron to drop a yellow TI over the built-up area in the hope of attracting some bombing. Some crews caught a glimpse of the target area through a chink in the cloud, while others carried out a time-and-distance run from the last visual pinpoint, before aiming at red skymarkers with green stars. Four 630 Squadron crews were unable to carry out satisfactory bombing runs and attacked a built-up area to the south of the target as an alternative, while another bombed the nearby city of Krefeld on a Gee-fix. At debriefing many crews reported that the Master Bomber's VHF transmissions had been jammed by someone in another aircraft leaving the transmit button on and it was evident that a lack of clear communication with the Master Bomber and the wide spread of the markers were major factors in the failure of the operation. Ultimately, the conditions rendered the whole attack ineffective, and although 159 aircraft released their bombs, it is unlikely that any hit the intended target, and the repair of flak damage would keep the airframe and engine fitters busy into the night. An attack by 3 Group on the following day using its G-H system was more successful, and large fires were reported.

Düsseldorf's turn to face a massive force came on the 2nd, when 992 aircraft were made ready for what would prove to be the final major raid of the war on this much-bombed city on the southern edge of the Ruhr. 5 Group put up 187 Lancasters, fourteen provided by 630 Squadron for this rare experience for the "Lincolnshire Poachers" to operate with the rest of the Command. They departed East Kirkby between 16.21 and 17.05 with F/L Archer the senior pilot on duty and each crew sitting on a cookie and six 1,000 and six 500-pounders, and all arrived at the target to find clear skies, moonlight and only ground haze to slightly mar the vertical visibility. The moonlight nullified the searchlights ringing the city, but of greater concern was the heavy flak bursting at 17,000 to 20,000 feet. The main force crews found the aiming-point to be well illuminated and marked with red and green TIs, which the East Kirkby participants bombed from 17,000 to 21,000 feet between 19.13 and 19.37. F/O McGuffie and crew had taken off late and were twelve minutes behind schedule as they approached the target alone, at which point common sense persuaded them to turn back. Returning crews reported fires beginning to take hold and a burgeoning thick pall of smoke rising through 2,000 feet as they turned away and were confident of a successful attack. Fierce night-fighter activity was reported from the target to 04.30° East homebound and six 630 Squadron crews reported inconclusive engagements. The success of the operation was confirmed by post-raid reconnaissance, which revealed that the northern half of the city had received the main weight of bombs, and that five thousand houses had been destroyed or seriously damaged.

The continuing campaign against Ruhr cities would be prosecuted by 749 aircraft of 1, 4, 6 and 8 Groups at Bochum on the 4th, while 5 Group renewed its acquaintance with the Dortmund-Ems Canal, which had been repaired following the successful breaching of its banks near Münster in September. Since Germany's railways had come under the spotlight during the pre- and post-invasion campaigns, the Dortmund-Ems and the nearby Mittelland Canals had taken on a greater significance as vital components in the transportation system, particularly with regard to supplying the front and the movement of raw materials like coal and coke to the steel works of the Ruhr region. A force of 168 Lancasters and two Mosquitos contained thirteen 630 Squadron aircraft, which departed East Kirkby between 17.34 and 17.44 with S/L Eyre the senior pilot on duty and fourteen 1,000-pounders in each bomb bay. They were heading for the familiar aqueduct section of the canal south of Ladbergen and hoped to sneak in under cover of the main operation sixty miles to the south and avoid the attentions of night-fighters. The first marker aircraft of 83 Squadron arrived at the target at 19.19, after making a GPI run (ground position indicated) by means of H2S from Münster and encountered clear skies with ground haze. A blind-dropped green TI burst on the canal bank four hundred yards short of the aiming-point, which the flare force crews employed as a reference for their runs between 19.20 and 19.28. Red TIs were observed to fall between the two aqueducts, after which, the Master Bomber cancelled the third wave of flares and sent them all home to leave the way clear for the main force. The first bombs tended to overshoot, but, thereafter, an accurate and concentrated attack was delivered from around 10,000 to 13,000 feet from 19.30 onwards and photo-reconnaissance confirmed that both branches of the canal had been breached and drained, leaving barges stranded and the waterway unnavigable. Meanwhile at Bochum, damage was immense, amounting to more than four thousand buildings destroyed or severely afflicted, with almost a thousand people killed, but night-fighters made contact with the bomber stream, and twenty-eight aircraft, mostly Halifaxes, were shot down.

To capitalise on 5 Group's success, an attack was planned on the 6th against the Mittelland Canal at Gravenhorst, a point about a mile north of Das Nasse Dreieck, the "Wet Triangle", at Bergeshövede. This is a triangular basin, where the two waterways converge about ten miles north of Ladbergen, and during the war facilities were on hand for loading and unloading cargo and replenishing fuel and other supplies. The Dortmund-Ems Canal exits the basin at its north-western corner and heads west, while the Mittelland exits to the north before swinging to the east. It was to be a 5 Group show involving 239 Lancasters and seven Mosquitos, seventeen from each of the East Kirkby squadrons receiving a war load of thirteen 1,000-pounders before taking to the air between 16.08 and 16.47 with no senior pilots on duty among the 630 Squadron contingent. All reached the target area to find clear skies but haze up to around 4,000 feet that affected the vertical visibility, and the Master Bomber called in the flare force to alleviate the situation, despite which, the low-level Mosquito markers experienced great difficulty in identifying the aiming-point. A single Mosquito piloted by F/L De Vigne eventually delivered its target indicator accurately onto the aiming-point, where it fell into the water and was extinguished. Only thirty-one aircraft had bombed before the Master Bomber called a halt to proceedings at 19.38, and all from East Kirkby withheld their loads, jettisoning the delayed-action 1,000 pounders before setting course for home and encountering not only night-fighter activity, but also very challenging weather conditions in the form of electrical storms and low cloud. Ten Lancasters failed to return, a high rate of loss with nothing to show for it, and among them was one from 57 Squadron.

Earlier on the 6th, a series of raids on Ruhr oil refineries had begun with an area attack by more than seven hundred aircraft from all but 5 Group at Gelsenkirchen, where the Nordstern plant (Gelsenberg A G) and the city centre were the aiming-points, and this was followed by smaller-scale operations against the Meerbeck plant at Homberg on the 8th, the Krupp Treibstoffwerke at Wanne-Eickel on the 9th and the Klöckner Werke refinery at Castrop-Rauxel on the morning of the 11th.

5 Group had remained off the order of battle after the 6th, and it was the 11th when it next went to war to attack the Rhenania-Ossag synthetic oil plant at Harburg, located on the South Bank of the Elbe opposite Hamburg. 237 Lancasters and eight Mosquitos were to take part in this all-5 Group show, while elements of 1 and 8 Groups targeted the Hoesch-Benzin plant 170 miles to the south in the Wambel district of Dortmund. Seventeen 630 Squadron Lancasters taxied to the runway in company with nineteen from 57 Squadron for the main event, with S/L Eyre the senior pilot on duty and each crew sitting on a cookie and fourteen 500lb Type-14 incendiary cluster bombs. Two additional 630 Squadron Lancaster and three from 57 Squadron were to join others to carry out mining sorties in the Eglantine garden in the Elbe estuary. East Kirkby dispatched its forty-one Lancasters between 16.09 and 17.04, but F/O Atkinson and crew were back on the ground within seventy-five minutes after losing their W/T. F/O Barnes and crew were over the North Sea when the bomb-aimer became indisposed and they, too, were compelled to turn back, while the others reached the target area to find largely clear conditions, with only a thin layer of stratus at 8,000 feet and another at 17,000 to 18,000 feet between them and the aiming-point. This they identified either by H2S or red and green TIs, before delivering their loads in accordance with instructions from the Master Bomber from around 16,000 to 19,000 feet. The defenders threw up a heavy flak barrage, which reached as high as 23,000 feet, and seven Lancasters failed to return. At debriefing, F/O Sassoon and crew reported that they had fallen behind schedule and were still short of the target when they picked up the Master Bomber's broadcast at 19.50 ending the operation and sending the force home. They dropped their cookie from 17,750 feet onto a searchlight concentration some thirty miles west of Hamburg and returned the rest of their payload to the station bomb dump. Many crews reported large explosions at 19.18. 19.22, 19.25 and 19.28, followed by an oil fire and a pall of black smoke from the storage tanks, and

local reports would confirm that heavy damage had been inflicted upon the town's residential and industrial districts. Meanwhile, the gardening duo of F/O Millar and F/L Archer and their crews planted a dozen Mk VI mines between them into the briefed locations during uneventful sorties.

The 16th was devoted to the erasure from the map of the three small towns of Heinsberg, Jülich and Düren, located respectively in an arc from north to east of Aachen, and close to the German lines upon which American ground forces were advancing. A total of 1,188 aircraft was involved, and 1, 5 and 8 Groups provided the heavy bombing and marking force of 485 Lancasters for the last-mentioned. 630 Squadron contributed nineteen Lancasters to the 5 Group effort of 214, loading each with eleven 1,000 and four 500-pounders before sending them on their way from East Kirkby between 12.24 and 12.59 with F/Ls Lewis and Nunns the senior pilots on duty. They climbed through the ten-tenths cloud which would accompany them most of the way to the target, before it thinned to three-tenths stratus above 6,000 feet as they approached the aiming-point in the final wave of the attack. Some heard the Master Bomber calling for them to descend to 1,000 feet, but most failed to pick up the signal in conditions of poor reception, and it is believed that all from East Kirkby carried out their attacks from around 10,000 to 13,000 feet between 15.31 and 15.42. They observed smoke rising through 9,000 feet as they turned for home confident in the success of the operation and waited for the bombing photos to be posted. Sadly, they were largely unplottable because of the smoke covering the area, but post-raid reconnaissance revealed that the town had been all-but erased from the map, and local reports gave a death toll in excess of three thousand inhabitants at a cost to 5 Group of four Lancasters. Many crews witnessed a Lancaster falling in flames at around 15.33 after its starboard wing had been hit by a bomb from a Lancaster with yellow fins. The victim Lancaster had a red letter painted on a black fin, but the squadron code letters could not be made out. In the event, unfavourable ground conditions prevented the American advance from succeeding.

Twenty-one 630 Squadron crews were called to briefing on the 21st, to be told, that the 55 Base squadrons were going back to the Gravenhorst section of the Mittelland Canal on a night of multiple operations involving 1,345 sorties. Three operations, each by 270 aircraft, were to be directed at railway yards at Aschaffenburg, situated about twenty miles south-east of Frankfurt, and oil plants at Castrop-Rauxel and Sterkrade in the Ruhr. 5 Group prepared two forces of 137 and 123 Lancasters respectively, with Mosquito support, for the Mittelland and Dortmund-Ems Canals, while a whole host of minor operations would complete the order of battle. The armourers worked magnificently to load all forty-one East Kirkby Lancasters, those of 630 Squadron with a dozen 1,000-pounders each, while the 57 Squadron aircraft received either the same or six American 1,900-pounders. They departed East Kirkby between 17.09 and 17.40 with S/L Eyre leading the 630 Squadron contingent and encountered a layer of six to ten-tenths cloud in the target area at between 4,000 and 8,000 feet. While this did not inhibit the accuracy of the marking, the instructions of the Master Bomber caused some confusion, a situation exacerbated by a week VHF signal. At first, he ordered the crews to come below the cloud base, to which some responded, before he changed his mind and told them to return to the briefed bombing height. He then issued instructions to aim for the more southerly of two red TIs, and most complied to deliver what appeared to be a good concentration of bombs. Post-raid reconnaissance revealed that the canal had been breached over a distance of fifty feet on the western bank, south of the road bridge, and had left a thirty-mile stretch drained with vessels stranded and damaged by direct hits. The attack on the Dortmund-Ems Canal was better organized and reconnaissance revealed the left-hand channel, which was the only one repaired since the last attack, to have been breached again where it crossed the River Glane. This had been unable to cope with the volume of water released and extensive flooding occurred on both sides of the canal. In contrast to the criticism of the master Bomber at Gravenhorst, the verdict by main force crews on the performance of the Master Bomber at Ladbergen was unanimously favourable.

The Germans recognised that repairing the canals was an open invitation to Bomber Command to return, and so vital were they to the transportation system, that they could not be abandoned. The answer was to complete repairs, but to leave the sections drained and apparently still under repair until sufficient traffic had built up to push through in one night. They would then be flooded and re-emptied to dupe RAF reconnaissance flights and maintain the deception.

On the following night, 5 Group assembled a force of 171 Lancasters and seven Mosquitos for an attack on the U-Boot pens at Trondheim in Norway, one of the few remaining havens for the craft since the capture of the French ports. It was a distant target, located 240 miles north of Oslo and a straight-line distance from East Kirkby of some eight hundred miles. 630 Squadron launched a dozen Lancasters into the air between 15.38 and 16.25 with F/L Lewis the senior pilot on duty and lost the services of F/O Barnes and crew to an undisclosed cause when well into the North Sea crossing. Those arriving in the target area after a five-and-a-half-hour outward flight through a major weather front found clear skies and excellent visibility. However, an effective smoke screen had been activated by the defenders on being alerted to the bombers' approach, and this prevented the marker force from finding the aiming-point. The Master Bomber was left with no option but to send the force home, the 630 Squadron participants landing between 02.23 and 03.36 after more than ten hours aloft. LL949 failed to return with the others and news soon came through that it had crashed onto a sandbank on the northern shore of the River Humber near Sunk Island. F/O Flood RNZAF and five of his mixed RNZAF/RAF crew died at the scene, and the flight engineer succumbed to his injuries a week later. This was the squadron's first operational casualty since Darmstadt in September.

The weather was mainly responsible for curtailing operations over the next few days until the 26$^{th}$, when briefings took place on 5 Group stations at 20.00, the twenty attending 630 Squadron crews and seventeen from 57 Squadron learning that Munich was to be their target for an all-5 Group maximum effort involving 270 Lancasters and eight Mosquitos. After the take-off time had been pushed back, they departed East Kirkby together between 23.00 and 23.52 with F/L Lewis the senior pilot on duty among the 630 Squadron element and each Lancaster carrying a 1,000 pounder and thirteen 500lb J-Type cluster bombs. Forming up and climbing to operational altitude was a time-consuming business, and it would be five hours before the target was reached, the force having been depleted by isolated aircraft turning back, including those of F/Os Langley and Billing because of W/T and starboard-inner engine failure. Some crews struggled with icing conditions and tried in vain to find clear lanes in the cloud, before abandoning their sorties because of sluggish controls. The others found the target area under clear skies with good visibility and confirmed their positions by means of H2S. Aside from one errant red TI, the low-level Mosquito marking was accurate, and the

Master Bomber ensured that the crews focused upon the reds and greens on and close to the planned aiming-point, calling on some to carry out a twenty-two second overshoot. The bombing took place from around 18,000 to 20,000 feet either side of 05.00 and a very large explosion was witnessed near the marshalling yards at 05.07. All from East Kirkby returned safely to praise the quality of the route, the target marking and the performance of the Master Bomber and reported smoke rising through 18,000 feet as they turned away and the glow of fires visible on the horizon for a hundred miles into the return flight. The confidence in a concentrated and effective attack was justified, when post-raid reconnaissance confirmed it as such, and a local report singled out railway installations as being particularly hard-hit.

During the course of the month, the squadron carried out ten operations and dispatched 154 sorties for the loss of a single Lancaster and crew.

## December 1944

There were no operations for 5 Group for the first three nights of the new month, largely because of the weather, and in the meantime, 1, 4, 6 and 8 Groups pounded the Ruhr town of Hagen on the 2/3rd. Worthwhile targets were becoming more and more scarce at a time when the Command was at its most powerful, and this final period of the war would bring the most devastating attacks to date on the German homeland. When East Kirkby returned to action in the early evening of the 4th, it was to launch twenty Lancasters from each squadron as part of a 5 Group force of 282 Lancasters and ten Mosquitos. Their target was the town of Heilbronn, situated thirty miles due north of Stuttgart, which had the river Neckar and a north-south rail link running through it, but was otherwise of no obvious strategic importance, and would not have been expecting an attack. The main operation on this night was actually by 535 aircraft of 1, 6 and 8 Groups at Karlsruhe, some fifty-six miles west-south-west of Heilbronn, and the concentration of aircraft in this area would be certain to bring out the night-fighters.

The 630 Squadron element departed East Kirkby between 16.04 and 16.52 with W/C Grindon the senior pilot on duty and each bomb bay containing a cookie and fourteen 500lb cluster bombs. The bomber stream made its way across France in good conditions to find three to five-tenths thin stratus over the target at around 12,000 feet and watched the illuminator flares falling ahead of them to light the way for the low-level Mosquitos seeking out the marshalling yards and city centre aiming points. They dropped red TIs for the heavy brigade visual marker crews to back up with yellows at the marshalling yards, but the main force element was unable to distinguish them in the burgeoning fires and turned their attention instead upon the town. The East Kirkby crews attacked from 7,300 to 15,000 feet between 19.30 and 19.43, adding to the general destruction, and as the force retreated westwards into electrical storms, 82% of the city's built-up area was in the process of being destroyed by what probably amounted to a firestorm. Returning crews had to battle through icing conditions on the way home, and twelve aircraft were absent from their stations when all of the returnees had been accounted for. The empty dispersal pan at East Kirkby belonged to a 57 Squadron aircraft. The post-war British Bombing Survey estimated 351 acres of destruction in Heilbronn, and a death toll of at least seven thousand people.

The town of Giessen and its marshalling yards were 5 Group's objectives on a night of heavy Bomber Command activity on the 6/7th, while other operations centred on the oil refinery at Leuna (Merseburg), the target for 475 Lancasters of 1, 3 and 8 Groups, and 450 aircraft from predominantly 4 and 6 Groups attacked railway installations at Osnabrück, north of the Ruhr. 630 Squadron briefed sixteen crews as part of an overall 5 Group heavy force of 255 Lancasters, and they set off from East Kirkby between 16.46 and 17.03 with S/L Eyre the senior pilot on duty, and each bomb bay containing a cookie and fourteen 500lb cluster bombs. Their destination lay some eighty-five miles south-east of Cologne in west-central Germany, and thirty-five miles north of Frankfurt, and although it may not have been known to the Allies at the time, it was home to a sub-camp of the infamous Buchenwald concentration camp. The main force crews had been assigned to two aiming-points, two-thirds of them to the town, and the remainder to the marshalling yards, and on arrival in the target area they found predominantly clear skies and good visibility. The flare force began illuminating three minutes early and to the west of the target, but the Mosquito-laid red TIs fell close to the aiming-point and the Master Bomber ensured that they were backed up by greens. The East Kirkby crews bombed from 9,500 to 12,200 feet between 20.14 and 20.35, and all from the 630 Squadron side of the station returned safely to report another successful raid, which would be confirmed by reconnaissance photographs. The gunners in the crew of Lt Lacey, one of a number of South African pilots serving with the squadron, claimed a Ju88 as destroyed. Among eight missing Lancasters were two more belonging to 57 Squadron.

The Urft Dam was one of a number of similar structures in the beautiful Eifel region of western Germany, close to the Belgian frontier, which stood in the way of an American advance into Germany. There was a fear that the enemy might strategically release flood water to hamper it, and it was decided to attempt to breach the dam, to allow time for any excess water to drain away. The first of a number of attacks on the region began on the 3rd at Heimbach, the small town nestling against the northern reaches of the reservoir, but the 1 and 8 Group force failed to identify it, and no bombs fell. On the following day, a small 8 Group effort against the dam was unsuccessful, as was a 3 Group attack on the nearby Schwammenauel Dam on the 5th. The job was handed to 5 Group on the 8th, and a force of 205 Lancasters assembled, which included a contribution from East Kirkby of fourteen from each squadron, all receiving a bomb load of fourteen 1,000-pounders. 617 Squadron was also on the order of battle and its nineteen Lancasters would be carrying Tallboys. The East Kirkby contingent took to the air in wintry conditions between 08.30 and 08.58 with W/C Grindon leading the 630 Squadron element and all reached the target to be greeted by moderate visibility and six to nine-tenths cloud at between 6,000 and 8,000 feet, which partially obscured the aiming-point for some as they ran in to bomb. The instruction at briefing had been to not orbit, and W/C Douglas of 467 Squadron RAAF took the decision to lead his squadron away from the target and head for home, as did W/C Tait, who refused to allow the 617 Squadron element to waste their Tallboys in such unfavourable conditions. The East Kirkby crews carried out their attacks from 9,000 to 10,500 feet between 11.00 and 11.11 and returned home to report bomb bursts around the aiming point and straddling the dam. The single missing Lancaster was 630 Squadron's LM637, which collided with another aircraft over the target and crashed with fatal consequences for F/L Lewis and all but the rear gunner, who got out in time and fell into enemy hands. An analysis of the operation revealed that 129 crews had carried out a scattered attack before the Master Bomber called a halt.

The conditions had prevented any assessment of results, which meant that another attempt on the dam would be necessary, and preparations were put in hand on the 10th to return with a force of 217 Lancasters. The East Kirkby squadrons detailed fourteen Lancasters each, which began to depart East Kirkby between shortly after 04.00 on a cold and frosty morning, only for the entire force to be recalled before it reached the English coast. The operation was rescheduled for early on the following morning, when 233 Lancasters and a Mosquito were to join five 8 Group Mosquitos at the target, but take-off was postponed until midday. The fifteen 630 Squadron participants got away between 12.21 and 12.32 with no senior pilot on duty and joined up with the rest of the force on the flight south to the Channel coast. They encountered icing conditions at the French coast and weather conditions in the target area that were barely an improvement on the previous day, with up to nine-tenths cloud with tops at 8,000 feet. This created challenges for the Master Bomber, who tried to bring the crews down below the 4,000-foot cloud base, some complying, while others remained at the higher altitude and were able to identify the aiming-point through a four-mile-long gap. It is believed that all from East Kirkby carried out an attack from 4,000 to 10,000 feet between 14.45 and 15.15, some after making two or three passes over the aiming point, but a few aircraft from other squadrons had not bombed before the Master Bomber issued the "Dewdrop" instruction to cease bombing and go home. The operation's only casualty was a 57 Squadron Lancaster, which crashed in Germany on the way home. Post-raid reconnaissance revealed a number of hits on the stepped apron of the dam, and cratering all around, but no actual breach had occurred.

A 5 Group contingent of ten Lancasters was sent mining in the Silverthorn III garden in the Kattegat on the 14th, and among them were four from East Kirkby, including the 630 Squadron crews of Lt Adams and W/O Thomas, who took off at 15.27 and 15.31 respectively and reached the drop zone between the east coast of northern Jutland and the north-western tip of Sjaelland Island some three hours later to find ten-tenths cloud at between 2,000 and 8,000 feet. They established their positions by H2S, before planting six vegetables each in the briefed locations from around 15,000 feet and returning safely after round-trips of six-and-a-half hours.

The main operation on the night of the 15/16th was directed at Ludwigshafen in southern Germany, home to a number of I G Farben factories, which were among the most blatant exploiters of slave workers in the production of synthetic oil. The attack by 327 Lancasters and fourteen Mosquitos of 1, 6 and 8 Groups landed 450 high explosive bombs and incendiaries in the Ludwigshafen plant, causing massive damage and fires, and was the greatest setback to production during the war. North of the city centre, the Oppau factory ceased production completely for an extended period, and five other industrial concerns also sustained severe damage, as did some residential areas. It was on the 16th that German ground forces began a surprise new offensive in the Ardennes, in an attempt to break through the American lines and reach the port of Antwerp in what would become known as the Battle of the Bulge. Facing inexperienced American troops, the Germans made major gains during a period of around ten days of complete and low cloud cover, which prevented the Allies from supporting the ground forces from the air.

Munich had become something of a 5 Group preserve during the year, and a further operation against it was planned for the night of the 17/18th, which would turn out to be another night of heavy Bomber Command activity. The main raid was to be by more than five hundred aircraft, predominantly of 4 and 6 Groups, on Duisburg, while 1 Group targeted Ulm with over three hundred Lancasters, leaving 5 Group to send 280 Lancasters some seventy miles beyond to the Bavarian capital city. 630 Squadron briefed seventeen crews, while out on the freezing dispersals their Lancasters were being loaded with a 2,000-pounder each and fourteen 500lb cluster bombs in preparation for the 1,300-mile round-trip. They departed East Kirkby ahead of the 57 Squadron contingent between 16.00 and 16.16 with S/L Eyre the senior pilot on duty. It turned out to be a night of poor serviceability for 55 Base, with six Spilsby crews and two from 57 Squadron among fifteen early returns with a variety of technical issues. The French coast was crossed near Berck-sur-Mer, and the bomber stream had to negotiate severe icing conditions before reaching the target to find generally clear skies and good visibility and bomb on red and green TIs from 12,000 to 15,000 feet between 21.17 and 22.13. The Master Bomber declared himself satisfied with the results and returning crews were confident that they had participated in an effective attack, citing as evidence the glow from the fires to be visible on the horizon from a hundred miles into the return journey. As usual at this target, no local report emerged, but Bomber Command claimed severe and widespread damage to the city.

On the following night it was the turn of the distant Baltic port of Gdynia to play host to 5 Group, for which a force of 236 Lancasters was assembled, thirteen of them belonging to 630 Squadron. The intention was to catch elements of the German fleet at anchor, in particular, the Hipper Class cruiser Lützow, and also to destroy harbour installations, as well as cause damage within the town. *(The original Lützow was actually never completed and had been sold to the Russian navy in 1940 as a hull minus superstructure. The "pocket battleship", Deutschland, was renamed Lützow, to avoid humiliation for the nation should she be lost in battle.)* While this operation was in progress, fourteen other 5 Group Lancasters were to take advantage of the main activity to deliver mines to the Privet and Spinach gardens in Danzig (Gdansk) Bay. 630 Squadron supported this undertaking also, detailing the crews of F/L Miller, F/O Millar and W/O Thomas, and the two elements departed East Kirkby together between 16.52 and 17.18 with F/L Nunns the senior pilot on duty among the bombing brigade and each crew sitting on nine 1,000-pounders. They reached the target area after an outward flight of almost five hours and found clear skies and good visibility in which the harbour and town could be picked out visually despite the activation of a smoke screen. Positions were established by H2S and the vessel spotted in its briefed berth, but not in time for those assigned to it to set up a good bombing run. Bombs were delivered from 11,000 and 16,000 feet shortly before 22.00 and were observed to straddle the vessel and the jetty, setting off a large explosion and an oil fire. The smoke screen eventually obscured the Lützow, and crews with bombs still to deliver turned their attention upon the port area and town, where the illumination and marking proceeded according to plan. The 630 Squadron crews assigned to the town delivered their payloads on red and green TIs from around 11,500 to 14,000 feet in a fifteen-minute slot from 22.00 in accordance with the Master Bomber's instructions and in the face of intense light flak. It was not possible to make an accurate assessment of results, but reconnaissance photos confirmed that damage had been inflicted upon shipping, port installations and residential property in the waterfront districts, at a cost of four Lancasters.

Meanwhile, the gardeners were experiencing some difficulties in identifying the drop zone by H2S, but two from 630 Squadron planted their vegetables into the briefed locations in the Spinach garden from around 15,000 feet, probably after pinpointing on Hel point, while F/O Millar and crew suffered the frustration of H2S failure and had to bring the six Mk IV mines home with nothing to show for a round-trip of more than ten hours.

Thick fog kept the crews on the ground on the 20th, and threatened to do so also on the 21st, but an operation was called on the belief that the weather over Scotland after midnight would be clear for returning aircraft, even if Lincolnshire remained fogbound. Six Lancasters each from 630 and 57 Squadrons were detailed for the 5 Group operation that night, and briefings took place while the ground crews did their best to winch a cookie and twelve 500-pounders into their bomb bays in time. In briefing rooms across southern and south-eastern Lincolnshire, crews learned that their target would require them to retrace their recent steps to Germany's eastern Baltic region, although the I G Farben-owned Wintershall oil refinery at Politz, situated fewer than ten miles north of the port of Stettin, was some two hundred miles short of their trip to Gdynia. *(This location is often wrongly spelled Pölitz, which is a town in Germany's Schleswig-Holstein region at the western end of the Baltic. Politz is now Police in Poland.)* A force of 207 Lancasters and a single Mosquito was assembled, and unusually, it included an element from 617 Squadron carrying Tallboys, a weapon never normally deployed against industrial targets and never at night. The 630 Squadron element departed East Kirkby between 16.55 and 17.01 with F/L Archer the senior pilot on duty, and as the bomber stream became elongated, many crews straightened the route in order to keep up. The target was found to be under clear skies with ground haze, which may have been a smoke screen, and this important war-industry asset was protected by around fifty searchlights and heavy flak batteries, which accompanied the Lancasters as they ran in on the aiming-point. The markers fell some two thousand yards north-north-west of the plant, a situation recognised by the Master Bomber, but he was unable to persuade the backers-up to shift the point of aim accordingly, and most of the bombing would miss the mark. The East Kirkby element bombed on red and green TIs from around 14,500 to 20,000 feet in a fifteen-minute slot from 22.00 and observed most of the bomb bursts to be around the markers. Fires remained visible for almost a hundred miles into the return journey, but the plant had not been destroyed and it would be necessary to mount further raids. Foggy conditions at home caused major difficulties and among five aircraft coming to grief while trying to land was 630 Squadron's NG258, which crashed at Scanfield Farm (untraced) at 02.50, killing F/O Stockhill and five of his crew and injuring the rear gunner. A 617 Squadron Lancaster also crashed causing a number of fatalities and injuries.

The final wartime Christmas period was celebrated on 5 Group stations in traditional style and undisturbed by operational activity between the 22nd and Boxing Day, which was not the case for some other groups. The peace came to an end on the 26th, when crews from all groups were roused from any resulting stupor to attend briefings for operations against enemy troop positions at St Vith in Belgium now that the skies had cleared. The German advance towards Antwerp had run out of steam after its earlier successes, and starved of fuel and ammunition, it was now attempting to withdraw back into Germany. 5 Group contributed twenty-six Lancasters to the force of 296 aircraft for the first joint operation since October, the crews of F/Os Roberts and Monk representing 630 Squadron and departing East Kirkby at 13.15 and

13.24 respectively with fourteen 1,000-pounders beneath their feet. After the sea crossing, they made landfall between Ostend and Dunkerque and found the target, situated within five miles of the German frontier, to be under clear skies with good visibility, and were able to identify the aiming-point visually and by a red TI. They bombed from around 14,000 feet at 15.00, before the aiming point became obscured by smoke, at which point the Master Bomber ordered the crews to descend to 10,000 feet and bomb the upwind edge of the smoke. The East Kirkby crews were diverted to St Eval in Cornwall, where they may have been among a number of crews reporting a four-engine bomber going down but not crashing, from which five parachutes emerged.

On the 28th, the 630 Squadron crews of F/L Archer, F/O Baker and W/O Cowan were told to join three others from 57 Squadron to fly over to Strubby, from where they would take off as part of a 5 Group force of sixty-seven Lancasters targeting shipping, specifically the light cruiser Köln, at Horten in Oslo Fjord. The Köln was one of three vessels in the Königsberg Class and was built in Wilhelmshaven between 1926 and 1928 before being commissioned into the Kriegsmarine in 1930. She participated in Operation Weserübung, the invasion of Denmark and Norway in April and May 1940, during which her sister ships were lost. The 55 Base element departed Strubby between 19.38 and 20.17 with thirteen 1,000-pounders in each bomb bay and reached the target area after an outward flight of four-and-a-half hours to find the skies relatively clear and the visibility good. However, a thin layer of alto-cumulus cloud at between 15,000 and 20,000 feet reduced the brightness of the moonlight and cast deceptive shadows on the water to prevent a clear identification of the target. The aiming-point was marked by Wanganui flares, but most crews followed the Master Bomber's instructions after establishing their own reference point. A patch of light flak to the north-east of the harbour mole was thought to be concealing a large naval unit, and this area was marked and bombed, while other crews would claim to have attacked a large vessel moving from this area in a southerly direction, and other shipping in the harbour, all in the face of intense shipboard and shore-based light flak. The East Kirkby crews bombed from 8,000 feet between 23.44 and midnight but claimed no direct hits and the operation produced inconclusive results.

The 29th dawned fine and frosty, and shortly after lunch, 5 Group sent eleven crews on daylight mining sorties in the Onion garden in Oslo harbour. The 630 Squadron crews of F/O Millar and F/L Nunns departed East Kirkby respectively at 15.57 and 15.58 and established their positions on the target area by H2S confirmed by a visual identification of landmarks. They returned safely after sorties of six-and-three-quarter-hours' duration having planted their vegetable according to brief.

The East Kirkby squadrons conducted their final operations of the year at either ends of New Year's Eve, beginning with the departure from East Kirkby of twenty-two Lancasters, a dozen representing 630 Squadron, as part of a 5 Group force of 154 assigned to attack an enemy supply line at Houffalize in the Ardennes region of Belgium. They became airborne between 02.12 and 02.47 with no senior pilots on duty among the 630 Squadron contingent and each crew sitting on twelve 1,000 and six 500-pounders. They found the target area to be under five to seven-tenths stratus cloud at 5,000 to 6,000 feet, with another layer of eight-tenths with tops at 9,000 feet, which rendered identification something of a challenge. The marking was punctual and accurate, but the red TIs cascading on the ground were observed only by a proportion of the crews who chanced upon a gap in the clouds directly over the aiming-point. While some withheld their bombs, those from East Kirkby mostly delivered theirs from around 9,000 to 12,000 feet between 05.00 and 05.15. A number of crews, including one from 630 squadron, descended to below the cloud base and bombed in clear visibility from 5,000 feet, confirming that the bombing was concentrated around the markers, in spite of which it would be deemed necessary to revisit this objective within a short time.

It was dusk when the crews of W/O Thomas and F/O Millar took off from East Kirkby in the wake of a 57 Squadron duo at 16.20 and 16.21 to head for the Yewtree garden, the channel in the Baltic between Læsø Island and the east coast of North Jutland. They established their positions by H2S and carried out timed runs at around 15,000 feet to deposit their mines into the allotted locations, before the year ended on a sour note with the failure to return of the Thomas crew in PB894, which disappeared without trace.

During the course of the month the squadron conducted fourteen operations and dispatched 127 sorties for the loss of two Lancasters and their crews. The New Year beckoned with the scent of victory in the air, but any thoughts that the enemy defences were spent were misplaced, and even though they were unable to protect every corner of the Reich, they would continue to provide stubborn opposition for a further three months. 630 Squadron could look back on a relatively good year once the winter campaign was over, and the loss of fifty-seven aircraft during the past twelve months was roughly the norm for a 5 Group squadron of the line in 1944.

## January 1945

The final year of the war began with a flourish, as the Luftwaffe launched its ill-conceived and, ultimately, ill-fated Operation Bodenplatte (Baseplate) at first light on New Year's Day. The intention to destroy the Allied air forces on the ground at the recently liberated airfields in France, Holland and Belgium was only modestly realized, as the entire day fighter strength was committed to low level bombing and strafing attacks into the teeth of the airfield flak defences, and those which survived then had to run the gauntlet of Allied fighters to make their escape. It cost the German day fighter force around 250 aircraft and 150 pilots killed, wounded or taken prisoner, and it was a setback from which the Tagjagd would never fully recover, while the Allies could make good their losses within hours from their enormous stockpiles.

5 Group was also active that morning, having roused the crews early from their beds to attend briefings for an attack on the recently repaired Dortmund-Ems Canal near Ladbergen, for which 102 Lancasters and two Mosquitos were made ready. The 630 Squadron element of ten departed East Kirkby with their 57 Squadron counterparts between 07.47 and 08.05 led by F/L Archer as the senior pilot on duty and each crew sitting on fourteen 1,000-pounders with half-hour delay fuses. After climbing out over their respective stations, the 54 Base squadrons from Coningsby and Metheringham fell in line behind 83 Squadron, with the 55 Base squadrons from East Kirkby, Spilsby and Strubby about three miles further back, and a third section, made up of 53 Base units from Waddington, Skellingthorpe and Bardney some twenty miles to the rear. The last-mentioned were allowed to catch up, putting the force two

minutes behind schedule at point C over the North Sea, and it was between points C and D that the fighter escort was expected to join them. Although it was not immediately apparent, the escort did eventually put in an appearance to shepherd the gaggles, which held together fairly well, although the controller would complain later that the legs were too short to keep them tight and some aircraft were seen to break formation. When about eight minutes from the target, smoke from a Mosquito-laid red TI could be seen, which was assessed as being on the southern tip of the island between the two branches of the canal. It was clearly visible to all crews, who were able to home in on it without difficulty. A six-gun flak battery greeted their arrival with accurate salvoes, but this did not inhibit the bombing runs, which were carried out by the East Kirkby crews from 9,000 to 11,000 feet between 11.15 and 11.25. The impression was of an effective operation, but at debriefings on 55 Base stations, some crews complained that the gaggle was too tight and put them at risk from "friendly" bombs. The use of delay fuses prevented an immediate assessment of the results, but photo-reconnaissance revealed later that the canal had been breached again and the surrounding fields had become flooded.

Operations for the day were not yet done for 5 Group, which now had an appointment with the Mittelland Canal at Gravenhorst, situated some twelve miles to the north of Ladbergen, for which 152 Lancasters and five Mosquitos were made ready. 630 Squadron loaded six Lancasters with fourteen 1,000-pounders each and dispatched them from East Kirkby between 17.03 and 17.26 with F/L Nunns the senior pilot on duty. They crossed the Dutch coast at 18.38 with a time-on-target of 19.15, and in a bombing band of 9,000 to 14,000 feet, their briefed height was 9,600 feet. All reached the target area to find that the clear conditions enjoyed during the morning raid had persisted, and so accurate were the initial TIs and illumination, delivered visually or by H2S, that the third flare force was not required and was sent home. The main force was called in ahead of H-Hour at around 19.10, and the 630 Squadron element bombed according to their brief on red TIs. One of the perils of operating on New Year's Day was the risk of falling victim to trigger-happy American flak gunners, who had been spooked by the German raids at dawn and now fired at anything that moved. Such "friendly fire" incidents would cost a number of 3 Group crews their lives. Large parts of eastern England were found to be fogbound on return and the East Kirkby contingent faced the long slog to spend the rest of the night at Kinloss, before straggling back home during the course of the 2nd. The employment of predominantly delayed-action bombs again prevented an immediate assessment of results, but a highly successful operation was confirmed later by photo-reconnaissance.

The old enemy of Nuremberg was posted on the 2nd as the first major urban target of the New Year and would face a main force of 445 Lancasters drawn from 1, 3 and 6 Groups with a further sixty-nine Lancasters representing 8 Group to provide the marking and bombing support. 8 Group also contributed twenty-two Lancasters to a simultaneous attack by 351 Halifaxes of 4 and 6 Groups on two I G Farben chemicals plants, one in Ludwigshafen and the other close by in Oppau. Now that mobile Oboe stations had been set up on the Continent, both operations would also benefit from a Mosquito presence, seven for Nuremberg and twenty-two for Ludwigshafen. The two forces were to follow a similar route until dividing shortly before reaching Ludwigshafen, where the Nuremberg force would continue on towards the east for a further 140 miles. The success of the Ludwigshafen operation was confirmed by local reports that five hundred high-explosive bombs had fallen within the confines of the two production plants, along with many thousands of incendiaries. This had put an end to all production of synthetic oil, and adjacent industrial buildings, residential property and railway installations had also been destroyed. Nuremberg was left devastated by the loss of 4,640 houses, a large proportion of them apartment blocks, and more than four hundred industrial units were destroyed, and eighteen hundred people killed.

5 Group had remained on the ground during the above and many of its crews were called to briefing on the evening of the 4$^{th}$ to learn of a controversial attack planned against the small French town of Royan in the early hours of the 5$^{th}$. The raid was in response to requests from Free French forces, which were laying siege to the town because of its location on the eastern bank at the mouth of the Gironde Estuary and in the way of an advance towards the port of Bordeaux. The proposal to attack the town, which was occupied by a German garrison, was put to SHAEF by an American officer, and it was incorrectly suggested that the only French civilians remaining in the town were collaborators. The garrison commander had offered the inhabitants an opportunity to evacuate the area but based on their belief that the town would not be attacked, around two thousand had declined and would suffer the consequences. SHAEF handed the job to Bomber Command, which planned a two-phase attack, the first to be carried out by 221 Lancasters and seven Mosquitos of 5 Group employing the standard low-level technique, and the second by 126 Lancasters of 1 and 8 Groups an hour later. 630 Squadron loaded each of its eighteen Lancasters with a cookie and sixteen 500-pounders and sent them on their way from East Kirkby between 00.42 and 01.32 with no senior pilots on duty but four belonging to the SAAF. It was approaching 04.00 as they lined up for the bombing run in cloudless skies and excellent visibility, but the start of the attack was delayed for two minutes to allow misplaced markers to be corrected. A red TI went down at 04.01 very close to the aiming point, and another fell in the middle of the town near the beach, at which point the Master Bomber called in the main force. The East Kirkby crews carried out their attacks from around 8,000 to 10,500 feet on Path Finder markers between 04.01 and 04.15 and witnessed a yellow oil fire at 04.08, which began to emit volumes of black smoke. This was just one of a number of large explosions created by the first phase of bombing, and the resultant fires would act as a beacon to the 1 Group force following behind. A total of 1,576 tons of bombs destroyed an estimated 85% of the town and cost up to eight hundred civilian lives. In the event, the town was not taken, and it would be mid-April before the garrison surrendered. Recriminations abounded, thereafter, the American officer involved in the discussions with the Free French forces was removed from his post and General Degaulle identified the Americans as responsible, exonerating Bomber Command from all blame.

A major attack was carried out by more than 650 aircraft of 1, 4, 6 and 8 Groups on Hannover on the night of the 5/6$^{th}$, the first large-scale raid on this northern city since the series in the autumn of 1943. Massive damage was inflicted, but twenty-three Halifaxes and eight Lancasters failed to return in a sharp reminder that the Luftwaffe was not entirely spent. 5 Group had not been intended to operate on this night, but a rushed battle order came through to 5 Group stations at 18.30, which would lead to another late briefing and take-off for 131 crews. Nine 630 Squadron Lancasters each received a bomb load of eleven 1,000-pounders before departing East Kirkby between 00.06 and 00.54 bound for a German supply column trapped at Houffalize in the Belgian Ardennes. The recently arrived new A Flight commander,

S/L Cuelanaere DFC, was the senior pilot on duty as they made their way south on a clear night above low cloud, which, over the target, formed thin layers of eight to ten-tenths cover at between 4,000 and 10,000 feet. The marker force crews were able to identify the aiming-point visually, and the first red Mosquito-laid TIs were seen to go down close together, followed by greens at H-3. They were backed up to leave a compact group of reds and greens visible by their glow through the clouds, at which point, the Master Bomber, who was circling at 10,000 feet, called in the main force to bomb. The East Kirkby crews complied from 5,250 to 11,000 feet between 03.00 and 03.10, while around a third of the force retained their bombs in accordance with instructions at briefing, if they failed to identify the aiming-point. Afterwards, one of the marker crews descended to 3,500 feet between the cloud layers, where they saw two large columns of smoke, the source of which could not be identified. Post-raid reconnaissance confirmed that the target had been bombed with great accuracy, and the success had been gained for the loss of two Lancasters.

5 Group would not be involved in the main event on the 6th, an operation by 482 aircraft of 1, 4, 6 and 8 Groups against railway installations in the town of Hanau, and instead detailed thirteen Lancasters for mining duties in the Spinach garden off the port of Gdynia and seven for the Privet garden off Danzig. The 630 Squadron crews of F/O Waterfall, Lt Turner and F/L Nunns departed East Kirkby in that order at 01.39, 01.43 and 02.15, each sitting on six Mk IV mines, and reached the target area to find a layer of seven to ten-tenths cloud with tops at 3,000 to 5,000 feet and good visibility above. They established their positions by H2S before planting their vegetables into the briefed locations from around 15,000 feet and returned safely after more than nine hours aloft to report a successful night's work.

A major operation against Munich was planned for the 7th, for which a two-wave force of 645 aircraft was drawn from all five of the Lancaster-equipped groups. 5 Group, which was unused to sharing this target, would lead the way with 213 Lancasters and three Mosquitos, leaving the second wave to follow on two hours later, the tanks of the heavy brigade containing sufficient fuel for a nine-hour round-trip. The 630 Squadron element of fourteen Lancasters departed East Kirkby as dusk was descending between 16.39 and 17.15 with W/C Grindon and S/L Eyre the senior pilots on duty, and a bomb load in each of a cookie and ten 500lb Type-14 cluster bombs. As PD317 climbed away its port-inner engine failed, forcing F/O Billings to head directly for the jettison area to dump the bombs, before returning to East Kirkby to land at 17.59. On touchdown the Lancaster bounced, and the pilot opened the throttles for a "go-around", only for the port wing to drop, dig in and send the aircraft cartwheeling across the airfield. The navigator and mid-upper gunner were killed, and the rest of the crew injured, F/O Billings ultimately losing an arm, while the other survivors made a full recovery. The rest of the force, meanwhile, had encountered broken medium-level cloud at 14,000 feet above the target, with haze or thin cloud below, by which time the Master Bomber had made a visual identification of the aiming-point. He sent the first two primary blind markers in to deliver their TIs at the same time thirty seconds ahead of the planned opening of the attack and the flare force immediately afterwards to illuminate the city very effectively and allow ground detail to be identified. Red TIs went down west and east of the river Isar, bracketing the aiming-point, and the Master Bomber ordered the backers up to drop their TIs between the reds, after which, the next batch of flares formed a circle around the aiming-point. The main force was then called in, and the East Kirkby participants delivered their loads accurately within the specified area from 15,000 to 20,000 feet from around 20.30. The city was seen to be burning well as the force withdrew, and the glow of fires was still visible on the horizon from up to 130 miles away. Two hours after the 5 Group attack, in what would become an established pattern, the 1, 3, 6 and 8 Group force arrived to complete the destruction of the central and some industrial districts, and this proved to be the final large-scale attack of the war on Munich. Fourteen Lancasters failed to return, but there were no further casualties from East Kirkby.

With the exception of 617 Squadron, 5 Group remained on the ground for the ensuing six days, with snow-clearing providing exercise for all capable of wielding a shovel. The crews were, therefore, no doubt relieved to be called to briefings on the 13th to learn that 5 Group would be operating alone against the Wintershall oil refinery at Politz near Stettin. The plant had sustained damage in the previous attack in December, but production had not been halted, and a force of 218 Lancasters and seven Mosquitos was assembled for the return, of which fifteen of the Lancasters were provided by 630 Squadron. Under cover of the main event, ten Lancasters, including three each from 630 and 57 Squadrons, were to mine the approaches to the area in the Geranium garden off the port of Swinemünde. All of the 630 Squadron Lancasters had a cookie winched into their bomb bays, ten supplemented with nine 500-pounders and five with twelve, before another dusk departure saw them and their twelve 57 Squadron counterparts depart East Kirkby between 16.04 and 16.32 with S/Ls Cuelanaere and Eyre the senior 630 Squadron pilots on duty. F/O Waterfall and crew had been the first of the gardening gang to take off at 16.11, and the crews of F/O Stemp and F/O Millar followed at 16.37 and 16.43 respectively, each carrying six Mk IV mines.

The bomber stream crossed the North Sea at 1,500 feet in accordance with instructions to not climb until approaching the Danish coast at 19.30, and they arrived in the target area on time to find clear skies with slight haze, by which time the blind marker crews had identified the target by means of H2S and delivered their green TIs shortly after 22.00. The illuminators then dropped their flares, which caused ground detail to stand out, highlighted by the snow on the ground. A blind-bombing attack had been planned, but aided by the excellence of the conditions, Mosquitos were able to go in at low level to be followed soon afterwards by the main force. The plant was protected by fifty to eighty searchlights which were not troublesome and were employed largely in co-operation with night-fighters. The East Kirkby crews bombed from 14,000 to 18,250 feet between 22.14 and 22.30 and a particularly large explosion at 22.17 sent a pall of black smoke into the air. Photographic reconnaissance confirmed that the plant had been severely damaged, while Bomber Command claimed it to be in ruins. Meanwhile, the gardeners had fulfilled their briefs and returned safely to complete a very satisfactory night's work. F/O Langley and crew failed to return with the rest of the squadron, but news soon reached East Kirkby via the usual channels that explained their absence. F/O Langley had been contending with a starboard-outer engine issue for some time, and while traversing the Baltic over the Danish Islands it burst into flames and defied all attempts to quell them. He steered PB880 into Swedish air space, where, from around 8,000 feet in the vicinity of Bastad, it was abandoned to its fate, sadly, the mid-upper gunner striking the tailplane as he left the aircraft and succumbing to his injuries on the following day. The others enjoyed the legendary hospitality of the Swedes under internment, before returning to the UK.

Oil targets would continue to dominate during the remainder of the month as the Allies sought to strangle the enemy's access to vital fuels. The German synthetic oil industry relied on two main production methods, the Bergius process, which involved the hydrogenation of highly volatile bituminous coal to manufacture high-grade petroleum products like aviation fuel, and the Fischer-Tropsch process, which produced lower-grade diesel-type fuels for vehicle, tank, U-Boot and shipping requirements. A two-phase attack was planned on the 14th for the I G Farbenindustrie A G Merseburg-Leuna refinery, which lay some 250 miles from the Dutch frontier and five hundred miles from the bomber bases of eastern England. This was one of many similar sites situated in an arc on the western side of Leipzig from north to south, was the second largest synthetic oil plant in Germany and was the one at which the Bergius process had been developed. At briefings at 13.30 crews learned that the first phase would be carried out by 210 Lancasters and nine Mosquitos of 5 Group and the second, three hours later, by 363 Lancasters and five Mosquitos of 1, 6 and 8 Groups. The thirteen 630 Squadron Lancasters each received a bomb load of a cookie and twelve 500-pounders, one of the latter with a twelve-hour delay fuse, before departing East Kirkby between 16.01 and 16.36 with no senior pilot on duty.

The squadrons formed into a bomber stream as they headed for the Sussex coast near Brighton to begin the Channel crossing for the southern approach to eastern Germany, and they reached the target area to find clear skies but poor vertical visibility due to a layer of haze. In the event, this proved to be no hindrance to the primary blind markers, whose job was to establish their position over the aiming-point by means of H2S and deliver their TIs from 18,000 feet as a guide to the flare force. The Master Bomber called for ground marking only, which was carried out by the low-level Mosquito element, and by 20.50 he was satisfied and sent the marker aircraft home. The main force crews produced what appeared to be concentrated bombing, those from East Kirkby aiming at the red and green TIs from 13,000 to 17,000 feet in a fifteen-minute slot from 21.00 with a fourteen-second overshoot in accordance with the Master Bomber's instructions. Returning crews reported explosions and smoke rising upwards as they turned for home, leaving behind them a beacon for the second wave force to exploit and complete the massive destruction that effectively put the plant out of action for the remainder of the war.

Three oil plants were selected for attention on the night of the 16/17th, at Zeitz, near Liepzig, Wanne-Eickel in the Ruhr, and Brüx in north-western Czechoslovakia (now Most in the Czech Republic), some 140 miles due south of Berlin. It was for the last-mentioned that fifteen 630 Squadron crews were briefed as part of a 5 Group force of 224 Lancasters and six Mosquitos, which would be accompanied by seven 101 Squadron ABC Lancasters for RCM duties. They were each loaded with a cookie and nine 500-pounders for what would be a nine-hour round-trip and departed East Kirkby between 17.45 and 18.19 with S/L Cuelanaere the senior pilot on duty. There were ten early returns from the force, leaving the rest to reach the target area and encounter nine to ten-tenths low cloud with tops at 3,000 feet, which interfered with the low-level marking system. The four primary blind markers identified the target by means of H2S, and dropped green TIs, and they were followed by the first illuminators, who also relied on H2S to deliver their flares. It seems that a number of Mosquitos managed to get below the cloud base to put red TIs onto the aiming-point and reported that the greens were among the oil tanks. However, the reds were not generally visible through the clouds, and the Master Bomber called for skymarking, while informing flare force 3 that it would not be required. The East Kirkby participants bombed either on the glow of the red TIs or on the cascading greens from 12,000 to 18,000 feet between 22.30 and 22.45, and observed many explosions and large columns of thick, black smoke emerging through the cloud tops. Photo-reconnaissance would confirm that massive damage had been inflicted upon the plant, and a severe setback delivered to the enemy's oil production.

Adverse weather conditions ensured that there were no further operations for 5 Group during the month, although a number would be posted before being cancelled. The squadron spent the period inducting new crews, attending lectures, training, and, during the last few days, clearing snow from the runways. During the course of the month, the squadron took part in ten operations and dispatched 111 sorties for the loss of two Lancasters, two crew members, and one crew in temporary internment.

## February 1945

The weather at the start of February provided difficult conditions for marking and bombing, particularly for 5 Group, and a number of operations would struggle to achieve their aims in the face of thick, low cloud and strong winds. 5 Group was back in harness immediately at the start of the new month following the long lay-off, and 271 Lancaster and eleven Mosquito crews were called to briefings on all 5 Group stations on the 1st to learn that their target was to be the marshalling yards in the town of Siegen, situated some fifty miles east of Cologne. This was a 5 Group show, and was one of three major operations planned for the night, the others, by larger forces, taking place at Ludwigshafen and Mainz further into southern Germany. A high wind during the night had helped to clear some of the snow, and the nineteen 630 Squadron Lancasters took off without incident between 15.48 and 16.07 with newly promoted F/Ls Ovens, Stemp Thompson and Waterfall the senior pilots on duty. They were carrying a cookie and fourteen deep SBCs of 4lb incendiaries (2,100) each as they climbed to 4,000 feet over the station, before setting course to the first turning point and climbing to 8,000 feet. They maintained that height until reaching 6° East, at which point they climbed again to a bombing height of 11,600 feet and dispensed "window" from 7° East, continuing that activity until arriving at 5° East on the way home. Conversations overheard between the Master Bomber and Deputy suggested that the flare and marker forces were experiencing difficulty in obtaining a clear H2S image on their screens, but eventually, one of the primary blind markers ran in and dropped green TIs at 19.05 from 15,000 feet, and their glow was visible through the clouds. This prompted the first flares, followed by an attempt to mark at low-level with red TIs, which were not visible through the clouds, and when the Master Bomber called for skymarking at 19.10, the remaining illuminators were superfluous to requirements and were sent home. The bombing phase was put back by four minutes until 19.20, forcing crews to either orbit or dogleg to waste time if they were still on approach, and then instructions were issued to aim at the skymarkers, which were being driven by the strong wind across the intended aiming-point and beyond the target. The 630 Squadron crews did not have to orbit or dogleg and went straight in to bomb on the faint glow of red and green TIs at around 19.20. A decoy fire site prepared by the Germans attracted many bomb loads, perhaps some from the East Kirkby participants, who, on return expressed the opinion that they had contributed to a widely scattered raid. Post-raid reconnaissance confirmed that much of the bombing had, indeed, fallen into open and wooded country, and although the railway station sustained damage, the marshalling yards escaped.

The next briefing at East Kirkby took place at 15.00 on the overcast and drizzly afternoon of the 2nd, in suitably dismal conditions to reveal to the assembled thirty-three crews the bad news that a tour of operations was to be increased again to thirty-six sorties. Whether or not that bombshell was delivered before or after the main briefing is not known, but by the time that the 231 participants filed out into the dank twilight to consume their pre-operational bacon and eggs, they knew that their target for that night was the city of Karlsruhe in southern Germany. This was to be another 5 Group effort involving 250 Lancasters and eleven Mosquitos, and was again, one of three major operations taking place. Wiesbaden was to receive its one and only major raid of the war at the hands of almost five hundred aircraft, while a 320-strong predominantly Halifax force dealt with an oil plant at Wanne-Eickel in the Ruhr. The sixteen-strong 630 Squadron element departed East Kirkby between 19.56 and 20.10 with F/Ls Baker, Kirkwood, Nunns and Stemp the senior pilots on duty and a cookie and SBCs of 4lb incendiaries in each bomb bay. They headed for the assembly point over Reading in winds that were lighter than forecast, and this caused a change in route, which now took the force directly from Reading to the target, straddling the Franco-Belgian frontier all the way to Germany, where they encountered heavy cloud at between 3,000 and 15,000 feet. The flare force arrived over the target at 17,500 to 18,500 feet between 23.03 and 23.28 and tried to perform their assigned tasks in difficult conditions, some with malfunctioning H2S boxes. The Mosquito crews attempted to establish an aiming-point, but the illumination provided by the flare force was not getting through to the ground, and even had they dropped red TIs, it is unlikely that they would have been visible. At 23.11 the Master Bomber called for skymarking, sent the Mosquitos and remaining illuminators home and ordered the main force crews to bomb on the southern edge of the glow from the descending green Wanganui flares. The East Kirkby crews complied from 12,000 to 17,000 feet between 23.16 and 23.31, and their pessimistic assessment of what would turn out to be the final raid of the war on this city proved to be correct. It had been a complete failure and cost fourteen Lancasters, four of them from 189 Squadron alone.

In preparation for an advance into Germany by the British XXX Corps in the Reichswald region, the Command was ordered to bomb the frontier towns of Goch and Cleves, situated six miles apart between the Rhine and the Dutch frontier and forming part of the enemy defences. 4, 6 and 8 Groups attacked the former, and 1 and 8 Groups the latter, and both were left heavily damaged. 5 Group took advantage of this activity to take another swipe at the Dortmund-Ems Canal at Ladbergen with a force of 177 Lancasters and eleven Mosquitos, the heavy brigade carrying a dozen 1,000-pounders each with one-hour delayed action fuses. 630 Squadron made ready a dozen Lancasters for the main operation and three others to be occupied by the crews of F/Ls Harris and Nunns and F/O Weston for mining duties in the Forget-me-not garden in Kiel harbour. The latter element departed East Kirkby first between 19.18 and 19.22, leaving the bombing brigade to follow them into the air between 20.38 and 21.03 led by S/L Eyre. The bombers reached the target area to find seven to ten-tenths cloud at between 6,000 and 9,000 feet and an absence of clear instructions from the Master Bomber, which left them uncertain as to which of the widely scattered red TIs should be their focus. They were left with little choice but to select a random red TI or at least its glow and release their payloads from between 9,000 to 12,000 feet in a fifteen-minute slot from midnight, before running the gauntlet of enemy night-fighters on the way home to report an inconclusive and probably ineffective night's work. Some crews were unable to identify the aiming point and brought their bombs home and photographic reconnaissance revealed later that the bombs had fallen into fields and had failed to cause any breach in what was a rare unsuccessful attack on this target,. Meanwhile, the gardeners had established their positions by H2S and delivered their six Mk VI mines into the briefed locations through a layer of thin cloud at 8,000 feet.

Nineteen crews from each squadron attended briefing on the 8th to learn of another long round-trip to the Wintershall oil refinery at Politz as part of a 5 Group force of 227 Lancasters and seven Mosquitos. They were to act as the first wave in a two-phase attack, which would be completed two hours later by 248 Lancasters from 1 and 8 Groups. They departed East Kirkby between 16.34 and 17.25 with F/Ls Baker and Stemp the senior pilots on duty, and all made it across northern Jutland to enter Swedish air space near Helsingborg before turning south on a direct heading for the target. It was not unusual to violate Swedish air space intentionally, and the Swedes would normally respond with inaccurate warning flak, but on this night, it brought down 57 Squadron's PB382, killing all but the pilot, who was interned. The blind marker and flare force crews went in at 13,000 to 14,500 feet between 21.03 and 21.15 to carry out their assigned tasks in the face of an ineffective smoke screen, which covered all ground detail but the tops of the tall chimneys. Fierce night-fighter activity was evident to the main force crews as they reached the target area to find clear skies and excellent visibility and those from East Kirkby identified the aiming point in the light of the illuminating flares before delivering their loads onto red TIs in accordance with the Master Bomber's instructions. A series of up to six violent explosions was witnessed including two of particular note at 21.18 and 21.23 and smoke was rising through 3,000 feet as they turned away to the west, confident in the quality of their work. 1 and 8 Groups completed the destruction of the plant, and no more synthetic oil would be produced before war's end. Of the eleven missing Lancasters, ten were from the 5 Group first wave, and they included 630 Squadron's ND554, which was lost without trace with the crew of F/O Knight RNZAF.

Briefings took place on the 13th for the first round of Operation Thunderclap, the Churchill-inspired offensive against Germany's eastern cities, which was devised partly to act in support of the advancing Russians, and also as a demonstration to Stalin of RAF air power, should he turn against the Allies after the war. The historic and culturally significant city of Dresden was selected to open the offensive in another two-phase affair, with a 5 Group force of 246 Lancasters and nine Mosquitos leading the way, to be followed three hours later by 529 Lancasters of 1, 3, 6 and 8 Groups. It had proved to be a successful policy thus far, with the 5 Group low-level marking system and main force attacks leaving a burning beacon for the second force, and should it be required on this night, 8 Group would provide any necessary marking for phase two from high level. The 630 Squadron contingent of seventeen Lancasters each received a bomb load of a cookie and up to fourteen 500lb cluster bombs before departing East Kirkby in advance of most of their 57 Squadron counterparts between 17.40 and 17.53 with S/L Cuelanaere the senior pilot on duty. To the crews, this was a standard operation, and they had absolutely no concept of its ramifications, both in terms of its outcome on the ground and the hysteria of its aftermath. Dresden was Germany's seventh largest city, and its largest remaining largely un-bombed built-up area, which, according to American sources, contained more than a hundred factories and fifty thousand workers contributing to the war effort. It was also an important railway hub, to the extent that the marshalling yards had been attacked twice in late 1944 by the USAAF.

The heavy force was two hours out when W/C Maurice Smith of 54 Base, the Master Bomber for the 5 Group attack, lifted off the Woodhall Spa runway at a few minutes before 20.00 hours in Mosquito KB401 AZ-E, a 627 Squadron aircraft, and he was followed away by eight others from 627 Squadron. The heavy brigade and the Mosquitos arrived in the target area at the same time to encounter three layers of cloud, between 3,000 and 5,000 feet, 6,000 to 8,000 feet and 15,000 to 16,000 feet, but otherwise good visibility. The first primary blind marker Lancaster delivered green TIs from 15,000 feet at 22.03, and was followed in by the flare force, which lit the way for the low-level Mosquitos. The main force Lancasters were carrying eight hundred tons of bombs, and these were delivered from around 13,000 to 15,000 feet onto the glow of red TIs in accordance with the Master Bomber's instructions. As far as the crews were concerned this was no different from any other attack, and the fires visible for more than a hundred and fifty miles into the return journey nothing out of the ordinary.

By the time the second force of 1, 3, 6 and 8 Group Lancasters arrived over Dresden three hours after 5 Group, the skies had cleared, and the fires created by the earlier attack provided the expected reference point. A further eighteen hundred tons of bombs rained down onto the historic and beautiful old city, setting off the same chain of events that had devastated parts of Hamburg in July 1943 and a number of other cities since. Dresden's population had been swelled by masses of refugees fleeing from the eastern front, and many were engulfed in the ensuing firestorm. On the following morning, three hundred American bombers carried out a separate attack under the umbrella of a fighter escort and completed the destruction. There were claims that RAF aircraft had strafed the streets and open spaces to increase the level of terror, and such accusations abound in the city to this day. In fact, American fighters were responsible and were trying to add to the general confusion and chaos. Initial propaganda-inspired reports from the Office of the Propaganda Minister, Joseph Göbbels, falsely claimed a death toll of 250,000 people, but an accurate figure of twenty-five thousand has been settled upon since.

The destruction of Dresden has been used even by some in this country as a weapon with which to denigrate Bomber Command and Harris, and label them as war criminals. Curiously, no accusations have been levelled at the Americans. It should also be understood that Harris had no interest in attacking Dresden and had to be nagged by Chief-of-the-Air-Staff Portal to fulfil Churchill's wishes. The aircrew simply did the job asked of them, and the Dresden raid was no different from any other attack on a city. The death toll at Hamburg arising out of the "firestorm" raid as part of Operation Gomorrah in July 1943 was much higher at forty thousand, and yet there has been no similar outcry. The legacy of this operation served to deny Harris and the men under his Command their due recognition for the massive part they played in the ultimate victory, and only in recent times has a monument been erected in Green Park in London and a campaign clasp awarded, sadly, far too late for the majority. Churchill, with his eyes set on a peacetime election, betrayed Harris and the Command in a typical politically motivated U-turn, in which he accused Harris of bombing solely for the purpose of inflicting terror. In the post-war honours, Harris was the only commander in the field to be denied recognition.

Round two of Thunderclap was planned for the following night, when Chemnitz was posted as the target for 717 aircraft drawn from 1, 3, 4, 6 and 8 Groups, while 224 Lancasters and eight Mosquitos of 5 Group targeted the Deutsche Erdöl (DEA Group) oil refinery in the small town of Rositz, situated twenty-five miles due south of Leipzig and thirty miles northwest of Chemnitz. Fourteen 630 Squadron Lancasters each had a cookie winched into its bomb bay, a dozen to be supplemented with twelve 500-pounders and two with nine, before departing East Kirkby safely between 16.44 and 16.57 with F/L MacLean the senior pilot on duty. They pushed on across Germany to be greeted by six to ten-tenths thin cloud in the target area in two layers, one at 6,000 to 8,000 feet, and the other at 10,000 to 12,000 feet, but the primary blind marker Lancaster made a good run on H2S at 15,000 feet at 20.48 to drop green TIs, and the illuminators followed up between 20.51 and 20.58 from a similar height. The main force crews arriving on time carried out support runs with the marker element, before being called in to bomb at 21.07, those from East Kirkby carrying out their attacks on red and green TIs or on their glow from 7,000 to 12,000 feet in a fifteen-minute slot from 21.00. Three or four large fires were evident in the oil plant, and black smoke was rising through 5,000 feet as the force turned away. Among four missing Lancasters was 630 Squadron's LL966, which came down somewhere deep inside Germany with no survivors, five of the crew having no known grave. The rear gunner lies in the 1939-1945 Berlin War Cemetery, while his pilot, Lt Lacey SAAF, is buried in Belgium, his remains having presumably been transferred there after the war. Post-raid reconnaissance established afterwards that the southern part of the refinery site had been damaged, but it would be necessary to return to finish the job. The Chemnitz raid had been compromised by adverse weather conditions, and it would be March before success was achieved against this target.

The Brabag (Braunkohlen Benzin A G) oil refinery at Böhlen was posted as the target on the 19th for a 5 Group force of 264 Lancasters and six Mosquitos. It was another of the collection of similar plants in the Leipzig area and some ten miles north of Rositz, for which 630 Squadron loaded fifteen of its Lancasters with a cookie, thirteen supplemented with twelve 500-pounders and two with nine. They departed East Kirkby ahead of their 57 Squadron counterparts between 23.30 and 23.45 with S/L Cuelanaere the senior pilot on duty and all completed the three-and-a-half-hour outward flight to meet up at the target with the later-departing Mosquito element, among which was the Master Bomber, 54 Base's W/C Benjamin, who was flying the same Mosquito used by W/C Smith at Dresden six nights earlier. They encountered ten-tenths cloud over the target in two layers at 5,000 to 8,000 feet and 10,000 to 14,000 feet, and this would introduce a challenging element to the operation. The illuminators went in at around 15,000 feet between 04.05 and 04.13, and the VHF chatter suggested that a Mosquito had been able to mark a factory building with a red TI, which had been backed up. The main force was called in, before W/C Benjamin's VHF was suddenly cut off, and his Deputy took over. It would be established later, that the Master Bomber's Mosquito had been shot down by flak, and that W/C Benjamin DFC & Bar had died alongside his navigator. The East Kirkby crews carried out their attacks from 9,000 to 13,000 feet between 04.15 and 04.35 in accordance with confusing instructions, aiming mostly at the glow in the cloud of red and green TIs. Post-raid reconnaissance revealed only superficial damage to the site, which would have to be attacked again.

The following night, the 20th, proved to be a busy one, with more than five hundred Lancasters targeting Dortmund, while 268 Halifaxes from 4 and 6 Groups provided the heavy elements for raids on Rhenania-Ossag oil refineries in Düsseldorf and Monheim. 5 Group, meanwhile, prepared itself for a further attempt on the Mittelland Canal at Gravenhorst, for which eleven crews from each of the East Kirkby squadrons were briefed as part of an overall force of 154 Lancasters and eleven Mosquitos. They took off between 21.35 and 21.53, the 630 Squadron element with F/Ls Baker and Thompson the senior pilots on duty and thirteen 1,000-pounders in each bomb bay, and all reached the target area to find ten-tenths cloud between them and the aiming-point. The primary blind marker succeeded in delivering two green TIs by H2S from 12,000 feet at 00.53, and they fell on the starboard side of the canal. After the flare force went in, the Mosquito element descended to 400 feet, but could not identify the aiming-point, and just before H-Hour, the Master Bomber sent the marker force home, to be followed almost immediately by the main force as he abandoned the operation.

The operation was rescheduled for twenty-four hours later, when the cities of Duisburg and Worms were also to be attacked by heavy forces of 362 and 349 aircraft respectively. 5 Group detailed 165 Lancasters and twelve Mosquitos, and among those attending the briefing at Coningsby was G/C Evans-Evans, the station commander, who would be taking the bulk of the 83 Squadron commanding officer's highly experienced crew with him. Evans-Evans was forty-three years old and a larger-than-life character, who had commanded 115 Squadron for a spell earlier in the war during its Wellington era and had never lost the enthusiasm to be "one of the boys" and take part in operations. A number of years of good living had widened his girth, and it must have been a struggle to fit into the cramped confines of a Lancaster cockpit. The thirteen 630 Squadron Lancasters departed East Kirkby in advance of their 57 Squadron counterparts between 17.05 and 17.55 with F/Ls Baker, Harris, Ovens, Stemp and Thompson the senior pilots on duty and a similar bomb load as for twenty-four hours earlier. They reached the target area to find moonlight beaming down from clear skies with some ground haze and one of the primary blind markers delivered his green TIs two minutes late because of a change in the wind, and they fell about a mile south of the aiming-point, quite close to the previously mentioned Wet Triangle meeting point of the Mittelland and Dortmund-Ems Canals. After the flare force had done its job, the Mosquitos delivered their red TIs, which were backed up successfully before the main force was called in at 20.25. The East Kirkby crews carried out their attacks from 8,000 to 11,000 feet between 20.30 and 20.45 but could not assess the outcome because of the use of long-delay fuses. The presence of night-fighters was clearly evident by the number of combats taking place, and among nine missing Lancasters was the one belonging to 83 Squadron containing G/C Evans-Evans and seven others. Only the rear gunner survived, and among those who died was the twenty-two-year-old navigator, S/L Wishart DSO, DFC & Bar, who had completed sixty-one operations in Lancasters with 97 (Straits Settlement) Squadron and eighteen in Mosquitos as navigator to Master Bombers. G/C Ingham was deeply saddened by the loss of his crew in an operation in which they did not need to take part. Another loss was that of G/C Forbes DSO DFC RAAF, the commanding officer of 463 Squadron RAAF.

55 Base did not take part in the 5 Group operation by seventy-four Lancasters to bomb what was believed to be a U-Boot base at Horten in Oslo Fjord on the night of the 23/24th. Whether or not a U-Boot base existed is uncertain, but no shipping was seen by the crews,

and a local report described heavy damage in the port area and a shipyard, and the sinking of a tanker and floating crane. While this operation was in progress, nine others from the group took advantage of the main event to mine the waters of the Onion III and IV gardens in Oslo harbour, a little further north. The 630 Squadron participants were the crews of F/Ls Waterfall and Harris, who had departed East Kirkby at 17.22 and 17.32 respectively and arrived in favourable weather conditions to establish their positions either visually or by H2S before delivering their six mines each into the briefed locations.

Meanwhile, some 770 miles to the south, a force of 366 Lancasters and thirteen Mosquitos drawn from 1, 6 and 8 Groups plus a lone 5 Group Lancaster in the form of a 463 Squadron RAAF aircraft from the Film Unit, had been sent against the city of Pforzheim, situated in southern Germany between Karlsruhe to the north-west and Stuttgart to the south-east. This would be the first area raid on the city, which was known as a centre for jewellery and watch manufacture but was believed by the Allies to be involved in the production of precision instruments in support of Germany's war effort. They were greeted by clear skies and bright moonlight in the target area, and the thin veil of ground haze proved to be no impediment as the first red Oboe TIs went down at 19.52, to be followed quickly by illuminator flares and salvoes of concentrated reds and greens. Fires rapidly took hold until the whole town north of the river looked like a sea of flames, and by 20.06, the fires were too dazzling for the TIs to be visible, after which, the Master Bomber ordered the smoke to be bombed. The raid lasted twenty-two minutes, during which 1,825 tons of bombs fell into the built-up area, reducing 83% of it to ruins and setting off a firestorm in which 17,600 people lost their lives. This was the highest death toll to result from a single attack on a German city after Hamburg (40,000) and Dresden (25,000). It was during this operation that the final Victoria Cross was earned by a member of RAF Bomber Command. It went posthumously to the Master Bomber from 582 Squadron, Captain Ed Swales of the South African Air Force, who continued to control the attack in a Lancaster severely damaged by a night-fighter, before sacrificing his life to allow his crew to abandon the stricken aircraft.

A daylight attack on the Dortmund-Ems Canal at Ladbergen was planned for the afternoon of the 24th, and would involve 166 Lancasters and five Mosquitos, eighteen of the former provided by 617 Squadron with Tallboys on board, while 630 and 57 Squadrons contributed thirteen each, their bomb bays containing fourteen 1,000-pounders. The 630 Squadron element departed East Kirkby first between 13.44 and 13.53 with W/C Grindon the senior pilot on duty and reached the target under the umbrella of an 11 Group fighter escort to encounter ten-tenths cloud with tops at between 4,000 and 9,000 feet, at which point, the Master Bomber abandoned the operation and sent the force home with its bombs. Once back home at their respective stations, crews complained about the unsatisfactory forming up of Base gaggles, which had been generally chaotic.

During the course of the month the squadron took part in a dozen operations, including those aborted, and dispatched 154 sorties for the loss of two Lancasters and crews.

# March 1945

The new month would see the Command bludgeon its way across Germany, concentrating on oil, rail and road targets, along with the few towns still boasting a built-up area. The new 5 Group A-O-C, AVM Constantine, visited 55 Base stations on the 1st, having succeeded AVM Cochrane on his departure after two years in the job to head the newly-forming Transport Command. Mannheim was raided for the last time in numbers by a large force from 1, 6 and 8 Groups on that day, while 5 Group remained at home. Later, on the 2nd, Cologne was pounded for the final time, first by a force of seven hundred aircraft, which inflicted huge destruction across the city, particularly west of the Rhine, and later by a 3 Group force, of which only fifteen bombed because of a faulty G-H station in England. The city ceased to function, thereafter, and was still paralyzed when American forces marched in four days later. Just when it seemed that German resistance to air attack might end, March would prove that the defenders were still capable of mounting a challenge, even though they were stretched beyond their capacity to protect every corner of the Reich.

5 Group opened its March account with a return to the Ladbergen aqueduct section of the Dortmund-Ems Canal on the evening of the 3rd, for which 212 Lancasters and ten Mosquitos were made ready. Thirteen 630 Squadron crews attended briefing for the main event, while those of F/Ls Waterfall and Ovens were assigned to mining duties in the Onion garden in Oslo harbour. The latter pair departed East Kirkby first at 17.17 and 17.21 respectively, to be followed into the air between 18.31 and 18.41, in advance of their 57 Squadron counterparts, by the bombing brigade with W/C Grindon and S/L Eyre the senior pilots on duty. Twelve crews had thirteen 1,000-pounders with long delay fuses beneath their feet and one had a dozen as they climbed away over the station and set course for the Dutch coast. They encountered eight to ten-tenths cloud in the target area at between 3,500 and 6,000 feet, and it was noted that the defences had been strengthened since the last attack and were throwing up a curtain of intense light flak as high as 15,000 feet. H2S allowed the two 83 Squadron primary blind markers to locate the canal and deliver their green TIs from 14,000 feet at 21.47 and 21.49, and the first illuminators went in a minute later to light the way for the Mosquitos, after which, a large red glow could be seen through the clouds. At 21.59, the Master Bomber called in the main force to bomb on the glow or on sight of the TIs through gaps in the thin cloud, and the East Kirkby crews complied from around 8,000 to 10,000 feet in a thirty-minute slot either side of 22.00. They contributed to the breaching of both branches, which rendered the waterway unnavigable and out of action for the remainder of the war.

Meanwhile, F/L Ovens and crew had found clear skies and good visibility over Oslo Fjord and had delivered their mines unopposed into the briefed location, while the Waterfall crew returned with their bombs to land at Bitteswell, an Armstrong-Whitworth manufacturing site two miles to the west of the town of Lutterworth on the Leicestershire/Warwickshire border. They had been airborne for eight-and-a-half hours and no explanation was offered to account for the failure to fulfil their brief. The Luftwaffe launched Operation Gisella on this night, sending two hundred fighters to stalk the bombers as they returned to their stations, and East Kirkby came under attack after ten 630 and four 57 Squadron Lancasters had landed safely. The rest were diverted to other airfields, including Bitteswell and Bruntingthorpe, the latter located five miles north-east of Lutterworth. Squadron offices and buildings were damaged by cannon shells and a squadron signals analysis officer was killed, while the WAAF commanding officer, the squadron gunnery leader and two others sustained wounds that required hospital treatment. Twenty bombers were shot down, and this demonstrated the possible impact on Bomber Command operations had Hitler not restricted this type of operation on the basis that it made better propaganda to show downed bombers on German rather than English soil.

Seventeen 630 Squadron crews joined twenty-one from 57 Squadron at briefing on the 5th, to learn that 5 Group would be sending 248 Lancasters and ten Mosquitos back to Böhlen for another crack at the Brabag synthetic oil refinery. A simultaneous operation by a Thunderclap force of 760 aircraft would attempt to redress the recent failure at Chemnitz, some thirty-five miles to the south. One can scarcely imagine the tumult of 152 Merlin engines making their way along the peri-track to the runway threshold, and the blare as each one throttled up to maximum revs for the take-off. The departure from East Kirkby was accomplished without incident between 16.51 and 17.21 with W/C Grindon leading the 630 Squadron contingent, and most bomb bays containing a cookie and twelve 500-pounders. The East Kirkby element remained beneath the 3,000-foot cloud base as far as Reading, before climbing to between 6,000 and 9,000 feet and joining the rest of the stream and climbing again to around 12,000 feet over the Channel and French coast, some venturing as high as 15,000 feet to escape icing conditions. Ten-tenths cloud lay over the target in layers between 2,000 and 11,000 feet, but uncertainty concerning the prevailing conditions on arrival had been anticipated and two marking plans prepared, low-level and skymarking, and the lead primary blind marker made his first run at 14,000 feet to drop green TIs at 21.40. He did not see them burst because of the cloud but thought that the illuminator flares were well-placed. Some of the Coningsby (marker) crews experienced H2S difficulties, and not all were able to pinpoint on Leipzig for the run-in. This meant that they were unsure of their position, and, when the Master Bomber called for Wanganui flares at 21.45, they withheld them rather than risk dropping them inaccurately and attracting some of the bombing. A large explosion was witnessed at 21.50, and three minutes later, Wanganui flares were observed by the approaching main force crews. The East Kirkby crews delivered attacks from 9,500 to 14,000 feet between 21.50 and 22.03, observing another large explosion at 21.57, before the Master Bomber called a halt at 22.01 and sent everyone home, leaving evidence of fires and smoke behind them. Post-raid reconnaissance revealed extensive damage to the coal-drying plant, and some hits in other areas of the site, but it was still not a knockout blow. Meanwhile, the Thunderclap force had succeeded in inflicting severe fire damage in central and southern districts of Chemnitz.

The target posted on 5 Group stations on the 6th was the town and port area of Sassnitz, located on the Baltic Island of Rügen, about thirty miles north of Peenemünde, a region with memories of heavy casualties sustained by 5 Group in the attack on the secret weapons site in August 1943. The two-fold purpose of the operation was to destroy the port installations and facilities and sink shipping to render it unusable as a refuge for escaping Kriegsmarine units. A force of 150 Lancasters and seven Mosquitos was assembled, eleven of the former by each of the East Kirkby squadrons, plus one from 630 Squadron with the crew of F/L Waterfall and five from 57 squadron to deliver mines to the Willow garden on the approaches to Sassnitz. The 630 Squadron bombing brigade had been briefed to act as Path Finder supporters, which meant that they were to accompany the marker force to beef up the numbers over the aiming point and make it more difficult for searchlight and flak batteries to latch on to individual aircraft. They were then to make a second pass to drop their ten 1,000-pounders each on shipping both in and outside of the harbour in the light provided by illuminating flares. They departed East Kirkby ahead of their 57 Squadron counterparts between 18.02 and 18.12 with W/C Grindon and S/L Eyre the senior pilots on duty and reached the target area to find five to nine-tenths drifting cloud with tops in places at 8,000 feet. An 83 Squadron blind marker Lancaster made a run at 22.50 to drop green TIs over the port from 12,000 feet, and the flare force maintained illumination of the town and outer harbour for the next twenty-five minutes. The 630 Squadron supporters made their first pass between H-16 and H-12 before orbiting to port and adopting vector headings for their bombing runs. Apart from a short break, when cloud slid across the aiming-point, the markers remained visible to the main force crews until bombing ceased at H+18, leaving those with bombs still aboard to take them home. A destroyer was observed to blow up after receiving a direct hit by a large bomb and may have been one of three large ships identified and attacked in the harbour, and according to post-raid reconnaissance, sunk, and there was also extensive damage in the northern part of the town. Meanwhile, the gardeners encountered five to seven-tenths cloud with tops at 9,000 feet and dropped their six mines each into the allotted location before returning safely.

It was back to the oil campaign for 5 Group on the following night, for an attack on the Rhenania-Ossag oil refinery at Harburg, south of Hamburg, for which a force of 234 Lancasters and seven Mosquitos was made ready. They would not be alone over Germany, however, as more than a thousand other aircraft would be engaged against similar targets at Dessau and Hemmingstedt and in minor and support operations. 630 Squadron's fifteen Lancasters each received a bomb load of a cookie and sixteen 500-pounders before departing East Kirkby between 18.10 and 18.46 with S/L Cuelanaere the senior pilot on duty. The force arrived over the target to find eight-tenths thin cloud and red and yellow target indicators clearly visible, which they bombed in accordance with the Master Bomber's instructions with a seven-second overshoot from 10,000 to 13,000 feet in a twenty-minute slot either side of 22.00. Bomb bursts were clearly observed, along with explosions and black smoke rising through 10,000 feet, and all but one 57 Squadron Lancaster returned safely, confident in the success of the operation. 5 Group distinguished itself on this night by claiming the destruction of seven enemy fighters, one of them, a FW190 shot down over the target by a 57 Squadron crew, but for the second time in a matter of weeks, 189 Squadron posted missing four crews. Post-raid reconnaissance confirmed further damage to this previously attacked target, with oil storage tanks taking the most hits, and revealed that a rubber factory had also been severely damaged.

An all-time record was set on the 11th, when 1,079 aircraft, the largest Bomber Command force ever for a single target, was assembled to attack Essen for the last time. 5 Group contributed 199 Lancasters and a single Mosquito, 630 Squadron loading its fifteen Lancasters with a cookie and sixteen 500 pounders each and dispatching them from East Kirkby between 11.49 and 12.10 with W/C Grindon and S/L Cuelanaere the senior pilots on duty. They found the target city covered by ten-tenths cloud with tops at 6,000 feet, which required the Path Finder element to employ skymarkers in the form of red and blue smoke puffs, and these were bombed by the East Kirkby crews from around 16,000 to 19,000 feet between 15.15 and 15.25. More than 4,600 tons of bombs were dropped into the already ravaged city and former industrial powerhouse and left it with smoke rising through 10,000 feet as the force turned away. It would still be in a state of paralysis when the American ground forces captured it unopposed on the 10th of April. The bombers' battle with Essen had spanned almost five years, and it was only during the last two that the bomber had prevailed. Many gallant crews had fallen during the various campaigns, but Essen now lay totally ruined, with seven thousand of its inhabitants having lost their lives in air raids.

Operations were not yet over for the 11th, as 5 Group sent eleven Lancasters that night to mine the approaches to Oslo harbour in the Onions III garden. The 630 Squadron crews of F/O McGuffie and F/L Waterfall departed East Kirkby at 17.42 and 17.48 and found the target area to be under clear skies with good visibility. They identified the drop zone by H2S, before making timed runs to deliver their stores in the briefed locations and return safely.

A little over twenty-four hours after the launching of the Essen raid, the short-lived record was surpassed by the departure from their stations in the early afternoon of 1,108 aircraft, which had Dortmund as their destination. This time 5 Group provided 211 Lancasters, sixteen of them from 630 Squadron, which departed East Kirkby between 13.29 and 13.44 with W/C Grindon the senior pilot on duty and a cookie and sixteen 500 pounders in each bomb bay. They arrived over the eastern Ruhr to find it still under a blanket of ten-tenths cloud, this time with tops at 6,000 feet and the Path Finders marking the aiming points with green and blue smoke puffs. The Master Bomber directed the main force element to aim for the blues, and the East Kirkby crews complied to the best of their ability from 13,000 to 17,000 feet between 16.45 and 16.50. On return they spoke of brown smoke climbing through the clouds to 8,000 feet from the northern end of the city, and also a ring of smoke encircling the area so dense, that it remained visible for 120 miles into the return flight. A new record of 4,800 tons of bombs was delivered, and photo-reconnaissance revealed that the central and southern districts of the city had received the greatest weight and had been left in chaos with all industry silenced permanently and railway tracks torn up.

The Group's next objective was the I G Farben-owned Wintershall oil refinery at Lützkendorf, another site to the west of Leipzig and south-west of Leuna in the Geiseltal region. *(Lützkendorf no longer exists on a map of Germany and is now known as either Mücheln or Krumpa)*. The briefing of 244 Lancaster and eleven Mosquito crews took place on the 14th, fifteen of the former representing 630 Squadron and departing East Kirkby ahead of the 57 Squadron contingent between 16.46 and 16.59 with W/C Grindon the senior pilot on duty. They headed out over the Wash and the bulge of East Anglia en-route to the Scheldt Estuary and crossed Belgium to swing south of Cologne, before pointing their snouts to the east for the long leg to the target. They were met on arrival by conditions described variously as ten-tenths cloud, no cloud, thin layer of cloud, thin banks of stratus with tops at 12,000 feet, a little medium cloud, poor visibility and good visibility, but there was unanimity with regard to the haze. Ahead, the primary blind marker aircraft could be seen delivering their green TIs at 21.49, followed by the illuminators immediately afterwards between 21.51 and 22.00 to drop flares and bombs. Finally, the low-level Mosquitos did their job to accurately mark the aiming-point before the main force crews were called in, and the East Kirkby participants bombed on red and green TIs in accordance with the Master Bomber's instructions from 8,000 to 11000 feet between 22.03 and 22.11. Returning crews claimed an accurate attack, reporting explosions and fires, and thick, black smoke drifting across the plant and ascending through 7,000 feet, which rendered impossible a detailed assessment. Night-fighters were very much in evidence over the target and during the return flight, and a hefty eighteen Lancasters failed to return, 7.4% of those dispatched, among them one from 57 Squadron. Post-raid reconnaissance revealed a partially successful operation, which meant that a further visit would be required.

Thirty-two crews assembled in the briefing room at East Kirkby at 14.00 on the 16th, to learn that they were to be part of a 5 Group force of 225 Lancasters and eleven Mosquitos for an attack on the virgin target of Würzburg, a small city on the river Main, situated some sixty miles south-east of Frankfurt in southern Germany. While this operation was in progress, a similar-sized force drawn from 1 and 8 Groups would be delivering the final attack of the war on Nuremberg, fifty miles to the south-east. The eighteen-strong 630 Squadron element got away in the wake of their 57 Squadron counterparts between 17.37 and 17.50 with F/L Nunns and Waterfall the senior pilots on duty, the former accompanied as second pilot by the newly posted-in S/L Flett, whose time with the squadron would be brief. There is a source suggesting that Flett was to succeed S/L Eyre as B Flight commander, but his posting to the command of 44 (Rhodesia) Squadron at Spilsby on the 1st of April suggests that he was gaining operational experience in preparation for his new role. They reached the target area to find clear skies with ground haze and saw the marking and flare forces ahead of them carrying out their assigned tasks between 21.25 and 21.34 to leave the way clear for the main force crews to exploit the favourable bombing conditions. They found red and yellow TIs marking the aiming-point and complied with the Master Bomber's call for a sixteen-second overshoot for their cookies and 4lb incendiaries. Six Lancasters failed to return, and 630 Squadron registered its first loss for a month, its first in 179 sorties, LM260 having crashed in southern Germany with no survivors from the crew of W/O Plumb. Crews had to wait for the reconnaissance reports to discover the extent of the destruction from a raid that had lasted just seventeen minutes. In that brief period, 1,127 tons of bombs had fallen into the historic old cathedral city, destroying an estimated 89% of the built-up area and killing four to five thousand people. The Nuremberg operation had also been highly destructive, but had cost 1 Group twenty-four Lancasters, thus proving, that the enemy defences were still capable of delivering a bloody nose.

There was still business to attend to at the Böhlen oil refinery, and 5 Group prepared a force of 236 Lancasters and eleven Mosquitos on the 20th, to deal what was hoped to be the knockout blow. Briefings began at 20.00, and at East Kirkby was attended by thirty-four crews, twenty-eight to take part in the main event and six to join six others for a small-scale diversionary raid on the town of Halle, situated some twenty miles to the north-west of Leipzig. All nineteen 630 Squadron Lancasters received a bomb load of a cookie and fourteen 500-pounders before taking off together between 23.16 and 23.50 with F/L Nunns the senior pilot on duty for Böhlen, accompanied again by S/L Flett, while the crews of F/Ls Ovens, Stemp and Thompson were Halle-bound. A few minutes after leaving the ground a 57 Squadron Lancaster crashed into a house in the village of Stickney some four miles south of the airfield, killing the pilot and three of his crew and injuring three others, one of whom would succumb on the 1st of April. The others set out on the now familiar path to eastern Germany and arrived in the target area to encounter reasonably favourable conditions with three to six-tenths cloud topping out at 6,000 to 8,000 feet. The bomber stream arrived early because of stronger-than-forecast tail winds, and the main force had to orbit while the first primary blind marker crew delivered green TIs at 03.33. They fell 750 yards south of the plant, to be followed at H-16 by a yellow TI bursting two miles short of the target. A cluster of illuminator flares ignited ahead, revealing that a smoke screen had been activated and was creating difficulties for the Mosquito low-level markers, despite which, they deposited red TIs on the button, allowing the Master Bomber to call in the main force. A few dummy TIs attracted a number of bomb loads, but the East Kirkby crews complied with instructions to bomb on specific reds and yellows from 10,500 to 15,500 feet between 03.44 and 03.55. The main weight of the attack was concentrated around the target, and numerous explosions were witnessed, as was smoke rising through 5,000 feet as they turned away. Meanwhile at Halle, thin cloud at 6,000 to 7,000 feet created some challenges and bombs were delivered largely on e.t.a, the outcome not important and not assessed. The Böhlen operation was successful in putting the oil plant out of action, and it was still idle when American forces moved in a few weeks later.

Briefings across 5 Group stations at 22.00 on the 21st informed 151 Lancaster and eight Mosquito crews that the Deutsche Erdölwerke synthetic oil refinery at Hamburg was to be their target that night. 630 Squadron loaded its sixteen Lancasters with a cookie and sixteen 500 pounders each and sent them into the air from East Kirkby between 01.20 and 01.39 with F/Ls Stemp and Thompson the senior pilots on duty. They pinpointed on the Danish coast to approach the target from the north and found thin stratus cloud at around 2,000 feet, through which the primary blind marker aircraft dropped green TIs on H2S from 14,000 feet at 03.55. The first illuminator Lancasters went in thirty seconds later and continued to light up the aiming-point until 04.01, by which time the Mosquitos had marked, allowing the main force element to be called in at 04.05. The East Kirkby crews bombed from 15,500 to 18,000 feet between 04.05 and 04.15, observing many fires and a large explosion at 04.11 that produced red flame and black smoke. Another was reported at 04.16, and it was clear to the homebound crews that the attack had been successful, a fact confirmed by post-raid reconnaissance, which revealed that twenty storage tanks had been destroyed in exchange for the loss of just four Lancasters.

The 55 Base squadrons were not involved in 5 Group's operations against railway bridges at Nienburg and Bremen on the 22nd and 23rd, but they were called to briefing on the afternoon of the 23rd to learn of their part in a raid that night on the town of Wesel. This had the misfortune to lie close to the Rhine and in the path of the advancing British 21st Army Group, which, since the 16th of February, had caused it to be systematically reduced to rubble by repeated air attacks, and now had one final onslaught to face, having already endured one by 3 Group earlier in the day. 195 Lancasters and eleven Mosquitos were made ready, the seventeen representing 630 Squadron loaded with either thirteen 1,000-pounders and one 500-pounder or eleven and three before departing East Kirkby between 19.02 and 19.28 with S/L Flett the senior pilot on duty and undertaking his one and only sortie with the squadron as crew captain. They found the target under clear skies with slight ground haze and were able to identify it visually, observing the aiming point to be well-marked by red and green TIs, which were bombed from 8,000 to 12,000 feet between 22.33 and 22.42 in accordance with the Master Bomber's instructions. It was noticed, that despite the Master Bomber ending the attack at H+8, bombing had continued. Post-raid reconnaissance confirmed the effectiveness of the raid, which left only 3% of Wesel's buildings standing, and after the war it would claim justifiably to be the most completely destroyed town in Germany.

During the course of the month the squadron undertook fifteen operations and dispatched 177 sorties for the loss of a single Lancaster and crew and was awarded its crest and motto by His Majesty King George VI. The crews could not have known that fewer than four weeks of operations remained ahead of them before the bombing war finally came to an end.

# April 1945

S/L Flett was posted to Spilsby on the 1st and S/L Pilgrim arrived at around this time to succeed S/L Eyre as B Flight commander. There would be a gentle introduction to April for 5 Group, with no operations posted until the evening of the 3rd, when briefings were held for an attack on what was believed to be a military barracks at Nordhausen, situated in the Harz Mountains between Hannover to the north-west and Leipzig to the south-east. The site was actually a pair of enormous parallel tunnels under the Kohnstein Hill, which had been developed originally by the BASF Company to mine gypsum between 1917 and 1934. Following the destruction of Peenemünde, smaller tunnels had been created as a link between them to form a horizontal ladder effect, and the site turned over to the Mittelwerk GmbH (Gesellschaft mit beschrenkter Haftung, or Limited Company) for the manufacture of V-2 rockets and other secret projects. The "barracks" were part of the Mittelwerk-Dora forced workers camp, where inmates existed under the most horrendous conditions and brutal treatment, while they were starved, worked to death or simply executed by an increasingly desperate regime seeking to change the course of the war. The site had been attacked by 1 Group on the previous day and heavy damage inflicted but it was decided to send 5 Group in to hit the barracks again and the nearby town.

There was an early start on the 4th for the 243 Lancasters, which were to be divided between the two aiming points, ninety-three to the barracks and 150 to the town, with the 55 Base squadrons assigned to the former and each of their Lancasters carrying a cookie and sixteen 500 pounders. The 630 Squadron element of seventeen departed East Kirkby between 06.15 and 06.31 with F/Ls Baker, Kirkwood, Nunns, Ovens and Roberts the senior pilots on duty and lost the services of F/O Hallett and crew to an unserviceable rear turret early on. Darkness prevented the forming up of a gaggle and it was only with the dawn that it became possible, by which time the force was over enemy territory, arriving at the target to encounter five-to-seven-tenths cloud with tops as high as 9,000 feet, through which they were able to establish a visual reference until smoke began to obscure the barracks. The East Kirkby participants mostly bombed the barracks, from 12,500 to 16,000 feet between 09.13 and 09.20, until smoke obscured the ground and persuaded others to attack the town as the designated alternative from 11,500 to 16,000 feet between 09.14 and 09.22. Some of the early bombing of the town was seen to undershoot, but the Master Bomber corrected this by calling for a five-second overshoot, and thereafter, the markers also became concealed by smoke. At debriefing, the crews were able to report a concentrated attack on both aiming-points, claiming severe damage, and the likelihood is that most slave workers were at work in the tunnel complex at the time of the attack and not exposed to the bombing in the barracks.

The only sizeable effort on the night of the 7/8th was by 175 Lancasters and eleven Mosquitos of 5 Group, which had a benzol plant at Mölbis as their target. Situated south-south-east of the city and fewer than two miles east of Böhlen, it was becoming a familiar destination for 5 Group via a well-trodden route across Belgium to pass south of Cologne. 630 Squadron made ready eleven Lancasters, which departed East Kirkby between 18.11 and 18.28 with W/C Grindon the first away and a cookie and twelve 500-pounders in each bomb bay. They found themselves delayed by wrongly forecast head winds and were reticent to increase speed and fuel consumption in case a diversion on return had them heading for Scotland. They eventually reached the target area, but not all would do so in time to participate in the attack. Two 83 Squadron primary blind markers formed the tip of the spear, and identified Zeitz on H2S, before making the ten-mile north-easterly run from there to the target. Green TIs were released from 15,000 feet at 22.48, and the flare force followed up between 22.50 and 22.57 to enable the low-level Mosquitos to drop red and green TIs among the chimneys of the plant. The approaching main force crews were greeted by clear skies with ground haze, or perhaps, a smoke screen in operation, but the highly accurate and visible marking was an invitation for them to plaster the aiming-point with high explosives. We do not know how many 630 Squadron crews bombed on red and green TIs from 10,000 to 15,000 feet from 23.03 until the Master Bomber called a halt at 23.10, leaving some with bombs still on board. Despite the fact that the oil plant was spared some of the bomb loads intended for it, photo-reconnaissance confirmed the operation to have been a complete success, which ended all production at the site. Later in the day, the length of a tour would be reduced from thirty-six to thirty-three sorties.

Two major operations were scheduled for the 8th, the larger one involving 440 aircraft from 4, 6 and 8 Groups to be directed at Hamburg's shipyards, where the new Type XXI U-Boots were under construction. 5 Group, meanwhile, would take on the Wintershall synthetic oil refinery at Lützkendorf, following a failed attempt on the 4th by 1 and 8 Groups to conclusively end production at the site. A force of 231 Lancasters and eleven Mosquitos was put together, of which the seventeen 630 Squadron participants departed East Kirkby between 18.00 and 18.37 with S/L Cuelanaere the senior pilot on duty and a cookie and up to sixteen 500-pounders in the bomb bays. Darkness fell as they crossed the Rhine and met no opposition either from the ground or in the air before reaching the target area, where conditions were as they had been twenty-four hours earlier, with clear skies and either ground haze or generated smoke. The primary blind markers ran in at 14,000 feet at 22.33 to deliver green TIs, and the illuminators followed between 22.35 and 22.42, after which, the main force was called in. The East Kirkby crews attacked in accordance with the Master Bomber's instructions to bomb the southerly red and yellow TIs after an eleven second overshoot, running in at 11,000 to 14,000 feet between 22.45 and 22.52. All were diverted on return, and possibly bound for one of the many airfields to the west of Lincolnshire, ND949 crashed at 03.10 at Foxton, three miles north-west of Market Harborough in Leicestershire, and the entire predominantly RAAF crew of F/O Richardson RAAF was killed. Returning crews were confident that it would not be necessary to return to that particular target and described their observations to the intelligence section at debriefing of many explosions, including a large one at 22.47, which was surpassed in size by another one two minutes later, and flames were said to have reached up to 3,000 feet. The complete destruction of the site was confirmed by photo-reconnaissance, and the plant would remain out of action for what rest of the war.

55 Base sat out a modest 5 Group raid on oil storage tanks and U-Boot pens at Hamburg in daylight on the 9th, and when its crews were called to briefing on the 10th, it was to discover that they would be going back to the Leipzig area for the third successive operation, this time to hit a stretch of railway track linked to the Wahren marshalling yards, situated to the north-west of the city. A larger operation on this night, involving more than three hundred aircraft from 1 and 8 Groups, was to be directed at the Plauen marshalling yards to the south-west of Dresden, and the two forces would adopt a similar route until shortly before reaching Leipzig. 5 Group contributed all seventy-six Lancasters for Leipzig and eleven Mosquitos, with 8 Group providing the other eight Oboe Mosquitos, and the eleven-strong 630 Squadron element departed East Kirkby between 18.20 and 18.32 with S/L Cuelanaere the senior pilot on duty and each Lancaster carrying ten or eleven 1,000-pounders. They reached the target area to find clear skies and excellent conditions for bombing, noting many ineffective searchlights and modest flak, probably because of a heavy night-fighter presence. The Oboe Mosquitos dropped green TIs as a reference for the 83 Squadron flare force crews, who provided the illumination between 22.51 and 22.57 for the low-level Mosquito element. The Mosquitos placed their red TIs accurately onto the aiming-point, before the main force bombed the southernmost red TI in accordance with the Master Bomber's instructions, those from East Kirkby from around 11,500 to 14,000 feet either side of 23.00. F/L Ovens and crew suffered the frustration of reaching the target only for the bomb doors to refuse to open over the aiming point.

Not since the raid on the railway junction at Revigny in July had 630 Squadron posted missing more than one crew from a single operation, but two failed to return on this night, ME739 abandoned over Germany by F/O Cameron RAAF and his crew. The pilot and three others were taken prisoner, the mid-upper gunner sadly fell to his death as his parachute burned away, but the bomb-aimer and rear gunner managed to evade capture. RF122 also went down over Germany, killing F/O Sassoon and four of his crew, while the bomb-aimer and rear gunner joined their squadron colleagues in some kind of limited and short-lived captivity. These were the final losses to be sustained by the squadron. Some crews commented on intense night-fighter activity over the target and on the way home and F/O Ramsey RNZAF and crew claimed the destruction of two FW190s. Photographic-reconnaissance would confirm that serious damage had been inflicted upon the eastern half of the targeted stretch of track.

A major attack on Kiel by elements of 3, 6 and 8 Groups was planned for the night of the 13/14th, while 5 Group took advantage of that activity to send eighteen Lancasters to lay mines in the Forget-me-not garden in Kiel harbour. The crews of F/O Cowan, F/O Weston, F/L Roberts and W/O Granger departed East Kirkby in that order between 20.30 and 20.32 each sitting on six Mk VI mines and reached the target area to encounter six to ten-tenths stratus with tops up to 7,000 feet, through which three of them fulfilled their briefs by H2S from an undisclosed altitude at some time around 23.30, while one was thwarted by H2S failure.

5 Group was used to being handed the most distant targets, and as the final days of the bombing war approached, it found itself facing three long-range trips on consecutive nights, all to railway targets. The first of these was at Pilsen in Czechoslovakia, for which a force of 222 Lancasters and eleven Mosquitos was made ready. The fourteen Lancasters from each Squadron departed East Kirkby between 23.21 and 23.53 with W/C Grindon leading the 630 Squadron contingent and a cookie and fourteen 500-pounders in each bomb bay. They found clear skies in the target area with only slight haze, and ahead watched the first primary blind marker Lancaster deliver green TIs at 03.38, before the flare forces followed between 03.51 and 03.56. The main force was called in at 03.58, and all but one of the East Kirkby participants bombed from around 13,000 to 16,000 feet either side of 04.00, aiming at the north-westerly red and yellow TIs with an eight-second overshoot in accordance with the Master Bomber's instructions. Several large explosions were observed, one of particular ferocity at 04.00½ followed by oily smoke, and it was concluded that the raid had been successful.

The East Kirkby squadrons were on the order of battle for the night of the 17th, for an operation against railway yards at Cham, close to the Czech border in south-eastern Germany, and there was good news to celebrate at briefing, when the length of a tour was reduced yet again to thirty sorties, releasing many crews to contemplate a long future. The bombing-up process was nearing completion by 18.00 hours, when a fire erupted underneath the bomb bay of a 57 Squadron Lancaster. Two 1,000lb bombs detonated, flinging burning debris in all directions, and soon other 57 Squadron Lancasters were on fire. The 630 Squadron ground crews abandoned their charges to take cover in the face of what was obviously a major incident, and the station's contribution to the operation was scrubbed. Ninety Lancasters and eleven Mosquitos ultimately took off and reached the target more than four hours later to be greeted by clear skies with slight ground haze. The primary blind marker Lancaster dropped the first green TIs on H2S from 14,000 feet at 03.47, and the flare forces went in between 03.51 and 03.54 to light the way for the Mosquito low-level markers. Their efforts were seen to be very concentrated, but the use of delay-fused bombs meant that no immediate assessment would be possible. Photo-reconnaissance later confirmed that tracks had been torn up and rolling stock damaged, and it was another success for the group.

By the following morning, East Kirkby was a shambles, bearing the shattered remains of six 57 Squadron aircraft and fourteen others displaying various degrees of damage. 630 Squadron escaped lightly, but the airfield would remain unusable for days. As a result, none of its aircraft participated in the massive assault by all groups on the island of Heligoland on the 18th, or the successful final 5 Group operation of the long-running railway campaign at Komotau in Czechoslovakia on the night of the 18/19th. It was not until the 23rd that the two squadrons could operate again, when twelve Lancasters from each were part of a 5 Group force of 148 Lancasters targeting railway yards and shipping in the port at Flensburg on Schleswig-Holstein's Baltic coast. The twelve 630 Squadron participants departed East Kirkby between 15.06 and 15.16 with S/L Cuelanaere the senior pilot on duty and fourteen 1,000-pounders in each bomb bay, and after climbing out formed up with the other 55 Base squadrons to fall in behind the 53 Base formation. As the force approached the target it encountered cloud at between 4,500 and 8,000 feet, which persuaded the Master Bomber to send them home with their payloads intact.

5 Group operated for the final time on the 25th, with an operation in the morning against the SS barracks and the Berghof, Hitler's Eaglesnest retreat, at Berchtesgaden in the Bavarian mountains, and later that night on an oil refinery at Tonsberg in Norway. 5 Group supported the former with eighty-eight Lancasters and a single Mosquito in an overall 1, 5 and 8 Group force of 359 Lancasters and sixteen Mosquitos. There was an early start, the 630 Squadron crews of S/L Pilgrim and F/Os Cowan, Gibson, Hoare and Scott and their 57 Squadron counterparts departing East Kirkby between 04.15 and 04.38 with twelve 1,000-pounders in each bomb bay. They all arrived in the target area to find clear skies, but despite the favourable conditions, the Master Bomber's instructions were not getting through and high mountains on the run-in hid the target almost until it was too late. It proved difficult to identify the barracks in the absence of visible markers, however, a nearby lake and the town stood out clearly, and the East Kirkby crews were able to establish their position before carrying out their attacks from around 15,000 to 16,000 feet either side of 09.00. It was difficult to assess the accuracy of this operation, but it appeared to be effective, and no local report emerged to provide clarity.

That night, 5 Group conducted its and Bomber Command's final offensive operation of the war involving heavy bombers, when sending 107 Lancasters and seven Mosquitos to attack the Vallø Oljeraffineri oil refinery at Tonsberg in southern Norway, situated close to the western shore of Oslo Fjord, a dozen or so miles south of the recently attacked Horten. The purpose of the attack was to cut off fuel supplies from its storage tanks, but they were largely empty, and some bombs hit civilian housing adjacent to the site, killing fifty-three people. At the same time, fourteen 5 Group Lancasters carried out the final mining sorties of the war in the Onion garden in Oslo Fjord, and it was for the latter that the East Kirkby squadrons each dispatched four Lancasters between 20.06 and 20.35. The 630 Squadron crews of F/Os Bathgate, Jacobs, Maclean and Weston all reached the target area to find a layer of eight to ten-tenths cloud and established their positions by H2S, before delivering their six Mk VI mines each into the briefed locations. When F/O Jacobs and crew touched down in NN774 at 02.53, they had the honour of bringing to a close the brief but effective offensive operational career of 630 Squadron. Six minutes later the last 57 Squadron Lancaster landed to bring down the curtain on East Kirkby's offensive contribution to Bomber Command's war.

The crews were unaware of the significance of the above operations, and others were posted over the ensuing days, only to be cancelled. On the 28th, and as testimony to his calibre as 630 Squadron's commanding officer, W/C Grindon was posted to Woodhall Spa to take Command of 617 Squadron. Later in the year he would be awarded the DSO in recognition of his wartime service, his citation reading; "In the course of numerous operational sorties, W/C Grindon has established an excellent reputation for leadership, energy and courage. The worst weather or the heaviest opposition have never deterred him from the accurate completion of his allotted tasks. Over such heavily defended targets as Königsberg, Bremen and Bergen he has braved intense anti-aircraft fire, and despite damage to his aircraft on more than one occasion, has always fulfilled his mission. On one occasion, during a daylight attack on Homberg severe damage was sustained and his aircraft became difficult to control, but, in spite of the danger, W/C Grindon continued to lead his formation with skill and determination. He has at all times set an outstanding example."

W/C Wild succeeded W/C Grindon to become the squadron's final wartime commander. During its eighteen months of operations, 630 Squadron served with distinction in 5 Group's front line and contributed to the success of Bomber Command's campaigns from November 1943, dropping 10,347 tons of bombs. Having completed its task in the finest traditions of the Command, the squadron undertook a humanitarian role, helping to repatriate Allied prisoners of war. By the end of May, 57 and 630 Squadrons had ferried a magnificent eighteen hundred former prisoners back to the UK. The Squadron was finally disbanded on the 18th of July 1945.

The wartime home of 630 Squadron, East Kirkby, is now the Lincolnshire Aviation Heritage Centre, established by the Panton brothers in memory of their brother Christopher, who was killed while flying with 433 (Porcupine) Squadron on the Nuremberg operation at the end of March 1944. Lancaster NX611 has been lovingly restored as the main attraction and is frequently taxied for spectators. The museum now also boasts a Mosquito and B25 Mitchell, and displays information on all of the wartime 5 Group squadrons, with many exhibits depicting this and later periods of the station's operational life. The control tower is very much as it was during 630 Squadron's residency, and the entire site stands as a memorial to the crews of Bomber Command in general, and those of 5 Group in particular.

# Postscript to the Story of P/O Barnes

Provided by his daughter, Amanda Burrows.

After the war Dad often wondered about the brave French people who had helped him but didn't know their names or where he had been hidden. Twenty-three years to the day (15/03/1967) after he was shot down, he received a telegram from France. He was perplexed as he didn't know anybody in France. It was from a French TV programme called 'Rendevous des Souvenir'. After Dad had left them in May 1944 the Coigne family, who lived in Fere-en-Tardenois, had hidden Dad's distress whistle, RAF wings and his address in a jam jar and buried it in the garden. They had tried to make contact after the war, but the house had been bombed two weeks after Dad got back and the Barnes family had moved. This TV programme reunited Dad with Leon and Madeleine Coigne and their two children Christiane and Jean who despite their young age had also played a part in the Resistance line. (Christiane aged 14 would cycle past German soldiers with secret messages smuggled in her socks!) As you can imagine this reunion was very emotional. The TV crew took our parents to the village of St Gilles where his two gunners were buried. For many years one grave had my Dad's name on it as one of the bodies had been identified as him due to his particular type of flying boot that could be cut down to look like ordinary shoes. Unknown to the crew the mid upper gunner, nineteen-year-old Jim Overholt RCAF, had been issued with a pair the morning of the raid. There he was also presented with parts of his crashed plane including his pilot's seat. The bond that exists between our two families is immense. so much so that my daughter is named Madeleine after Madame Coigne. Further details can be found on www.630 squadron.co.uk. This website was set up by the son of my father's bomb-aimer.

*Len Barnes, Curly, Florentino, and Catalina.*

# Roll of Honour

| | | | |
|---|---|---|---|
| Sgt | Peter | ACKLAND | 17.03.45 |
| Sgt | Kenneth | ADAMS | 19.07.44, |
| F/L | Robert | ADAMS | 22.06.44. |
| P/O | Charles | AGNEW | 22.11.44. |
| Sgt | John Archer | AKERS | 30.08.44. |
| Sgt | Raymond George | ALEXANDER | 31.08.44. |
| P/O | Clifford Leslie Eldridge | ALLEN | 25.03.44. |
| Sgt | Philip | AMIES | 12.05.44. |
| F/L | Clifford Harold | ARMOUR | 20.02.45. |
| Sgt | Frederick Robert | ARNOLD | 27.07.44. |
| F/Sgt | Paul Druce | ARTHUR | 31.08.44. |
| F/Sgt | Kenneth James | ASPELL | 22.11.44. |
| P/O | Ronald Walter | BAILEY | 22.05.44. |
| F/O | Ambrose | BAIN | 27.07.44. |
| Sgt | James Stuart | BAIN | 22.12.44. |
| Sgt | John David | BAKER | 17.03.45. |
| F/Sgt | Richard Hooton | BANKS | 02.12.43. |
| Sgt | Norman | BARKER | 19.07.44. |
| P/O | William John | BARR | 10.06.44. |
| F/Sgt | George Henry | BARRINGTON | 29.01.44. |
| P/O | Harold John | BARRONS | 29.01.44. |
| F/O | Harold Knowles | BATTYE | 20.02.44. |
| P/O | William | BAXTER | 22.05.44. |
| F/Sgt | Gordon Edwin | BECKHOUSE | 19.07.44. |
| F/Sgt | Reginald Joseph | BENNETT | 08.12.44. |
| Sgt | James | BINNIE | 23.05.44. |
| F/Sgt | Ronald William | BISHOP | 18.08.44. |
| F/O | William Egbert Trevor | BLADEN | 02.03.44. |
| Sgt | Thomas Walter | BLANC | 23.11.43. |
| Sgt | George Rex | BODEN | 01.01.45 |
| Sgt | William James | BOTT | 10.06.44. |
| Sgt | Roy Stuart | BOURNE | 25.03.44. |
| F/L | Evelyn George William | BOWERS | 27.08.44. |
| F/Sgt | Anthony Ellis | BOWMAN | 09.04.45. |
| P/O | Donald McMillan | BOYD | 12.09.44. |
| P/O | Dennis George | BRADD | 22.06.44. |
| Sgt | Harold | BRADLEY | 05.07.44. |
| F/O | Dennis Archibald | BRAMMER | 18.10.44. |
| F/Sgt | Frederick George | BREZINA | 18.07.44. |
| W/O | Albert Edward | BROOMFIELD | 29.01.44. |
| Sgt | Leslie Alfred | BROOMFIELD | 12.09.44. |
| P/O | Vivian William | BROWN | 23.05.44. |

| Sgt | Raymond Athol | BRUCK | 22.12.44. |
| P/O | Gordon Alan | BULLOCK | 18.08.44. |
| F/Sgt | Herbert Eric | BURTON | 09.04.45. |
| F/O | John Francis | BUSH | 19.07.45. |
| F/Sgt | William Albert | BUTCHER | 29.02.44. |
| Sgt | John Adams | BYARS | 20.02.44. |
| F/O | Herbert Laurence Wray | CAIRNS | 29.01.44. |
| Sgt | James Alexander | CALDER | 18.07.44. |
| F/O | George | CAMERON | 18.08.44. |
| Sgt | John Charles | CAMERON | 10.06.44. |
| Sgt | Stanley Laidler | CAMERON | 09.02.45. |
| P/O | Derek Reginald | CARLILE | 15.02.44. |
| W/O | William John | CARRIER | 27.08.44. |
| Sgt | Alexander | CARSON | 15.02.45. |
| P/O | Daniel Newton | CARTER | 17.08.44. |
| Sgt | Richard Matthew | CARTLIDGE | 12.05.44. |
| F/L | Dennis Edward | CAUDREY | 23.11.43. |
| P/O | Edward Frank | CHAMPNESS | 23.05.44. |
| W/O | Leslie | CHRISTIE | 29.01.44. |
| P/O | John | CLAPPERTON | 23.11.43. |
| P/O | Ronald Leslie | CLARK | 31.03.44. |
| P/O | William Alfred | CLARK | 02.12.43. |
| Sgt | Winston Pescod | CLOUGH | 18.03.44. |
| F/Sgt | Raymond | COATES | 22.05.44. |
| Sgt | Harry Morley | COFFEY | 31.03.44. |
| Sgt | Thomas William | CONNOR | 23.05.44. |
| Sgt | Cyril | COOK | 08.12.44. |
| Sgt | Leonard George | COOK | 18.10.44. |
| Sgt | Leon Harvey | COOPER | 23.11.43. |
| Sgt | Robert Frederick | COUSIN | 29.07.44. |
| F/Sgt | William Edwin John | COX | 31.08.44. |
| P/O | Robert Arthur Godwin | CRANEFIELD | 12.09.44. |
| F/O | John Stanley | CROSS | 20.02.44. |
| F/Sgt | John Harold | CROUCHER | 17.03.45. |
| Sgt | George Alfred | CROWE | 02.12.43. |
| Sgt | Herbert George | DAVIES | 15.02.45. |
| P/O | William Alfred Cyril | DAVIES | 22.06.44. |
| P/O | Billy | DAVIS | 20.01.44. |
| W/O | Gerlad Joseph | DAVIS | 18.10.44. |
| F/O | Leonard George | DAVIS | 22.06.44. |
| F/Sgt | John Leslie | DAVISON | 27.04.44. |
| F/Sgt | Dennis Arthur | DAWSON | 20.02.44. |
| Sgt | Eric Charles | DAY | 05.07.44. |
| W/C | William Inglis | DEAS | 08.07.44. |
| F/O | Peter Buck | DENNETT | 19.07.44. |

| Rank | Name | Surname | Date |
|---|---|---|---|
| P/O | Rusel Edward | DENNIS | 10.06.44. |
| W/O | Frederick Sayre | DEWIS | 22.06.44. |
| Sgt | John Radford | DICKEN | 10.04.45. |
| Sgt | Kenneth | DICKINSON | 22.05.44. |
| F/O | John Christopher | DOHERTY | 04.12.43. |
| F/Sgt | Eric Colston | DORAM | 27.04.44. |
| Sgt | Stephen Nelson | DOUGAN | 27.04.44. |
| F/Sgt | George | DOVE | 29.01.44. |
| F/Sgt | Alan George | DRAKE | 31.03.44. |
| Sgt | Robert Edward | DUCK | 22.06.44. |
| Sgt | James | DUFFETT | 22.12.44. |
| F/Sgt | Maxwell | DUNBAR | 25.04.44. |
| F/Sgt | Peter James | DUTCHAK | 18.03.44. |
| Sgt | Richard John Harry | EASTER | 16.03.44. |
| W/O | Ernest James | EDWARDS | 14.01.45. |
| F/L | Leopold (Leo) | EHRMAN | 29.01.44. |
| F/L | William | ENGLISH | 15.02.44. |
| Sgt | Clifford John | EVANS | 18.10.44. |
| F/O | John Emlyn | EVANS | 15.02.44. |
| F/L | George Grafron Haig | FARARA | 08.07.44. |
| F/Sgt | Ernest Arthur | FARNELL | 31.03.44. |
| F/O | Charles Robson | FAULKNER | 12.09.44. |
| F/O | Joseph | FELDMAN | 12.05.44. |
| F/O | Walter Geroge Frederick | FILBY | 17.08.44. |
| P/O | Wilfred James | FINGLAND | 27.08.44. |
| Sgt | John Christopher | FITZPATRICK | 18.10.44 |
| F/O | George Ross | FLOOD | 22.11.44. |
| F/Sgt | Kevin Gregory | FOGARTY | 15.02.45. |
| Sgt | David Jack Ervin | FONTAINE | 27.07.44. |
| Sgt | John | FORD | 02.12.44. |
| F/O | William | FORRESTER | 09.04.45. |
| S/L | Arthur Edgar | FOSTER | 22.06.44. |
| Sgt | Thomas Austin | FOX | 16.03.44. |
| Sgt | William Edward | FRANCE | 31.03.44. |
| Sgt | Thomas Douglas Safely | FRASER | 22.06.44. |
| W/OII | Alexander McCowan | FREEMAN | 16.03.44. |
| P/O | Llewellyn Vivian | FUSSELL | 15.02.44. |
| Sgt | Charles William | GARNER | 30.08.44. |
| F/Sgt | John Thomas | GEOGHEGAN | 04.04.44. |
| Sgt | Bernard | GIBBONS | 09.04.45. |
| Sgt | Ronald | GILES | 20.02.44. |
| Sgt | Percy Arthur | GILLIATT | 27.07.44. |
| F/O | Jack Norman | GILL | 18.03.44. |
| P/O | Vernon Alfred | GOODWIN | 22.05.44. |
| Sgt | William John | GOODYEAR | 05.07.44. |

| | | | |
|---|---|---|---|
| Sgt | Norman James Yates | GOULDING | 23.11.43. |
| P/O | Alfred Frederick | GRANT | 12.05.44. |
| Sgt | Kenneth Howard | GREENFIELD | 17.03.45. |
| F/Sgt | Kelvin Carlyle | GREEN | 31.03.44. |
| P/O | Percy Wilfred | GREEN | 02.03.44. |
| Sgt | George Henry | GRIFFITHS | 20.02.44. |
| F/Sgt | William Edward | GRIFFITHS | 19.07.44. |
| P/O | John Reginald Cecil | GUTCHER | 27.07.44. |
| Sgt | David Beattie | HAIG | 23.05.44. |
| F/O | Bernard | HALL | 17.05.45. |
| F/Sgt | Leslie | HALL | 16.03.44. |
| Sgt | James | HANNA | 07.06.44. |
| Sgt | Frederick Hubert | HARD | 05.07.44. |
| F/Sgt | Frank | HARTLEY | 05.07.44. |
| P/O | Thomas George | HART | 22.06.44. |
| F/Sgt | Raymond Guy | HARWOOD | 22.06.44. |
| F/O | Ronald Thomas | HAYES | 24.07.44. |
| Sgt | Frank | HELLIWELL | 18.07.44. |
| Sgt | John Alfred | HELLIWELL | 24.07.44. |
| F/Sgt | Alastair Millar | HENDERSON | 07.06.44. |
| F/Sgt | James Mitchell | HENDERSON | 22.05.44 |
| Sgt | Maurice Benjamin | HENLEY | 22.11.44. |
| F/L | Alfred George | HENRIQUEZ | 17.08.44. |
| Sgt | James | HERON | 04.12.43. |
| F/O | Frank Leonard | HEWISH | 22.06.44. |
| Sgt | Leslie Bertram | HEWITT | 08.08.44. |
| P/O | William Philip Revenall | HEWITT | 15.02.44. |
| F/Sgt | Frank James | HOBBS | 16.03.44. |
| F/Sgt | Arthur | HOBSON | 07.01.45. |
| Sgt | Denis Albert | HOLLOWAY | 07.01.45. |
| F/Sgt | Dennis Gordon | HOLYOAK | 18.10.44. |
| F/Sgt | John Walter | HOMEWOOD | 22.01.44. |
| P/O | Robert Cecil | HOOPER | 22.06.44. |
| F/O | John | HOPWOOD | 10.04.45. |
| P/O | Claud Morley | HOUGHTON | 10.06.44. |
| F/Sgt | Burton Dix | HOWARD | 21.02.44. |
| P/O | Joseph | HOWE | 23.11.43. |
| Sgt | James Napier | HOWIE | 19.07.44. |
| F/Sgt | Frederick James | HOWLETT | 09.04.45. |
| Sgt | Eric | HUBBERT | 04.12.43. |
| Sgt | Aereon | HUGHES | 31.08.44. |
| Sgt | Elwyn Rees | HUGHES | 21.02.44. |
| Sgt | Frederick | HUGHES | 22.11.44. |
| Sgt | Robert | HUGHES | 02.12.43. |
| Sgt | Thomas | HUGHES | 31.03.44. |

| | | | |
|---|---|---|---|
| P/O | Leslie Raymond | INGELL | 25.03.44. |
| Sgt | Robert | INGLIS | 23.11.43. |
| F/Sgt | William Ritchie | INGRAM | 22.11.44. |
| Sgt | Horace | ISON | 11.06.44. |
| P/O | Alfred Thomas | JACKSON | 12.05.44. |
| Sgt | Douglas Edward | JAMES | 29.01.44. |
| F/O | William McPherson | JAMES | 22.12.44. |
| Sgt | William John | JARMAN | 19.07.44. |
| F/Sgt | Peter Woolvin | JARVIS | 17.08.44. |
| Sgt | George William | JEFFERY | 31.03.44. |
| Sgt | Roy | JEFFERY | 17.03.45. |
| Sgt | Wallace Henry (Wally) | JENKINS | 27.04.44. |
| Sgt | William Howard Roger | JENKINS | 10.04.45. |
| F/Sgt | William | JENKINS | 02.01.44. |
| F/Sgt | Cedric Raymond | JERWOOD | 19.07.44. |
| F/L | George Russell | JOBLIN | 29.07.44. |
| F/O | Allan George Garth | JOHNSON | 31.03.44. |
| Sgt | John Peacock Craig | JOHNSTONE | 23.05.44. |
| Sgt | David Daniel | JONES | 01.01.45 |
| F/Sgt | Joseph Henry | JONES | 01.01.45. |
| Sgt | William Donnan | JONES | 31.03.44. |
| Sgt | Ronald Merrick | JORDAN | 22.06.44. |
| F/O | Rayner Francis | JOWETT | 02.03.44. |
| Sgt | Peter Hogan | KANO | 22.06.44. |
| Sgt | henry George | KEMBER | 22.06.44. |
| Sgt | Percy George | KEMPEN | 29.01.44. |
| F/O | Harold | KIDD | 20.02.44. |
| P/O | Joseph Seddon | KILGOUR | 27.04.44. |
| Sgt | Alexander Murphie | KILTIE | 18.03.44. |
| Sgt | John Kenneth | KIMBERLEY | 22.06.44. |
| F/O | William Leopold Carver | KIRKPATRICK | 02.03.44 |
| F/O | Robert Baines | KNIGHT | 09.02.45. |
| Lt. | Gordon Ramsey | LACEY | 15.02.45. |
| Sgt | James | LAMBELL | 31.08.44. |
| F/O | Donald Bell | LAMBTON | 29.07.44. |
| F/Sgt | John | LAMONT | 09.02.45. |
| P/O | Leslie George | LANE | 15.02.44. |
| Sgt | Alan Ambrose Michael | LANGRIDGE | 27.08.44. |
| F/Sgt | Leonard | LAWRENCE | 22.06.44. |
| Sgt | Ronald Victor | LAWRENCE | 22.05.44. |
| Sgt | George Law | LAWRIE | 12.09.44. |
| F/Sgt | Eric | LEESE | 01.01.45. |
| Sgt | George | LEGGOTT | 04.12.43. |
| F/Sgt | Kenneth Frank | LENTON | 08.12.44. |
| F/L | Rendel Forrest | LEWIS | 08.12.44. |

| | | | |
|---|---|---|---|
| F/O | Alexander | LINDSAY | 27.07.44. |
| Sgt | James | LINDSAY | 22.05.44. |
| Sgt | Stanley Robert | LOADES | 29.01.44. |
| P/O | Roland James | LOCKE | 08.07.44. |
| P/O | Ross William | LOUGH | 25.07.44. |
| Sgt | Ernest Albert | LOUIS | 12.05.44. |
| F/L | Douglas Allister | MACDONALD | 02.01.44. |
| P/O | Harold Charles Leeton | MACKINTOSH | 21.02.44. |
| Sgt | Michael John | MACNAUGHTON-SMITH | 22.06.44. |
| F/Sgt | Morris Slock | MARKS | 22.01.44. |
| F/Sgt | William Henry McDonald | MARSHALL | 01.01.45. |
| F/O | Robert | MARTIN | 09.04.45. |
| P/O | Arthur James | MATTHEWS | 23.11.43. |
| F/O | Gordon Edward | MAXWELL | 19.07.44. |
| Sgt | Duncan Kennedy Watson | MAYES | 15.02.45. |
| F/Sgt | Alexander Ernest | McCORMICK | 25.03.44. |
| F/Sgt | Arthur Henry | McGILL | 31.03.44. |
| P/O | John Leo | McKENNA | 22.06.44. |
| Sgt | Alan | McKENZIE | 17.08.44. |
| Sgt | Clarence Ray | McLAREN | 02.12.43. |
| F/O | Burton | McLAUCHLIN | 27.08.44. |
| P/O | William James | McMEEKAN | 25.03.44. |
| F/O | Victor Francis Dobell | MEADE | 17.05.45. |
| Sgt | David Victor | MENELL | 31.03.44. |
| F/Sgt | Arthur | MICHAELS | 17.03.45. |
| Sgt | Robert | MIDDLETON | 27.04.44. |
| Sgt | Norman Harold | MITCHELL | 15.02.44. |
| Sgt | David Drylie | MOFFATT | 19.07.44. |
| F/Sgt | James | MONTAGUE | 09.02.45. |
| Sgt | John Desmond | MORRIS | 22.01.44. |
| Sgt | Philip Gascoyne | MOTTRAM | 20.02.44. |
| F/Sgt | Denis Walter | MUDDIMAN | 12.05.44. |
| F/Sgt | Murray Swanson | MUNRO | 10.04.45. |
| P/O | Edgar John | MURRAY | 20.02.44. |
| F/Sgt | James Francis Joseph | MURRAY | 24.07.44. |
| Sgt | Martin Ernest | MURTON | 22.05.44. |
| P/O | Peter Albert | NASH | 15.05.44. |
| P/O | Gerlad Melbourne | NAUGLER | 23.05.44. |
| F/L | Thomas | NEISON | 22.06.44. |
| F/Sgt | Kenneth | NELSON | 19.07.44. |
| Sgt | Arthur Ronald | NEWBY | 09.02.45. |
| F/Sgt | Thomas George | NOTTINGHAM | 17.08.44. |
| F/O | Ronald James | O'DONNELL | 17.05.45. |
| P/O | Kenneth Watson | ORCHISTON | 18.03.44. |
| Sgt | James Henry | OVERHOLT | 16.03.44. |

| | | | |
|---|---|---|---|
| Sgt | Harold Edgar Frank | OWEN | 12.05.44. |
| Sgt | Leslie | OYSTON | 08.12.44. |
| Sgt | Leonard Augustus Alfred | PAGE | 08.07.44. |
| Sgt | Jack | PALMER | 18.03.44. |
| P/O | George Vernon Bently | PATTERSON | 08.08.44. |
| P/O | Francis James | PEACOCK | 29.01.44. |
| P/O | Kenneth | PEACOCK | 25.03.44. |
| F/Sgt | Derek Charles | PEARSE | 18.03.44. |
| F/Sgt | Robert Edward | PEARSON | 02.03.44. |
| Sgt | Charles Harry | PELL | 23.11.43. |
| F/L | Frederick Leonard | PERRERS | 23.11.43. |
| F/Sgt | Ernest John | PHILIPSON | 16.03.44. |
| Sgt | Bernard John | PHILLIPS | 01.01.45. |
| Sgt | Alan Leslie | PICKERING | 23.05.44. |
| F/O | Peter Jojn | PIGGIN | 02.03.44. |
| Sgt | Ian Alistair | PLACE | 22.06.44. |
| P/O | Donld Ivan | PLUMB | 17.03.45. |
| F/Sgt | Leonard | PRIOR | 30.08.44. |
| F/O | Robert Edward | PROUDLEY | 15.02.45. |
| Sgt | John Henry | QUINLIVAN | 22.12.44. |
| Sgt | Ronald Charles | QUINN | 12.09.44, |
| Sgt | Gordon Leonard | RABBETTS | 17.05.45. |
| Sgt | John | RAE | 19.07.44. |
| F/Sgt | Alexander William | REEDMAN | 22.01.44. |
| Sgt | Douglas William | REMOLE | 20.02.44. |
| P/O | John Leslie | RICHARDS | 15.02.44. |
| F/Sgt | Charles Henry | RICHARDSON | 22.05.44. |
| F/O | Colin Robert Moore | RICHARDSON | 09.04.45. |
| Sgt | Thomas Richard | RILEY | 12.09.44. |
| F/O | Leonard Rodmond | RINN | 02.12.43. |
| F/Sgt | William Joseph | ROCHE | 02.01.44. |
| P/O | Kenneth | RODBOURN | 16.03.44. |
| W/C | John Dudley | ROLLINSON | 29.01.44. |
| F/Sgt | William John | ROSSER | 29.01.44. |
| F/Sgt | James Louis | ROSSITER | 04.12.43. |
| Sgt | Peter Robert | ROWTHORN | 12.05.44. |
| F/O | Alexander James | SARGENT | 19.07.44. |
| F/O | Richard Joseph | SASSOON | 10.04.45. |
| Sgt | William John | SAXBY | 23.05.44. |
| P/O | John Joseph | SCULLY | 22.06.44. |
| Sgt | Arthur William | SEAGO | 12.05.44. |
| Sgt | Philip Donald | SECRETAN | 17.08.44. |
| F/Sgt | Norman Eric | SHARPE | 09.02.45. |
| F/O | William Joseph | SHEARSTONE | 18.08.44. |
| P/O | Archie Harry | SIEMINS | 22.06.44. |

| Sgt | John Alfred | SILLS | 17.05.45. |
| W/O | Kenneth Arthur | SINCLAIR | 23.05.44. |
| F/Sgt | Geoffrey | SLATER | 21.02.44. |
| Sgt | Robert Francis | SMALE | 02.01.44. |
| F/O | Howard Wallace | SMITH | 22.05.44. |
| Sgt | John George | SMITH | 23.11.43. |
| P/O | John Henry George | SMITH | 22.06.44. |
| F/Sgt | Owen Preston | SMITH | 21.02.44. |
| Sgt | Reginald Henry | SMITH | 17.05.45. |
| Sgt | Vincent Reginald Woodburn | SOUTHWORTH | 17.05.45. |
| Sgt | Alan | SPENCE | 20.02.44. |
| Sgt | Harold Raymond | SPENDELOW | 29.07.44. |
| P/O | Leonard | SPENSLEY | 22.05.44. |
| Sgt | Samuel | STANTON | 30.08.44. |
| F/L | Ernest | STEAD | 20.02.44. |
| P/O | Walter | STEAD | 24.07.44. |
| F/Sgt | George Edward | STENNER | 29.07.44. |
| F/O | Arnold | STOCKILL | 22.12.44. |
| F/O | Frederick Richard | STONE | 22.06.44. |
| Sgt | Alexander Charles | STOPP | 22.01.44. |
| P/O | Donald William | STORY | 29.01.44. |
| Sgt | Guy Raymond | STOTT | 27.08.44. |
| Sgt | Kenneth | SWINCHATT | 04.12.43. |
| P/O | John | SYME | 04.12.43. |
| Sgt | Daniel Felix Oliver | SYNNOTT | 22.06.44. |
| P/O | Ralph Norman | TAFT | 05.07.44. |
| F/Sgt | Stephen | TATAI | 21.02.44. |
| F/O | Joseph Thomas | TAYLOR | 08.07.44. |
| F/Sgt | William Irving | TAYLOR | 23.05.44. |
| P/O | Edward Ainsley | THOMAS | 01.01.45. |
| Sgt | Leslie St.Clair | THOMPSON | 12.05.44. |
| Sgt | Leslie | THOMPSON | 27.08.44 |
| F/O | Albert Edward (Bertie) | TRUESDALE | 22.05.44. |
| F/Sgt | John Mowbray | TURNBULL | 02.01.44. |
| F/O | Douglas George | TWIDLE | 30.08.44. |
| Sgt | George Herbert | TYLER | 05.07.44. |
| Sgt | William Richard | TYRIE | 02.01.44. |
| F/O | Reginald Harold William | USHER | 08.12.44. |
| S/L | Kenneth Frederick | VARE | 02.01.44. |
| LAC | Robert Charles | VICKERS | 06.05.44. |
| P/O | Reginald Charles H | WAKELEY | 07.06.44 |
| Sgt | William | WALLACE | 24.07.44. |
| Sgt | Kenneth James | WALLBEY | 20.02.44 |
| F/O | Albert | WALLWORK | 15.02.45 |
| Sgt | Edward John | WALTON | 30.08.44. |

| | | | |
|---|---|---|---|
| P/O | Richard John | WALTON | 22.06.44. |
| Sgt | Stanley Charles | WALTON | 10.04.45. |
| Sgt | Ernest Nelson | WATSON | 08.08.44. |
| P/O | Wilfred Arthur | WATT | 12.05.44. |
| F/O | Niels Erik | WESTERGAARD | 02.01.44. |
| W/O | James | WHITE | 25.03.44. |
| P/O | John Freebairn | WHITE | 23.11.43. |
| Sgt | Melvyn | WHITE | 27.04.44. |
| Sgt | Peter Sigston | WHITE | 02.03.44. |
| F/Sgt | William Albert | WHITE | 18.10.44. |
| P/O | Jack Maxwell | WHITING | 22.05.44. |
| Sgt | Harold Walter | WICKENDEN | 30.08.44. |
| F/O | Norman Bunker | WILCOCK | 22.06.44. |
| Sgt | Albert Henry | WILKINSON | 16.03.44. |
| P/O | Buce Gordon | WILKINSON | 31.08.44. |
| Sgt | Dennis | WILKINSON | 08.08.44. |
| Sgt | Ronald Ernest | WILLIAMS | 17.08.44. |
| P/O | Alan William | WILSON | 07.06.44. |
| F/O | Harold Earl | WILSON | 27.07.44. |
| Sgt | David | WITHERS | 19.07.44. |
| Sgt | Leslie Thomas | WOODWARD | 01.12.44. |
| Sgt | Norman | WORBOYS | 31.03.44. |
| Sgt | Eric Stanley | WORDEN | 22.06.44. |
| P/O | Charles Norman | WRIGHT | 08.07.44. |
| P/O | Wilson Birwell | YATES | 20.02.44. |
| Sgt | William George | YORKE | 22.01.44. |
| Sgt | Leonard | YOUNG | 09.02.45. |
| Sgt | Leslie Alfred | YOUNG | 20.02.44. |

# 630 Squadron

Motto; Nocturna More (Death by night)　　　　　　　　　　　　　　　　Code **LE**

## Station

**EAST KIRKBY**　　　　　　　　　　　　　　　　　　　15.11.43. to 18.07.45.

## Commanding Officers

| | |
|---|---|
| **WING COMMANDER** M CROCKER DFC | 15.11.43. to 12.12.43. |
| **WING COMMANDER** J D ROLLINSON DFC | 12.12.43. to 28.01.44. |
| **WING COMMANDER** W DEAS DFC | 01.02.44. to 07.07.44. |
| **WING COMMANDER** L M BLOME-JONES DFC | 12.07.44. to 14.10.44. |
| **WING COMMANDER** J E GRINDON DFC | 14.10.44. to 28.04.45. |
| **WING COMMANDER** F W L WILD DFC | 28.04.45. to 18.07.45. |

# Aircraft

**LANCASTER I/III**  15.11.43. to 18.07.45.

## Operational Record

| OPERATIONS | SORTIES | AIRCRAFT LOSSES | % LOSSES |
|---|---|---|---|
| 202 | 2453 | 59 | 2.4 |

### CATEGORY OF OPERATIONS

| BOMBING | MINING |
|---|---|
| 180 | 22 |

11 further Lancasters were destroyed in crashes.

# Aircraft Histories

| | |
|---|---|
| **LANCASTER.** | **From November 1943.** |

| | |
|---|---|
| **ED308** | From 57 Squadron. To 1661 Conversion Unit. |
| **ED413** LE-T | From 57 Squadron. To 207 Squadron. |
| **ED655** LE-J | From 57 Squadron. Crashed in Lincolnshire during operation to Berlin (619 Squadron crew) 15/16.2.44. |
| **ED698** | From 57 Squadron. To 207 Squadron. |
| **ED758** | From 57 Squadron. To 207 Squadron. |
| **ED777** LE-Q | From 57 Squadron. FTR Berlin 2/3.12.43. |
| **ED920** LE-D | From 57 Squadron. FTR Leipzig 3/4.12.43. |
| **ED944** LE-Z | From 57 Squadron. To 5LFS. |
| **JA872** LE-N | From 57 Squadron. To 61 Squadron. |
| **JB135** LE-L | From 57 Squadron. FTR Berlin 23/24.11.43. |
| **JB236** LE-O- | From 57 Squadron. FTR Berlin 23/24.11.43. |
| **JB288** LE-H | From 1660 Conversion Unit. FTR Nuremberg 30/31.3.44. |
| **JB290** LE-C/D | From 1660 Conversion Unit. |
| **JB294** | From 1660 Conversion Unit. FTR Berlin 21/22.1.44. |
| **JB532** LE-X | From 61 Squadron. FTR Berlin 1/2.1.44. |
| **JB546** LE-A | From 57 Squadron. FTR Braunschweig 22/23.5.44. |
| **JB556** LE-Y | Crashed on take-off from East Kirkby when bound for Munich 24.4.44. |
| **JB561** | From 61 Squadron. To 12 Squadron. |
| **JB597** | From 61 Squadron. Crashed while landing at Holme-on-Spalding-Moor on return from Berlin 27.11.43. |
| **JB654** LE-C | FTR Berlin 28/29.1.44. |
| **JB665** LE-B | FTR Berlin 15/16.2.44. |
| **JB666** | FTR Berlin 28/29.1.44. |
| **JB672** LE-U/F | FTR Duisburg 21/22.5.44. |
| **JB710** LE-W | From 49 Squadron. FTR Leipzig 19/20.2.44. |
| **LL886** LE-I | FTR Berlin 24/25.3.44. |
| **LL949** LE-E | Crashed in the Humber Estuary on return from Trondheim 22/23.11.44. |
| **LL950** LE-Y | FTR from mining sortie 21/22.5.44. |
| **LL966** LE-P | FTR Rositz 14/15.2.45. |
| **LL972** LE-T | FTR Stettin 16/17.8.44. |
| **LM117** LE-J | FTR Revigny 18/19.7.44. |
| **LM118** LE-V | FTR Wesseling 21/22.6.44. |
| **LM216** LE-K | To 186 Squadron. |
| **LM259** LE-F | To 227 Squadron. |
| **LM260** LE-S | FTR Würzburg 16/17.3.45. |
| **LM262** LE-G | FTR Secqueville 7/8.8.44. |
| **LM269** LE-I | FTR Bordeaux 18.8.44. |
| **LM287** LE-O | To 1651 Conversion Unit. |
| **LM537** LE-X | FTR Revigny 18/19.7.44. |
| **LM637** LE-V | FTR Urft Dam 8.12.44. |
| **LM649** | From 49 Squadron. |

| | |
|---|---|
| **LM673** | From 57 Squadron. Returned to 57 Squadron. |
| **LM680** LE-Z | From 50 Squadron. |
| **ME312** LE-A | To 1661 Conversion Unit. |
| **ME532** | To 207 Squadron. |
| **ME650** LE-B | FTR Königsberg 26/27.8.44. |
| **ME664** LE-T | FTR Nuremberg 30/31.3.44. |
| **ME717** LE-G | Crash-landed in Corsica following operation to Munich 24/25.4.44. |
| **ME729** | Crashed in Scotland while training 18.7.44. |
| **ME737** LE-E/S | FTR Bourg Leopold 11/12.5.44. |
| **ME739** LE-F/T | FTR Leipzig 10/11.4.44. |
| **ME782** LE-N | FTR Wesseling 21/22.6.44. |
| **ME795** LE-G | Abandoned over Henlow on return from Wesseling 21/22.6.44. |
| **ME796** LE-S | FTR Revigny 18/19.7.44. |
| **ME843** LE-U | FTR Wesseling 21/22.6.44. |
| **ME845** LE-Q | To 57 Squadron. |
| **ME867** LE-N | FTR St-Leu-d'Esserent 4/5.7.44. |
| **ND335** LE-L | To 1668 Conversion Unit. |
| **ND337** LE-S | FTR Nuremberg 30/31.3.44. |
| **ND338** LE-T/Q | FTR Stuttgart 20/21.2.44. |
| **ND412** LE-H | From 405 (Vancouver) Squadron RCAF. |
| **ND527** LE-O | FTR Givors 26/27.7.44. |
| **ND530** LE-P | From 207 Squadron. FTR Stuttgart 15/16.3.44. |
| **ND531** LE-K | FTR Wesseling 21/22.6.44. |
| **ND532** LE-N | FTR Leipzig 19/20.2.44. |
| **ND554** LE-A | From 617 Squadron. FTR Politz 8/9.2.45. |
| **ND561** LE-R | FTR Stuttgart 1/2.3.44. |
| **ND563** | Crashed on take-off from East Kirkby bound for Stuttgart 20.2.44. |
| **ND580** LE-G | FTR Bourg Leopold 11/12.5.44. |
| **ND583** LE-V | FTR Stuttgart 15/16.3.44. |
| **ND655** LE-J | FTR Braunschweig 22/23.5.44. |
| **ND657** LE-W | FTR Berlin 24/25.3.44. |
| **ND685** LE-Q | FTR Caen 6/7.6.44. |
| **ND686** LE-M | FTR Frankfurt 18/19.3.44. |
| **ND688** LE-R | FTR St-Leu-d'Esserent 7/8.7.44. |
| **ND788** LE-U | FTR Berlin 24/25.3.44. |
| **ND789** LE-I | FTR Schweinfurt 26/27.4.44. |
| **ND793** | To Flight Refuelling Ltd. |
| **ND797** LE-W | FTR Stuttgart 28/29.7.44. |
| **ND949** LE-Z | Crashed in Leicestershire on return from Lützkendorf 9.4.45. |
| **ND982** LE-Y | From 405 (Vancouver) Squadron RCAF. FTR Königsberg 29/30.8.44. |
| **NF961** LE-L | Crashed in Yorkshire while night-flying training 18.10.44. |
| **NG123** LE-U | |
| **NG125** LE-F/N | |
| **NG145** | To 57 Squadron. |
| **NG258** | Crashed in Lincolnshire on return from Politz 22.12.44. |
| **NG259** LE-N | |

| | | |
|---|---|---|
| **NG413** LE-M | From 1661 Conversion Unit. | |
| **NN702** LE-J | To 617 Squadron. | |
| **NN703** | | |
| **NN774** LE-L | | |
| **PA322** LE-V | | |
| **PA992** LE-Y | FTR Stuttgart 24/25.7.44. | |
| **PB121** LE-F | FTR Etampes 9/10.6.44. | |
| **PB211** LE-H | From 9 Squadron. Crashed in North Sea during mining sortie 23/24.7.44. | |
| **PB236** LE-F | FTR Revigny 18/19.7.44. | |
| **PB244** LE-N | FTR L'Isle Adam 18.8.44. | |
| **PB344** LE-R | | |
| **PB742** | To 189 Squadron. | |
| **PB865** | To 1661 Conversion Unit. | |
| **PB880** LE-B | FTR Politz 13/14.1.45. | |
| **PB894** | From 57 Squadron. FTR from mining sortie 31.12/1.1.45 | |
| **PD253** LE-D | | |
| **PD254** LE-W | | |
| **PD283** LE-G | FTR Darmstadt 11/12.9.44. | |
| **PD317** LE-G | Crashed on landing at East Kirkby on early return from Munich 7.1.45. | |
| **PD327** LE-E/Y | To 75(NZ) Squadron. | |
| **RA520** LE-E | | |
| **RF122** LE-S | FTR Leipzig 10/11.4.45. | |
| **RF124** LE-S | From 57 Squadron. | |
| **RF194** | From 207 Squadron. | |
| **RF266** | | |

## HEAVIEST LOSS

21/22.6.44. Wesseling 4 Lancasters FTR, 1 abandoned on return.

18/19.7.44. Revigny   4 Lancasters FTR.

www.ingramcontent.com/pod-product-compliance
Lightning Source LLC
Chambersburg PA
CBHW082119230426
43671CB00015B/2740